*Metre Gauge Railways
in South and East Switzerland*

RAILWAY HISTORIES OF THE WORLD SERIES

Hungarian Railways
by P. M. Kalla-Bishop

Italian Railways
by P. M. Kalla-Bishop

Mediterranean Island Railways
by P. M. Kalla-Bishop

Railways of Canada
by Robert F. Legget

Railways of New Zealand
by David B. Leitch

Railways of North Africa
by E. D. Brant

Railways of Rhodesia
by Anthony H. Croxton

METRE GAUGE RAILWAYS IN SOUTH AND EAST SWITZERLAND

by
JOHN MARSHALL

DAVID & CHARLES

NEWTON ABBOT   LONDON   NORTH POMFRET (VT)   VANCOUVER

0 7153 6408 1

Set in 11/13 point Linotype Plantin
and printed in Great Britain
by John Sherratt & Son Limited
Park Road Altrincham Cheshire WA14 5QQ
for David & Charles (Holdings) Limited
South Devon House Newton Abbot Devon

Published in the United States of America
by David & Charles Inc North Pomfret
Vermont 05053 USA

Published in Canada by Douglas David &
Charles Limited 3645 McKechnie Drive
West Vancouver BC

Contents

6   *Contents*

tender engines · Rhaetian Railway rolling stock ·
snow ploughs

List of Illustrations

Introductory Note on Metric Units and Diagrams

As this is a book about Swiss railways, and as Great Britain is changing to metric units, these measurements are used throughout. In the first chapter, however, both metric and Imperial units are used to accustom the British reader to the relationship. For reference, conversion tables are given on pp 253 and 254. From these, or easily obtainable tables, any measurements can be converted. For rough conversions 1 kilometre (km) is about ⅝mile, or 8km are roughly 5 miles. Weights are in metric tons of 1,000kg (2,204.6223lb).

The gradient profiles should be self-explanatory. Figures after station names indicate height above sea level. Those above tunnels indicate length; those above bridges and viaducts indicate numbers and lengths of span: eg $2 \times 20m + 3 \times 8m$ means two spans of 20m and three of 8m. Rack sections are indicated by a thick line. Gradients are 'pro Mille' or per thousand, indicated by $\%_0$: eg 25 pro Mille or $25\%_0$ means that the line rises 25 in 1,000, or at 1 in 40. On the Gornergrat Railway the steepest gradient is $200\%_0$, the line rising at 200 in 1,000, or 1 in 5. A conversion scale is given on p 252.

Money values are in Swiss Francs. During the period when these railways were being built the exchange rate for Swiss Francs was about 25 to £1 Sterling and about 5 to the US Dollar, and £1 was worth about ten times its value in 1971.

Except where otherwise stated maps, diagrams and drawings are by the author.

11

CHAPTER 1

Geographical and Historical Background

THE cantons of Graubünden, Uri and Wallis in south and east Switzerland embrace some of the grandest scenery in Europe and have justifiably become one of its most popular tourist regions. Historically their importance arose from their situation between Germany and Italy. North–south trade routes were established in very early times along the Rhine and through Graubünden via the Splügen and St Bernhardin passes.

Despite some losses of traffic following the opening of the road over the Brenner Pass in 1772 and that over the Arlberg, 1785–1824, the routes retained some importance. The construction of the Simplon road in 1801–7 and the St Gotthard in 1820–30, however, while bringing a measure of prosperity to Cantons Wallis and Uri, led to a severe decline in the importance of Graubünden, in spite of the construction of roads over the St Bernhardin and Splügen passes in 1820–3. The opening of the Brenner railway in 1867 and the Arlberg railway in 1884 caused further loss of traffic to the district.

The development of Graubünden as a tourist region and its consequent revival was largely brought about by the Rhaetian Railway. Known to the Romans 2,000 years ago as Rhaetia, Graubünden or the Grisons (Land of the 'Grey Confederates') is the largest of the twenty-five Swiss cantons, occupying more than a sixth of the confederacy, with an area of 7,113 sq km (2,736 sq miles). With a population of 137,000, it has the lowest population density, 20 per sq km (50 per sq mile). It compares in size with the English county of Lincolnshire, 2,646 sq miles, which, however, has a population of 624,600. Its capital, Chur, population 17,000, compares with the 19,600 of Buxton in Derbyshire.

It is a land of unbounded interest and scenic beauty. Rivers from its '150 valleys' drain to the North Sea, the Adriatic and the Black Sea. Altitudes range from 300m (984ft) in the Misox or Mesolcina valley to the 4,055m (13,292ft) of Piz Bernina, and its range of flora is immense. Although German is the principal language, Italian is spoken in the Puschlav and Mesolcina valleys while in the lower Engadin and one or two other parts, Romansch survives as a relic of the Roman conquest in 15 BC.

The main feature of canton Wallis or the Valais as it is called in French is the valley of the upper Rhone running west from the Rhone Glacier at the foot of the Furka Pass, and bounded to the north by the great range of the Bernese Oberland and to the south by the Lepontine and Pennine Alps. To the west of Visp or Viege, French is the main language; to the east, German.

Lying between these cantons is the southern tip of Uri, bounded on the east by the Oberalp Pass, by the St Gotthard in the south and the Furka in the west, and drained to the north by the River Reuss. Its capital is Altdorf, famous in the legend of William Tell.

Linking the three cantons is the route over the Furka Pass from the Rhone valley to Andermatt and over the Oberalp Pass into the valley of the Vorder Rhine, to Disentis and Chur. Using this route the Romans annexed Wallis to Graubünden. Mule traffic continued this way until 1850–67 when the road was built between Brig and Chur, 179km or 111 miles. The Furka, 2,431m or 7,990ft, remained the highest road in the Alps until the Great St Bernhard, 2,485m in 1894, and Umbrail, 2,503m in 1910. Its magnificent views of the Rhone Glacier, then much larger than today, attracted numerous tourists.

Railway penetration into this mountain fastness was at first along the fairly flat valleys of the Rhine and Rhone. As early as 1838 and 1841 Zurich merchants were actively striving for a railway from Zurich to Chur and Wallenstadt under the engineer

METRE GAUGE RAILWAYS IN SOUTH AND EAST SWITZERLAND

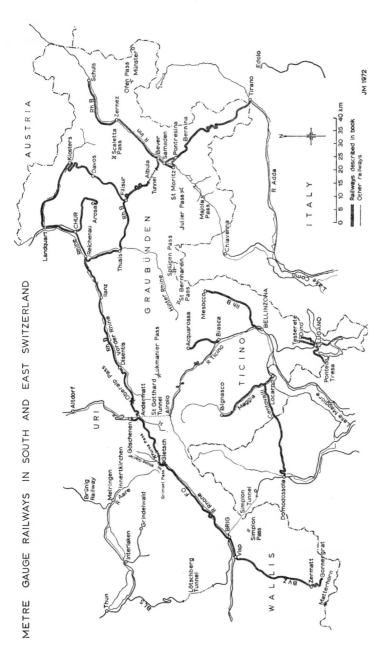

Map of metre gauge railways in south and east Switzerland

La Nicca who, for thirty years, was leader in the struggle for an east Alpine railway. It was not until 1858, however, that the standard gauge railway reached Landquart and Chur. Further west, in 1878, the Simplon Railway was extended up the Rhone valley to Brig in Canton Wallis. The opening of the Gotthard tunnel in 1882 established the first north–south railway through the region. They remained the only standard gauge lines until the opening of the Simplon tunnel in 1906 and the completion of the Lötschberg Railway in 1913.

Characteristic of the upper portions of glaciated valleys are the abrupt steps in the floor. It was the scale of engineering work necessary to overcome them, and the enormous expense on such standard gauge railways as the Gotthard and Lötschberg lines that led to the adoption of the metre (39.37in) gauge for the lines forming the subject of this book. This allowed sharper curves and a narrower formation, and hence cheaper construction. Despite this, engineering works are tremendous by any standards. Although several of these lines were built as widely separated, isolated units, considerable foresight was shown in the adoption of uniform standards which made through running possible when the final links were forged, to form one of the largest metre gauge networks in Europe.

The town of Davos in Graubünden, at an altitude of about 1,550m (5,100ft), lies in the Landwasser valley sheltered by high wooded mountains from the north and east winds while exposed to the full sun. With its dry climate, and temperature varying from a mean of 8.33°C (47°F) in summer to −3.33°C (26°F) in winter, it became popular as a health resort. In 1850, before the railway reached Landquart, it had a population of only 1,680; by 1920 it was 10,000.

It was to connect Davos with the standard gauge line at Landquart that the first of these metre gauge lines was built, in 1888–90, forming the nucleus of the Rhaetian system. It was extended to Chur and Thusis in 1896 and through the Albula tunnel to St Moritz in the upper Inn valley, known as the Engadin, in 1903–4. At the same time a branch was built from Reichenau up the Vorder Rhine as far as Ilanz, forming the first portion of the route to Brig, extended in 1912 to Disentis.

There was considerable competition in 1898 from the promoters of an 'Engadin Orient Railway', a standard gauge line from Chur to the Tirol frontier, with tunnels of 12km ($7\frac{1}{2}$ miles) beneath the Albula and 10.7km (6.65 miles) near Ofenberg, but the vast expense of this scheme prevented any progress.[1]

Davos was connected to the Albula line at Filisur in 1909; branches were also opened to Pontresina in 1908 and from Bever down the Inn valley to Schuls in 1913.

To complete the Graubünden lines the Bernina Railway from St Moritz to Tirano in Italy, the highest through railway in Europe, was opened in 1908, and the Chur-Arosa Railway in 1914. The projected extensions from St Moritz over the Maloja Pass to Chiavenna, and from Schuls down the Inn to the Arlberg Railway at Landeck, to form an international route from Italy to Austria, were killed by the 1914–18 war.

By the second half of the nineteenth century the valleys of Wallis entering the Rhone from the south were becoming popular with the more adventurous tourists. Chief among these valleys was that of the Visp leading up to Zermatt. This little town lying at the foot of the Matterhorn, almost surrounded by 4,000m peaks, and itself at an altitude of over 1,600m (5,300ft), and with a population today of only about 1,100, became famous overnight in July 1865 with the conquest of the Matterhorn and the tragedy which followed. But it was remote and inaccessible until the coming of the Simplon Railway in 1878, and even then required a long uphill trek from Visp. In 1838 visitors numbered 10–12, in 1867 4,400, in 1880 9,300.[2] Even today Zermatt is inaccessible by road, though this is the result of a deliberate policy to keep the town free from motor traffic.

The Visp–Zermatt Railway, metre gauge with mixed rack and adhesion, was opened in 1891. Three years later the number of visitors had jumped to 20,507. Those with energy to accomplish the $4\frac{1}{2}$–5 hour climb to the 3,136m (10,289ft) summit of the Gornergrat were rewarded with one of the finest views in the Alps. In 1898 a metre gauge rack railway was opened from Zermatt to the summit, with the distinction of being the world's first electric rack railway and, at the time, the highest railway in Europe.

This and the vz used the Abt double rack. This system, invented in 1882 by Roman Abt (1850–1933) has two (sometimes three) flat parallel toothed rails with teeth so staggered that the cog wheels are in constant mesh. Switches at turnouts for this system were first made in 1887 for the treble-rack line up the Bolan Pass in north-west India, and were first used in Switzerland on the double-rack Generoso Railway, Ticino, in 1890.

Following their penetration into Wallis, tourists began to explore the upper Rhone valley and to cross the Furka Pass to Andermatt and the Oberalp Pass to Graubünden. With the completion of the road in 1865 over the Oberalp Pass a horse postal service began between Chur and Andermatt and in 1867 via the Furka Pass between Brig and Hospenthal on the Gotthard road. From 1871 it became possible to travel through from Brig to Chur, with an overnight stop at Andermatt. After the opening of the St Gotthard Railway in 1882 this service called at Göschenen at the north end of the tunnel. First proposals for a railway up the wild Schöllenen gorge from Göschenen to Andermatt were made in 1890, and a concession for a metre gauge rack railway was obtained in 1904 but the line was not completed until 1917.

The importance of Brig as a railway centre was increased by the opening of the Simplon tunnel in 1906 and still further by the completion of the Berne–Lötschberg–Simplon Railway in 1913. By then work was well advanced on the Furka Railway between Brig and Disentis where it was to connect with the Rhaetian Railway. As on the vz mixed rack and adhesion was used, and it was opened from Brig to Gletsch in 1914. Here work was stopped by the war and it was not until 1926 that it was completed by the newly formed Furka-Oberalp company. The FO and the Schöllenen, like the vz and the Gornergrat, used the Abt double rack.

The missing link in this chain of metre gauge lines, the 8.5km ($5\frac{1}{4}$ miles) between Visp and Brig, was completed in 1930, making possible the introduction of the famous Glacier Express between Zermatt and St Moritz. It was now possible to travel by metre gauge lines from Tirano in Italy to the top of the Gornergrat, 339km or 211 miles, with only two changes, at St Moritz and Zermatt.

In 1910, when the Rhaetian Railway was beginning its extension down the Inn valley, the decision was made to electrify the Engadin lines at 11,000 volts single phase ac, $16\frac{2}{3}$ hertz (Hz—cycles per second)—a test in electric working at high altitudes. After the war the electrification was rapidly extended over the rest of the RhB network and was completed, to Disentis, in 1922. When the vz was electrified in 1930 and the FO in 1940–2 the same system was used to facilitate through working. Since, however, both these railways have rack sections while the Rhaetian system is entirely adhesion, locomotives are changed at Disentis.

To the south of Graubünden and Uri is Canton Ticino (Tessin in German), fifth in order of size, with an area of 2,769 sq km (1,069 sq miles) and population 179,500. Geographically it is part of Italy; place names, architecture, customs and language are all Italian. It was taken by Switzerland from Italy in 1512 and became part of the Federation in 1803. Though its scenery lacks the immensity of that in Graubünden and Wallis it has a charm of its own making it one of the most delightful parts of Switzerland.

Its main drainage system centres on the Ticino River which rises at the foot of the Gries Pass west of Airolo and flows southwards through Lake Maggiore. The two principal tributaries join from the left, the Brenno at Biasca and the Mesolcina, or Moesa, at Bellinzona. Although the Mesolcina valley lies largely within the boundary of Graubünden, it belongs geographically to Ticino. At Locarno another large drainage system, the Maggia River, flows into Lake Maggiore.

The Gotthard Railway makes use of the Ticino valley from Airolo to Bellinzona, the capital of the Canton. This old town of 12,600 inhabitants commands the ancient trade routes over the Gotthard into Uri and the Lukmanier and St Bernhardin passes into Graubünden. The years 1907–12 saw the opening of six short metre gauge electric railways in Ticino, three of them traversing these tributary valleys. In 1907 a line was opened up the Mesolcina valley from Bellinzona to Mesocco which, but for two world wars, might have become part of a through route over the St Berhardin Pass to Thusis. With the Chur–Arosa and

Bernina railways it became part of the Rhaetian system in 1942, making the total Rhaetian Railway route length 394km, or 245 miles.

Later in 1907 another line was opened from Locarno up the Maggia valley to Bignasco. In 1911 a third was opened from Biasca up the Brenno valley to Acquarossa. In the south of Ticino three short local lines radiated from Lugano; to Tesserete opened in 1909, to Dino in 1911 and to Ponte Tresa in 1912.

To connect the Gotthard Railway at Locarno with the Simplon Railway at Domodossola in Italy another metre gauge electric railway was built through the Centovalli (Hundred valleys) and the Valle di Vigezzo. It was planned as early as 1905 but not opened until 1923. While the Centovalli Railway survives, of the other Ticino lines only the Biasca–Acquarossa and Lugano–Ponte Tresa remain in full operation. The Bellinzona–Mesocco, or Misox, Railway now carries freight only.

Two metre gauge systems, both mixed rack and adhesion, are not included in this book. The Brünig Railway was opened from Alpnachstad on Lake Lucerne to Meiringen and Brienz on 14 June 1888, to Lucerne on 1 June 1889 and from Brienz to Interlaken Ost on 23 August 1916, making a total of 82km (51 miles). It uses the 'ladder' type of rack invented by Nicholas Riggenbach (1817–99) in 1863. In 1941–2 it was electrified at 15,000 volts $16\frac{2}{3}$Hz to conform with the standard Swiss Federal Railways (sbb) system with which it was amalgamated on 1 May 1903.

The Bernese Oberland Railway, another mixed adhesion and Riggenbach rack line, opened from Interlaken Ost to Lauterbrunnen and Grindelwald on 1 July 1890, a total of 24km (15 miles), and was electrified in 1913–14 using 1,5000 volts dc.

Proposals to link the Brünig and Furka railways from Meiringen to Gletsch via the Grimsel Pass were first made in 1915 at a time when construction of the Furka Railway between Gletsch and Disentis was suspended. Earlier standard gauge railways had been projected via the Grimsel in 1851–2 and 1862–4, and a street tramway in 1896. In 1903–4 a metre gauge adhesion railway was projected from Meiringen over the Grimsel to Brig and Visp (Ch 11).

In 1911, in connection with the construction of a power

station in the Grimsel, a railway along part of this route was opened from Meiringen to Innertkirchen, 4.9km, tunnelling the ridge through which the Aare cuts in its famous gorge. The FO was then being completed and although a post bus had been operating between Meiringen and Gletsch since 1921, the Grimsel railway project was again examined. The incompatibility of the Riggenbach and Abt rack systems was a major obstacle and another was the braking systems. The Brünig uses the Westinghouse air brake and the Rhaetian, FO and VZ use the Clayton–Hardy vacuum. Although the voltage difference could be overcome on the locomotives, the project was shelved once more and is unlikely to be revived.

CHAPTER 2

Brig-Visp-Zermatt and Gornergrat Railways

VISP–ZERMATT RAILWAY

THE attractions of the Zermatt valley and its increasing number of visitors have been mentioned. The first hotel at Zermatt was opened in 1861 by Alexander Seiler, but the difficulty of access along a rough track for 16km from Visp to St Niklaus and for 19km from there to Zermatt along a narrow road, very steep in places, was such that the Post Office charged a delivery rate as for 43km. By foot it could take all day and the hire of a horse could cost 25–40Fr. Yet despite these difficulties the annual total of tourists had reached 12,000 by 1886.

In that year a railway to Zermatt was surveyed and a concession was granted to two banking firms in Basel and Lausanne. A definitive survey was carried out in 1887 under an engineer named Perey who presented an estimate of 5,850,000Fr. This was for a purely adhesion railway 35.885km long with maximum gradients of 45%₀, as on the Landquart–Davos Railway being projected at the same time (Ch 3), minimum radius curves of 60m and tunnels totalling 1,017m.[1]

The following year a new survey was made for a route incorporating six rack sections which reduced the tunnelling, shortened the line by 500m and reduced the cost by 498,925Fr. This, however, had to be set against an increase of 8,375Fr in annual maintenance and operating costs.[2]

The choice of a mixed rack and adhesion line was absolutely

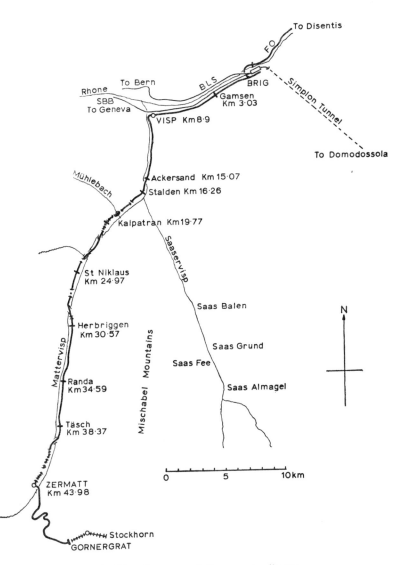

Map of Brig–Visp–Zermatt and Gornergrat railways

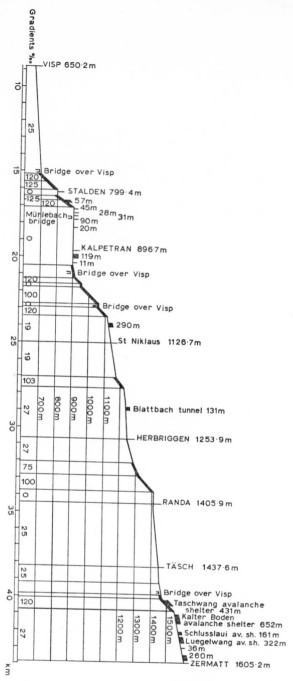

Gradients ‰

VISP 650·2m

Bridge over Visp

STALDEN 799·4m
57m
45m 28m 31m
90m
20m

Münlebach
bridge

KALPETRAN 896·7m
119m
11m

Bridge over Visp

Bridge over Visp
290m

St Niklaus 1126·7m

Blattbach tunnel 131m

HERBRIGGEN 1253·9m

RANDA 1405·9m

TÄSCH 1437·6m

Bridge over Visp
Taschwang avalanche
shelter 431m
Kalter Boden
avalanche shelter 652m
Schlusslaui av. sh. 161m
Luegelwang av. sh. 322m
36m
260m
ZERMATT 1605·2m

km

Profile of Visp–Zermatt Railway (Brig–Visp, 8.9km, omitted)

correct: the steps in the Zermatt valley are particularly steep and the narrowness of the valley precluded any satisfactory development for an adhesion line.

The contract was let at the end of 1888 to H. H. Chapuis & Stockalper, and work began in 1889.[3] In addition to several bridges over the Visp River, and a spectacular span over the Mühlebach 55m long and 44m above the stream, about 1.5km above Stalden, there were eight short tunnels totalling 263m. Bridges were mostly of steel.

On 1 July 1890 the section from Visp to Stalden was opened. From here it was planned to build a branch up the Saaser Visp valley as far as Saas Grund to serve the increasingly popular mountain resort of Saas Fee, but this was never carried out, and in the early 1950s a new motor road was built instead.

The next section, from Stalden to St Niklaus, was opened on 28 August 1890. The more difficult section from here to Zermatt came into use on 18 July 1891. The various features of the line are shown on the map and gradient profile, pp 23 and 24. The total rise from Visp to Zermatt is 955m, and the length 35.3km of which 27.61km is adhesion worked and 7.44km is equipped with Abt double rack. The steepest adhesion gradient is 20%o and rack 125%o. The original track was laid with 24kg/m rails on steel sleepers 1.85m long. Rack rails were 20mm thick on inclines up to 100%o and 25mm on steeper pitches.

The views from the train all the way up the valley are somewhat restricted. There are many delightful views of the river, sometimes only a few metres below the railway, at other times far below in a deep gorge, but not until the train is almost in Zermatt does the traveller get his first glimpse of the Matterhorn, a majestic peak and one of the most thrilling sights in the Alps.

Eight steam locomotives were built by Schweizerische Lokomotiv & Maschinenfabrik (SLM), Winterthur, to a design by Roman Abt. They were 0–4–2 tanks as shown in the drawing on p 26, with separate two-cylinder engines, one for the running wheels and one for the rack. Driving wheels were 900mm diameter. The rack mechanism was mounted on a separate frame independent of the springs so that the depth of contact with the rack was unaffected. The two rack wheels, 688mm pitch circle

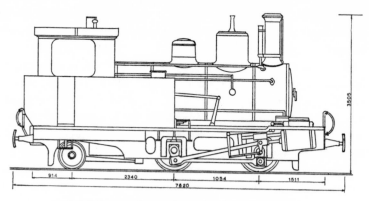

0–4–2T steam locomotive, Visp–Zermatt Railway

diameter, were connected by coupling rods. The engines had a maximum speed of 40kph on adhesion and 12kph on the rack and could pull 45 tons or three bogie coaches. Particulars of the engines were as follows:

No	Name	Date	Works No	Superheated	Wdn
1	*Matterhorn*	1890	609		1929
2	*Monte Rosa*	1890	610	1913	1929
3	*Mischabel*	1890	611	1925	1929
4	*Gornergrat*	1890	612		1929
5	*St Theodule*	1893	796	1916	1929
6	*Weisshorn*	1902	1410	1924	1929
7	*Breithorn*	1906	1725	1921	
8	*Lyskamm*	1908	1947	1915	1935

Principal dimensions:	1–6	7–8
Cylinders, adhesion engine, diameter mm	320	320
rack engine	360	360
stroke, mm	450	450
Tubes, before superheating, number	166	166
after superheating, small, number	92	92
large	10	10
Grate area, sq m	1.2	1.2
Heating surface, total before superheating, sq m	64.8	64.8
superheater, sq m	10.8	10.8
total with superheater, sq m	63.5	63.5
Water capacity, cu m	2.5	2.5
Coal capacity, tons	1.3	1.3
Length over buffers, m	7.624	7.636
Weight in working order, tons	29.0	31.7

Braking on descents was by air pressure in the cylinders. A hand brake operated on all wheels and a Hardy–Schmidt continuous air brake controlled the train.

All passenger and goods vehicles ran on bogies, one of which had a rack wheel for braking. On adhesion stretches a maximum speed of 40kph was maintained, and on the rack 6.5kph up and only 5kph down. The total journey time up or down was about $2\frac{1}{2}$ hours.

In 1924 the VZ became a partner in a syndicate to rescue the Furka–Oberalp Railway (Ch 11) and in 1925 the VZ, Gornergrat, FO and Schöllenen railways combined in an operating partnership which continued until 31 December 1960.

In its early years the railway operated above St Niklaus from 1 May to 15 September only. Three trains ran each way daily with extras at the height of the tourist season. The first winter trains to Zermatt ran in December 1928, but it was not until 1933 that a regular all-year-round service was established.

THE GORNERGRAT RAILWAY (GGB)

As mentioned in Chapter 1, with the opening of the vz the number of tourists increased rapidly and soon engineers were busy with schemes for railways to the summit of the Gornergrat, 3,136m, and even the Matterhorn, 4,481m. In fact six days before the first train steamed into St Niklaus, on 22 August 1890, a concession for these railways was sought by Leo Heer-Bétrix, a book printer in Biel.

In a report on Wallis railway projects in 1891 the engineer Xaver Imfeld (1853–1909) gave details of the schemes.[4] Both railways were to have a common section from Zermatt to a station at Moos, 1,670m. From here a funicular would take Gornergrat passengers to the Riffelalp where they would change to an electric track railway to the summit. Matterhorn passengers would travel by funicular railway to the Schafbergsee, 2,320m, then by an electric track railway to the Whymper Hut, 3,140m. From here another funicular in a tunnel with a gradient of 75.5 per cent (1 in 1.3), which the editor of *Schweizerische Bauzeitung* described as a lift shaft rather than a tunnel, would take passengers to the summit, 4,477m, where there would be galleries, a restaurant and sleeping cabins. The cost of the Gornergrat railway was estimated at 1,887,000Fr and of the Matterhorn railway 4,132,000Fr, both for construction only and excluding the common section to Moos, buildings and rolling stock. As Heer-Bétrix had by then died, a concession was granted to Imfeld on 20 June 1892.

While there could be little objection to a railway up the Gornergrat which, after all, was accessible to anyone with the energy to walk up, the Matterhorn was different, and the idea of this formidable stronghold being taken over by wealthy pleasure seekers aroused furious opposition from alpine climbers. However, the project was defeated by its cost and was officially abandoned in February 1895.

A portion of the concession was taken up in February 1894 by August Haag of Biel and in the same year the building contractors Haag & Greulich undertook to finance the construction of the Gornergrat railway. During the following winter the project was fully worked out, for a continuous metre gauge rack railway from Zermatt station to the summit and, in view of the abundant

GORNERGRAT RAILWAY

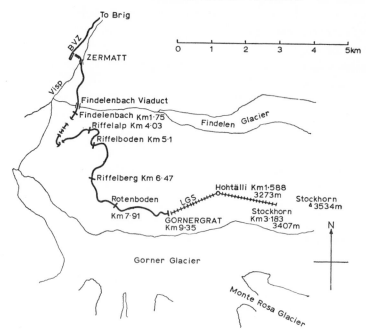

Map of Gornergrat Railway

water power, electric operation was decided upon. Construction costs were estimated at 3,500,000Fr and operation costs at 84,000Fr a year. In 1895 a Zurich banking consortium provided the building capital, 1,500,000Fr in debentures and Fr2 million in shares. Following a decision to harness the Findelenbach for hydro-electric power a further sum of 100,000Fr was granted for electrification. On 11 June 1896 the contract for construction was awarded to Haag & Greulich for Fr3 million with the stipulation that the line was to be ready with electrical equipment and rolling stock by 1 July 1898. Karl Greulich (1847–1907), one of the leading European railway engineers, was appointed to supervise construction.

The wet summer of 1896 caused delays, but progress was made with foundations for the bridges over the Visp and Findelenbach. During the following winter the tunnels were bored, entirely in hard rock, about 150 workers being housed in barracks at about 2,000m. The following summer was better and over 1,100 workers, mainly Italians, were engaged.

The biggest job was the Findelen viaduct at km1.9, shown in the drawing below. The piers and abutments, erected in two and a half months, were founded on rock and built entirely in

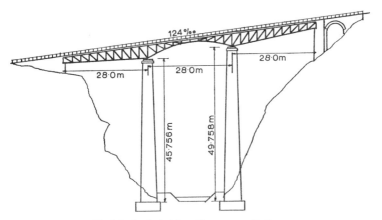

Findelenbach bridge, Gornergrat Railway

ashlar, consuming some 2,300cu m. Work had already begun on the original design for a stone arched viaduct when, on the advice of Arbenz-Zollikofer and Edward Locher (1840–1910, engineer of the Pilatus Railway and designer of the horizontal double rack named after him), a steel superstructure with centre cantilever span was substituted to facilitate rapid erection during the very short summer season. This was begun on 11 August 1897. The two complete halves were erected on timber staging and then pushed out over the piers until the short centre span could be secured. On 18 October the first material train crossed the bridge and on 31 October construction was completed. The viaduct is straight, and on a gradient of $124\%_0$.

The first three tunnels were left unlined. The curved Unteralp tunnel, in broken rock and rubble and on a $200\%_0$ gradient, was a difficult job and had to be bored from the lower end and lined throughout. Timber, sand and cement had to be carried on mules from Zermatt so that every cubic metre of sand cost 62Fr at the tunnel. Between km1 and 4.8 about 36,000cu m of dry stone footing walls had to be erected. The four straight tunnels totalled 168m and the Unteralp tunnel 171m, making only 3.6 per cent of the length of the railway. The GGB boasts of being the highest railway in Europe *unter freiem Himmel* (out in the open).

Permanent way material was supplied by Roman Abt of the Union Dortmund. Rails were 26kg/m and as all curves were laid to a uform 80m radius only three lengths were required, 10.8m on straights and others for inside and outside curves. Steel sleepers were used on ballast 30cm deep.

During construction an 0–4–2 steam locomotive was obtained (SLM 748, 1892) from the Aix-les-Bains Railway, France. It was numbered 8 on the GGB in 1905 and was retained as a service or assistance engine. Cylinders, 300mm diameter by 550mm stroke beside the boiler, drove the outside cranks by vertical levers in front. Other principal dimensions were: wheels 653mm and 520mm; coupled wheelbase 1,410mm, total 3,000mm; heating surface 36.5sq m; grate area 0.67sq m; tubes 156, 1,920mm long; working pressure 14atm; weight in working order 16.5 tons; maximum speed 9kph.

In 1912 it was transferred to the Villars–Chesières–Bretaye Railway, Switzerland, as a construction engine, and in 1918 was sold to the Monistrol–Monserat Railway, Spain, becoming No 6. It was withdrawn in 1957.[5]

In January 1896 the principal European electrical firms were invited to compete for the supply of electrical equipment and rolling stock. Five schemes were submitted, four dc and one three-phase ac, and were examined by Professor H. J. Weber in Zurich on whose advice the contract for three-phase ac equipment was awarded to Brown Boveri & Co (BBC), hydraulic equipment, turbines and alternators to Theodor Bell & Co of Kriens, and the mechanical portion of the locomotives and cars to SLM in conjunction with Schweizerische Industrie Gesellschaft (SIG), Neuhausen.

The power house was situated beside the Findelenbach 100m below the railway where the water has a fall of 105m at a rate of 1,000 litres a second, and provided space for four turbines and generators. Three were provided by Bell, each of 250hp at 400rpm, driving three-phase alternators producing current at 5,400V, 40Hz. Three 180kW transformers, at km2, 5 and 8, provided line current at 540V. Feeders and the twin contact lines were 8mm thick. The rails formed the third phase. Feeder lines took a more direct route. Electrical installation began as soon as trains could cross the Findelenbach viaduct, on 18 October 1897, and was completed in four weeks, current being supplied on 20 November.

Each of the three four-wheeled locomotives, weighing 10.5 tons, had two 500V three-phase motors each giving 90hp at 800rpm. Two hand brakes, on running wheels and rack, were

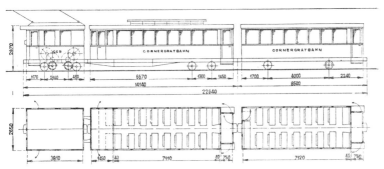

Original Gornergrat Railway train (*GGB Brig*)

fitted in addition to an electric brake operated automatically if speed exceeded the permitted maximum of 7kph. When descending the motors acted as generators, and a bank of resistances was automatically switched in at the power station to take up excess current. The motors were rigidly mounted on an unsprung chassis, the locomotive forming the lower bogie of the closed sixty-seat car. This pushed the open four-wheeled fifty-seat car.[6] Dimensions are shown in the diagram on p 31. A fourth locomotive was obtained in 1902 and a fifth in 1930.

The first experimental runs were made on 20–25 November 1897, but heavy snow early in 1898 delayed the opening, fixed for 1 July, until 20 August.[7] Trains took 1½ hours in each direction. At the end of its first season, on 3 October 1898, the railway had carried 10,590 passengers. The operating season extended from 1 June to about the end of September.

From the lower terminus, immediately outside the vz station at a height of 1,604m, the railway climbed 1,414m in 9.029km. The summit station, however, at 3,018m, was still 118m below the mountain summit. In 1905 it was decided to raise the upper terminus, lengthening the line by 310m to a new station at a height of 3,089m, only 47m below the summit. This was opened on 1 June 1909, making the total length of the line 9,339m. Passing loops were provided at Findelenbach, Riffelboden and Rotenboden, the last opened in 1917 at the request of the Swiss Alpine Club. The first hotel at the summit, with forty-three rooms and seventy beds, opened in 1910.

To connect the railway with the Hotel Riffelalp an electric tramway 468m long with a gauge of 80cm was built by A. Seiler & Co at a cost of 50,000Fr and opened in July 1899. It was unique in being a three-phase system and both the highest and the shortest in Switzerland. The journey took three minutes.[8] The hotel was burnt down in February 1961 and the tramway was abandoned.

For thirty years the GGB ran only in summer. From 25 December 1928 to 11 February 1929 the first winter service was established between Zermatt and Riffelalp. The following winter it was extended to Riffelboden and continued to the end of March.

In connection with the electrification of the vz in 1929–30

Page 33. (Above) Zermatt
train leaving Brig behind
locomotive No 14. On
the left is FO electric baggage
car No 51 *Disentis;* (left)
Gornergrat Railway single-unit
railcars on the 1963 double
track section near the summit,
with a view of the Matterhorn
(p 37)

Page 34. (Above) Mixed train from St Moritz to Chur, behind a 2–8–0 steam locomotive, crossing Schmittentobel viaduct on the Albula railway. Landwasser viaduct beyond; (below) a view of the spirals between Bergün and Preda on the Albula railway (p 73)

the electrical equipment of the GGB was reconstructed. The voltage was increased to 725 and the frequency to 50Hz. The power station was modernised and each turbine drove two generators, one supplying three-phase current at 50Hz, the other single-phase at $16\frac{2}{3}$Hz. So power not needed for the GGB could be transferred to the VZ by an arrangement with the SBB, from which the VZ obtained its main supply (p 39).

Locomotives 1–4 were rebuilt with motors giving a total output of 260hp, raising the speed to 8.5kph. No 5 (1930) was supplied for 725V, with two motors totalling 250hp. These made possible a reduction in journey time from ninety to seventy minutes. The cars were rebuilt with larger windows. In 1935 two special wagons for skis were placed in service and in 1945 a third, each carrying 120 pairs of skis.

In June 1939 work began on a 770m snow gallery between Riffelboden and Riffelberg under the engineer Paul Schneller. Four-fifths were completed by September, the remainder in 1946 after various wartime interruptions. From the winter of 1941–2 the gallery roof was used as a ski run, but for the 1951–2 season a new ski run was built just below the railway, passing through a 72m rock tunnel below the Riffelberg.[9] This track frequently arouses the curiosity of visitors who wonder if it is an earlier course of the railway.

In March 1942 a service to the summit was established for the first time so early in the year. To maintain a winter service to the summit a powerful snow plough was needed, and in 1943 one, No 3931, was constructed by SLM/MFO (Maschinenfabrik Oerlikon); it has two electrically driven rotary snow ploughs but is not self-propelled. The body swivels on the chassis and does not, therefore, require a turntable.

The first of the new single railcars, by SLM/BBC, was delivered in 1947. There are now twelve, numbered 3011–22, the last entering service in 1961. The two motors give a total 260hp at 4.8kph, and the cars have a maximum speed of 14.5kph. They carry fifty-six passengers seated and fifty-four standing, a total equal to that of the old locomotive combinations, and have a tare weight of only 17.7 tons. Two close-coupled double railcars, 3041–2, appeared in 1966; mechanically and electrically they

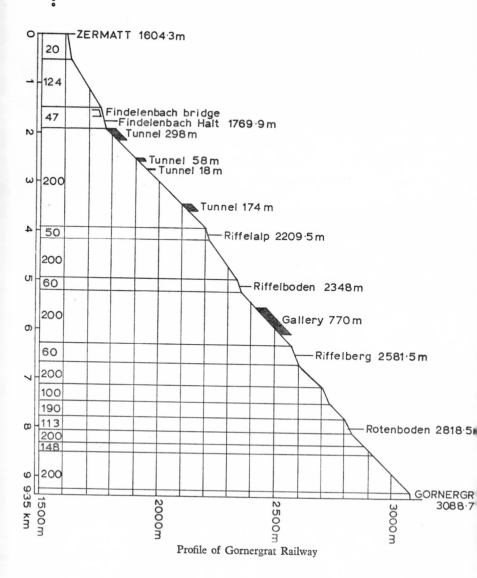

Max gradient ‰

ZERMATT 1604·3m
20
124
47 — Findelenbach bridge
— Findelenbach Halt 1769·9m
Tunnel 298m
Tunnel 58m
Tunnel 18m
200
Tunnel 174m
50 — Riffelalp 2209·5m
200
60 — Riffelboden 2348m
200 Gallery 770m
60 — Riffelberg 2581·5m
200
100
190
113 — Rotenboden 2818·5
200
148
200
935 km GORNERGR
1500m 2000m 2500m 3000m 3088·7

Profile of Gornergrat Railway

are identical with the single cars, and can make the journey to the summit in forty-one–fifty minutes. Like the old stock, they are painted light brown. All the old cars were scrapped, together with locomotives 4 and 5. The remaining locomotives were renumbered 3001–3 in 1966; the end which supported the passenger car was loaded with a concrete block, and they are now used for shunting at Zermatt and for works trains.

In 1963 the section from Riffelberg to the site of the old summit station was doubled (see photograph p 33). A second snow plough, 3032, was built in 1970 by Martin Beilhack, Rosenheim, West Germany; it is similar to 3931, but the plough unit can be raised or lowered.

Mountain railway operation

On Swiss mountain railways of the rack type where speeds are low, perhaps no more than 8–15kph up or down, signals are hardly required. However, a clearly defined operating code is employed to ensure safety on single lines. The motive power unit is always at the lower end of the train where non-powered coaches are used. Sometimes several trains may be operated to one timetabled service. When this happens a green head disc with a slanting white stripe is carried on the front of each portion except the last so that at passing places the station staff and train crews know that there is more than one train to cross. On practically all mountain lines of this type timetable and train order working is the general rule.

A journey up the Gornergrat Railway is one of the most rewarding mountain railway trips in Switzerland. The Matterhorn dominates the scene throughout most of the journey, with increasingly magnificent views of the surrounding peaks as the train climbs. At the summit is a glorious 360 degree panorama in which the most striking feature is the gleaming mass of Monte Rosa, 4,638m, to the south-east. The Gorner and Grenz glaciers sweep down on either side of it. To the south are Lyskam and Breithorn, and the east face of the Matterhorn rears up above the Furgg Glacier to the west. In the north the great range of the Bernese Oberland is partly hidden by the Mischabel range which separates the valleys of the Saaser Visp and Matter Visp.

If the visitor has the time and energy to spare he is recommended to return on foot to Zermatt via the Findelen valley, with views of the Findelen Glacier, eventually emerging above the great Findelen viaduct.

ELECTRIFICATION OF THE VISP–ZERMATT RAILWAY
AND EXTENSION TO BRIG

The slow journey between Visp and Zermatt with the small 0–4–2 steam locomotives led to early proposals for electrification using, for economy reasons, the chassis of the steam locomotives on which to build electric power units. This idea fortunately came to nothing. In November 1926 new proposals were made to electrify the line at 2,000 or 3,000V dc using motor coaches but, after further discussion and in view of the possibility of a future link via the Furka–Oberalp with the Rhaetian Railway which had then electrified its network at 11,000V single-phase ac, $16\frac{2}{3}$Hz, it was decided to adopt a similar system using current at 10,500V. An order was placed with MFO for six locomotives, Nos 11–16, the first of which was delivered in August 1929.

The specification posed some interesting design problems, requiring about 650hp and a maximum axle load of 12 tons. A Bo-Bo type was produced, as shown in the drawing below.[10] Four 230V ac motors gave a total of 640hp (one hour rating) or 560hp (continuous rating). Wheels are 926mm diameter, bogie wheelbase 2,010mm, total wheelbase 8,720mm, length over buffers 14,100mm. For working on both adhesion and rack sections the motors drive on to a common shaft through a friction clutch. The intermediate shaft carries two pinions, one engaging with a gear wheel on the driving axle of the running wheels with a

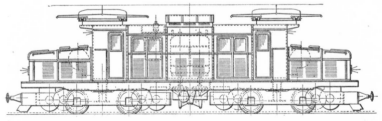

Bo–Bo electric locomotive, Visp–Zermatt Railway
(*The Engineer*)

ratio of 1:6.2, the other through a ratio of 1:5.6 with a gear wheel bolted to the rack wheel, rotating freely on the driving axle. On adhesion sections the rack wheel rotates idly, and on rack sections both adhesion and rack wheels drive. The bogies and other mechanical parts were supplied by SLM.

The locomotives weighed 48 tons and could haul 60 tons on adhesion stretches at a maximum speed of 45kph. Speed up the racks was greatly increased: 20kph up to 70‰, 18–15kph up to 110‰ and 14kph up to 125‰. A photograph of No 14 is shown on page 33.

The superstructure included two cabs, a centre transformer compartment and a small compartment for two tons of luggage behind one of the cabs. The Hardy vacuum brake was provided together with two hand brakes and an electric rheostatic brake for controlling speed on descents. To apply this the four motors were connected in series and separately excited by a direct current varied by the master controller. The braking resistances were cooled by the transformer air cooling system. The dead man safety device when released brought into operation both rim and rack brakes and opened the main circuit breaker.

Electric power was obtained from the SBB at Visp. The first test trains ran on 9 August 1929 when it was found that the overall journey time could be cut from 2hr 5min to 1hr 35min.[11] Locomotives 11–14 were delivered in 1929, No 15 in 1930 and 16 in 1939. Full electric services began on 1 October 1929.

Steam locomotives 1–5 and 8 were sold to Rumania and Ethiopia. No 6 was sold in 1941 to HOVAG, Ems, Chur. No 7 is retained at Zermattt as a spare and it is occasionally used on specials.

By 1941 all six electric locomotives had been rebuilt to give a total output of 800hp, and by 1960 this had been increased to 928hp. On 25 January 1952 locomotive No 16 was wrecked in an avalanche between Zermatt and Täsch. A new locomotive was built in replacement, outwardly resembling the Furka–Oberalp locomotives (Ch 11) but utilising the original transformer, controllers, motors and other salvaged material. It thus still has the same power rating, but a maximum speed of 50kph on adhesion.

RECONSTRUCTION AND MODERNISATION
In conjuction with the electrification the vz was extended to Brig alongside the SBB to link with the Furka–Oberalp Railway. The electrified extension of 8.5km was opened on 6 June 1930, making possible the running of through trains between Zermatt and St Moritz. In 1931 the Glacier Express was introduced, always so named, in English, running in summer only between Zermatt and St Moritz. For these services the Brig–Visp–Zermatt (BVZ) introduced some fine modern corridor coaches 15m long, seating ten first and twenty-four second class passengers, yet weighing only 15 tons tare. Large windows gave unobstructed views and folding tables allowed refreshment to be served to passengers in their seats.[12]

The development of Zermatt as a winter sports centre made it necessary to reconstruct the railway above St Niklaus for operation throughout the year. This was stimulated by an avalanche in the winter of 1931–2 which buried the line between Täsche and Zermatt. A bridge over the Blattbach which had to be dismantled every winter was replaced by a section of line in the Blattbach tunnel, 130.78m, at km27.55. Two concrete avalanche shelters 200 and 250m long were followed by a third smaller gallery and a fourth of 150m joined to an artificial tunnel of 110m. The work was completed in the autumn of 1933 at a total cost of 900,000Fr, making possible the establishment of an all the year round service.[13]

A vast programme of renewals and reconstruction was undertaken after the war. All the galleries were lengthened and are now as follows: Tschongbach gallery, 115.3m (1962) at km19.7; Täschwang gallery, 430.7m (1932, 1953–4) at km40.36; Kalter Boden gallery, 652m (1933, extended 1953), and Schilten gallery, 652.42m (1946, 1952–3) from km41.24; Schusslaui gallery, 160.9m (1933, 1937, 1955) from km42.4; and Lugelwang gallery, 322.5m (1932, 1955–6) from km42.7.

In 1945 the steel Kipfen bridge at km21 was destroyed by an avalanche and was replaced in 1947 by a new bridge. The steel Mühlebach bridge at km17.86 was renewed in concrete in 1959, and in 1960 the two bridges over the Faulkinn Ravine were replaced by pre-stressed concrete beams. Selli bridge was renewed in reinforced concrete in 1961 and the Visp bridge above Täsch at km40 by pre-stressed beams in 1963–4.

Renewal of the entire track with rails of 36 and 30kg/m, with additional sidings and passing loops, was completed in 1965. The workshops at Visp were modernised in 1956 and a new locomotive depot was built in 1961.

From 1950–5 the number of passengers increased from 317,000 to 536,000 and by 1964 was 1,055,000. To cope with this increase two six-axle articulated railcars, 2031–2, were obtained from SLM/SIG/SAAS (Ateliers de Sécheron SA, Geneva) in 1960. The six motors give a total output of 1,200hp with a maximum speed of 55kph on adhesion and 30kph on racks. The cars measure 32.3m over buffers, weigh 69 tons and seat twelve first and eighty second class passengers. In 1965 three eight-axle double railcar units, 2041–3, were obtained from the same makers. They have eight motors with a total output of 1,600hp, measure 36.1m over buffers, weigh 86 tons and have twelve first and ninety-six second class seats. The railcar units have enough power to haul ordinary coaches to form normal length trains. For shunting at Visp and Zermatt two diesel tractors were obtained, 2921 in 1957 and 2922 in 1959.

The renewals and reconstruction were undertaken only on a guarantee from the Federal and Cantonal authorities that no road would be built up the Visp valley above Stalden, but this undertaking lapsed in 1952. On the granting of a concession, in July 1961, for the construction of a motor road from St Niklaus to Täsch the BVZ sought to turn this to its advantage and obtained a concession to run a bus service between Visp and Herbriggen. Since 30 May 1965 the BVZ has maintained an hourly local bus service between Visp and St Niklaus and runs a school bus between Visp and Stalden.

A road is now open to Täsch where there is a vast car park. Motorists travel from there to Zermatt by train. It is possible that the odd one might even walk. Further proposals to continue the road into Zermatt, although receiving local and Federal approval, were rejected by referendum in 1973. Zermatt has now grown beyond recognition, and for those of us who knew and loved the place as a quiet mountain village before 1950 it is ruined. For the sake of monetary gain one of Europe's treasures has been destroyed. But the BVZ has no cause to complain: in 1971 revenue was 12,088,000Fr, against an expenditure of 8,910,000Fr. It is the only one of these metre gauge main lines which makes a profit.

At Brig the trains run into the south side of an island platform —a dead end as far as passenger trains are concerned—in the middle of the broad street outside the main line station, with road traffic rushing past on both sides and at both ends. FO trains use the north face of the platform. Beyond this is a connection to the SBB goods yard belonging to the FO and worked by its four-wheeled electric shunting locomotives. A pedestrian crossing leads directly to the booking hall of the main station and to the subway beneath the platforms. Connections between the BVZ and FO trains and and those of the SBB and BLS are excellent.

In 1962 BVZ placed a contract with Integra Ltd of Wallisellen for the installation of a centralised traffic control system extending from Brig to Zermatt, with a control office at Brig. Work began in 1963 and the Brig–Stalden section came into operation on 16 November 1965, Stalden–St Niklaus on 17 May 1966 and the remainder during that autumn.

The railway is divided into eleven block posts and nine automatic crossing stations and is controlled by sixty-seven main signals. For shunting operations any station can be switched to a local control desk.

THE STOCKHORN AERIAL ROPEWAY

On 18 August 1954 a concession was obtained for an aerial ropeway from the Gornergrat to the Stockhorn, 4.5km to the east. Work began at the end of May 1955 and the 1.6km section from the Gornergrat to Hohtälli station, 3,273m, was opened on 9 August 1956 for materials and on 8 March 1957 to the public. The journey takes $5\frac{1}{2}$min.

The second section of 2.6km to the Stockhorn terminus at a height of 3,407m was begun at the end of August 1957 and opened on 23 October 1958; journey time is 8min. The total cost was 2,300,000Fr. The Stockhorn cable line is the highest open air transport in the Swiss Alps exceeded only by the Jungfrau Railway. From the end of the ropeway an interesting walk of about an hour to the summit of the Stockhorn, 3,534m, is rewarded by unrivalled mountain views. The Luftseilbahn Gornergrat-Stockhorn (LGS), like the Gornergrat Railway, is operated by the BVZ. The administration of the BVZ and its operating subsidiaries is now centred at a fine new building in Brig, opened in 1965.

In the summer of 1972 there were eight expresses from Brig to Zermatt and six from Zermatt to Brig, taking from 1hr 21min to 1hr 25min. Also there were nine stopping passenger or mixed trains from Brig to Zermatt and twelve back to Brig, taking 1hr 36min to 1hr 43min, and from six to nine goods or service trains each way, these mostly terminating at Visp where freight traffic is exchanged with the SBB. On the GGB there were twenty return trips taking 40–45min, and a similar number of return trips on the LGS.

CHAPTER 3

The Beginnings of the Rhaetian System

THE Rhaetian Railway owes its origin to a Dutch businessman, Willem Jan Holsboer, born on 23 August 1834, founder of the spa of Davos. Since the opening of the main line railway through Landquart in 1858 traffic between there and Davos had increased steadily, and in 1872 Holsboer conceived the idea of a standard gauge branch from Landquart to Davos. Two years later the engineer Bavier of Chur worked out a scheme with a ruling gradient of 40‰ and minimum curves of 180m radius at an estimated cost of 12,500,000Fr. Traffic prospects were insufficient to justify such an outlay, so a cheaper project was evolved in 1876 by the engineer Lutz, but again nothing more was done.

By 1886 the number of people travelling from Landquart to Davos had reached 59,330, of which 19,982 used the horse postal service, about 5,000 used private vehicles and the remainder, about 35,000, walked. Goods handled at Landquart for Klosters and Davos amounted to 13,870 tons, worth 459,763Fr in terms of railway traffic.

It was now decided to economise by building a metre gauge railway and to extend it to become an international line from Landquart to Chiavenna in Italy via Davos and the Scaletta and Maloja passes. The German engineer C. W. Wetzel (1857–1928) was placed in charge of the Landquart–Davos section and on 15

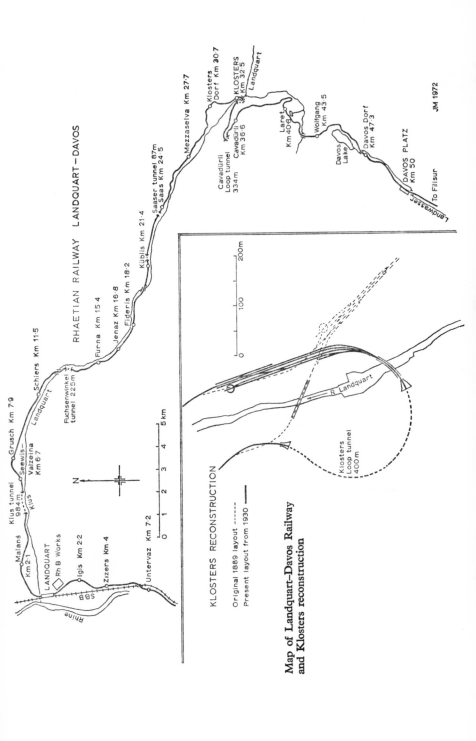

RHAETIAN RAILWAY   LANDQUART–DAVOS

Rhine

LANDQUART
Rh B Works
SBB

Malans Km 2·1
Klus tunnel 984m
Seewis–
Klus
Grusch Km 7·9
Valzeina Km 6·7
Schiers Km 11·5
Landquart
Fuchsenwinkel tunnel 225m

Igis Km 2·2
Zizers Km 4
Untervaz Km 7·2

N

0 1 2 3 4 5 km

Furna Km 15·4
Jenaz Km 16·8
Fideris Km 18·2
Kublis Km 21·4
Saaser tunnel 87m
Saas Km 24·5
Mezzaselva Km 27·7
Klosters Dorf Km 20·7
KLOSTERS Km 32·5
Landquart
Cavadurli Loop tunnel 334m
Cavadurli Km 36·6
Laret Km 40·9
Wolfgang Km 43·5
Davos Lake
Davos Dorf Km 47·3
DAVOS PLATZ Km 50
To Filisur
Landwasser

JM 1972

KLOSTERS RECONSTRUCTION

Original 1889 layout ------
Present layout from 1930 ——

0   100   200m

R Landquart

Klosters Loop tunnel 400m

**Map of Landquart–Davos Railway
and Klosters reconstruction**

October 1886 he submitted a project including three rack sections, of $91\%_0$ between Klosters and Laret, of $100\%_0$ between Laret and Wolfgang and $81.9\%_0$ between Wolfgang and Davos Lake. Subsequently it was decided that the saving in distance by rack sections was insufficient to justify the additional maintenance costs and the complexities of locomotives and operation. So an adhesion scheme was adopted with maximum gradients of $45\%_0$ which was worked out by May 1887.

There was virtually no choice of route; the railway had to follow the Landquart valley, through the narrow gorge known as the Klus into the Prättigau (in Romansch, Val Pratens, or valley of meadows). Beyond Küblis came a stiff climb to Klosters and an even stiffer one to cross the 1,634m watershed into the Davos valley.

The terrain was unfavourable to railway construction. The Klus gorge, about 1.5km long about 5km from Landquart, with sides towering 600m above, was barely wide enough for the river and road, and the railway had to be built out of the river bed along the right bank. Above here the valley floor consisted of compacted scree, and around Klosters treacherous beds of schist were to prove troublesome. Beyond in the Stützalpbach valley friable serpentine rock had to be overcome. Although little trouble was expected from snow, which in most years did not exceed 0.7m, cuttings were avoided as much as possible.

On 15 October 1887 the contract for the entire line was awarded to Thomas Holzmann & Co and Jakob Mast of Zurich and by the end of the year drawings to a scale of $1:2,000$ were completed. The route is shown on the map on p 45 while heights, tunnels, etc are shown on the gradient profiles on pp 48 and 49.

Of the total estimated cost of Fr7 million the local communities contributed 1 million through the subvention of 12 September 1886. Annual traffic receipts were estimated at 700,000Fr. By the concession of 7 February 1888 the Landquart–Davos Narrow Gauge Railway Company was formed in Basle under the direction of Achilles Schucan.

Schucan, who was to become the presiding genius of the Rhaetian Railway for the next thirty years, was born in Arignon in southern France on 1 March 1844. After moving to the Engadin, he completed his education at Zurich, achieving distinction in engineering. He began his railway career with the Swiss Railway Department and from 1885 spent three years setting the poverty stricken Seetal Railway on its feet.

Schucan and Wetzel set up headquarters at Küblis on 1 May 1888 and on 29 June work began. The formation through the Klus was carried out in the winter, while the water was low, using 35,000cu m of dry stonework. Halfway through the gorge a halt was provided for Felsenbach. Between Landquart and Küblis the railway crosses the Landquart River in three places by plate girder bridges, that beyond Schiers leading straight into the Fuchsenwinkel tunnel. Beyond here the valley opens out, to close in again at the Fidiser gorge. Here again the line was built close beside the river, crossing it again just before Küblis.

A far as this the gradients were kept down to a maximum of $35\%_0$, but beyond Küblis a gradient of $43\%_0$ had to be used on the climb to Klosters. Along this treacherous slope drainage is a perpetual problem. Tremendous footing and retaining walls were needed. Between Sernius and Klosters Dorf the Saaser Alpbach is crossed at a height of 22m by the longest span bridge on the line, 40m.

Klosters is an attractively situated little town of about 2,100 population. Its name, meaning Cloisters, derives from the convent of St Jakob which was suppressed in 1528. The original station here was a terminus on a site south east of the present station. Trains had to reverse, and then leave by a lattice girder bridge over the Landquart, of two outer spans of 22m and two inner ones of 28.6m, crossing the river at a height of about 21m on a gradient of $21\%_0$. (Plan, p ·45.)

Considerable development work was needed above here to keep the gradient to a maximum of $45\%_0$. In the Cavadürli Loop tunnel, on a radius of 100m, the gradient is eased to $35\%_0$. Boring this tunnel was a wicked job, with ventilation problems from the lower end and drainage from the upper. Here the line leaves the Landquart and climbs the valley of the Stützalpbach.

At km39.7 is a further loop of 100m radius in the open, on a gradient of $40\%_0$, leading into Davos Laret station. At Wolfgang the summit is reached and the line descends past Davos

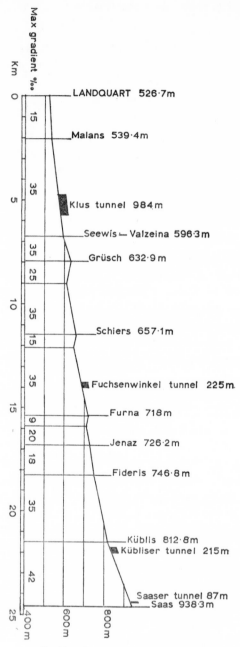

Max gradient %

Km

LANDQUART 526·7m

15

Malans 539·4m

35

Klus tunnel 984 m

Seewis — Valzeina 596·3m

35

Grüsch 632·9 m

25

35

Schiers 657·1m

15

35

Fuchsenwinkel tunnel 225m

Furna 718 m

9

20

Jenaz 726·2m

18

Fideris 746·8 m

35

Küblis 812·8m

Kübliser tunnel 215m

42

Saaser tunnel 87m

Saas 938·3m

400 m   600 m   800 m

Profile of Landquart–Davos Railway 1

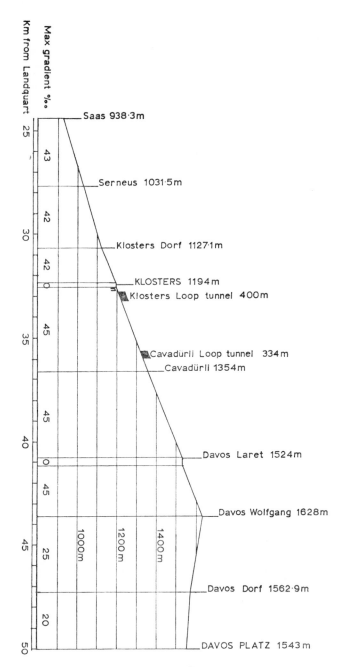

Profile of Landquart–Davos Railway 2

Lake through Davos Dorf to Davos Platz on a ruling gradient of 24%oo.[1]

The total cost of the railway, excluding locomotives and rolling stock, was 5,641,000Fr, or 112,500Fr per km. When opened, from Landquart to Klosters on 9 October 1889 and to Davos on 20 July 1890, it was the highest adhesion worked railway in Europe, and one of the steepest. At the same time the head offices were transferred to Davos with A. Schucan as managing director.

The original track consisted of Vignoles section rail weighing 23.5kg/m in 10m lengths, on sole plates on sleepers of larch or oak 1.8m × 0.2m × 0.15m, mostly from local forests. These sleepers soon proved indequate and by the end of 1904 all curves, and by 1912 the whole line, had been relaid with steel sleepers.

Station buildings were of the chalet type, in keeping with the district. Engine sheds were built at Landquart, Küblis, Klosters and Davos. All buildings were by Kuoni & Co of Chur. The steam locomotives and rolling stock will be described in Chapter 6.

During the first years of operation expensive protection, strengthening and renewal works were needed, in particular against rock falls in the Klus. The necessity for more snow protection works became apparent in February 1892 when 2.6m fell in Laret. The heavy Mallet locomotives of 1891 (Ch 6) required the strengthening of steel bridges. Worst of all, a flood on 14–15 June 1910 between Küblis and Landquart damaged about 1,650m of railway formation, deposited material along a further 3,000m, and destroyed the bridges over the Schraubach.

ENGADIN EXTENSION SCHEMES

As mentioned earlier, this railway was intended as the first section of a route through Graubünden to Italy. In 1888 two alternative schemes were prepared for a railway from Davos to St Moritz, as shown on the map on p 53. One passed beneath the Sertig Pass and the other beneath the Scaletta Pass. Maximum gradients were to be 45%oo and the curves of a minimum radius of 100m. Estimated costs were 18,500,000Fr for the Sertig and 17,500,000Fr for the Scaletta.[2]

During 1889 a third scheme was prepared for a line via Chur,

Page 51. (Above) Filisur–Davos train crossing the Wiesen viaduct. C–C type electric locomotive No 408 (p 88); (below) Robert Maillart's bridge at Klosters as built in 1930, before the strut was placed between the abutments (p 59)

Page 52. (Above) RHB Bo–Bo–Bo locomotive No 704 with a Chur–St Moritz train on the double track section between Chur and Reichenau. Notice the third rail for SBB standard gauge freight trains between Chur and Domat/ Ems works (p 135); (below) RHB C–C locomotives 413 and 407 on a Disentis– Chur train at Trun

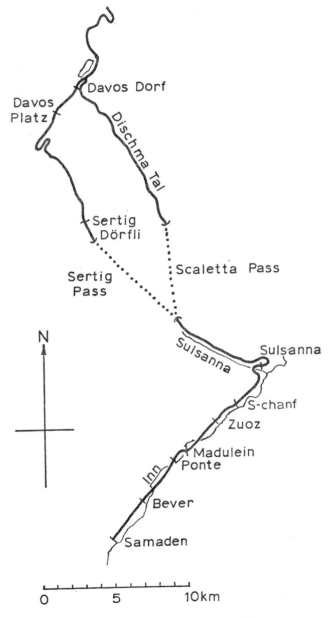

Davos Dorf

Davos
Platz

Dischma Tal

Sertig
Dörfli

Sertig
Pass

Scaletta Pass

N

Sulsanna

Sulsanna

S-chanf

Zuoz

Madulein
Ponte

Inn

Bever

Samaden

0   5   10km

Map of Davos–Samaden projects, 1888

M.G.R.—D

Thusis, Filisur and under the Albula Pass. This line would serve many more people, and by a connection from Davos to Filisur could also serve the Davos valley.

The section from Chur to Filisur was planned by Robert Moser who was to become one of the outstanding engineers of the Rhaetian Railway. He was born at Herzogenbuchsee, between Basle and Berne, on 4 April 1838 and gained his engineering diploma at Zurich in 1859. After achieving distinction with municipal works in Basle and Berne he began his railway career in 1869 on various Swiss railways including the Gotthard where he supervised construction of the northern ramp.

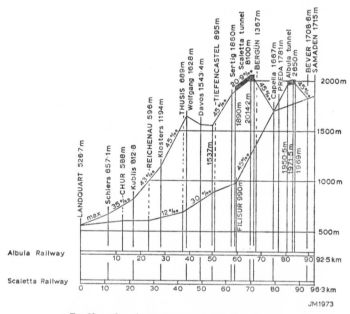

PROPOSED SCALETTA RAILWAY   Landquart - Davos - Samaden 96·3 km
ORIGINAL ALBULA RAILWAY PROJECT   Chur - Filisur - Samaden 78·8 km
1889

Profiles of early Scaletta and Albula schemes

The Albula and Scaletta projects (the Sertig was rejected) are compared in the table on p 55.

Estimates showed that the Scaletta route would cost more than the whole Albula line from Chur to Samaden plus the Davos–Filisur link.[3] Further the Scaletta route traversed high, unpopu-

	Albula Railway Chur–Samaden	Scaletta Railway Landquart–Samaden
Length of railway, km	78.5	96.35
Maximum height above sea level	1,971.5m	2,014.2m
Total rise and fall from Landquart	1,820m	2,070m
Length of tunnels (excluding summit)	2,650m	8,100m
Length of railway above 1,500m asl	22.6km	55.0km

lated valleys with heavy snowfalls. By popular vote on 24 November 1889, of 12,308 to 4,379, support was gained for the Filisur route.[4] This, however, was not the end of the matter.

Graubünden had become a victim of conflicting railway interests which caused considerable delay to further progress. A long article in *Schweizerische Bauzeitung* (9–16 May 1891) compared these struggles with those of Switzerland as a whole in the early 1850s when disputes between rival local interests made any coordination of railway schemes impossible. Many projects were fully worked out, at great expense, by eminent engineers, often with considerable danger, but could not be realised. As the above article commented, it needed a foreigner, Holsboer, to get things moving.

LANDQUART–CHUR–THUSIS

At the end of 1890 Moser prepared a long report in which he discussed the eight different schemes and strongly supported the Albula route, with a Davos–Filisur link, for constructional, financial and social reasons.[5]

At this stage Holsboer gave support to the Albula scheme as part of a united cantonal narrow gauge system, and through the enterprise of the Swiss Railway Bank in Basle the financial means became available. The bank united with the so-called Swiss Central Railway Committee which sought and obtained concessions in December 1890 (Chur–Thusis) and April 1891 (Landquart–Chur) as part of the Albula route. The line was worked out by Wetzel and Moser at an estimated cost of Fr6 million.

An exchange crisis now resulted from a referendum against the purchase of the proposed 'Swiss Central Railway', and the consequent fall in the value of railway shares caused the bank to withdraw support until the Landquart–Davos Railway had produced a dividend of $4\frac{1}{2}$ to 5 per cent for three years. In 1894

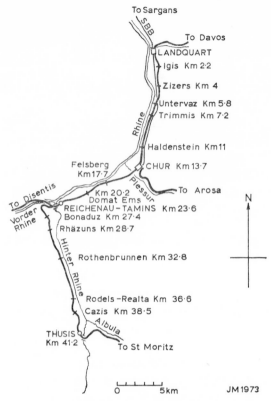

Map of RhB Landquart–Thusis

however, agreement was reached for cantonal support and construction began in that autumn.

Compared with the Davos railway the new line, following the Rhine valley through Chur to Reichenau and the Hinter Rhine from there to Thusis, presented few problems. The biggest engineering work was the bridge over the Hinter Rhine at Reichenau, built in 1895 by Theodor Bell & Co, Kriens, with spans of 44, 63 and 44m and containing 381 tons of steel. As far as Chur the railway duplicated the existing standard gauge line. The ruling gradient was 25‰ and the sharpest curves 120m radius. There were forty-one bridges of which only eight were over 10m span. The total cost was 6,283,000Fr, or 153,200Fr per km.

The section from Chur to Thusis was opened on 1 July 1896

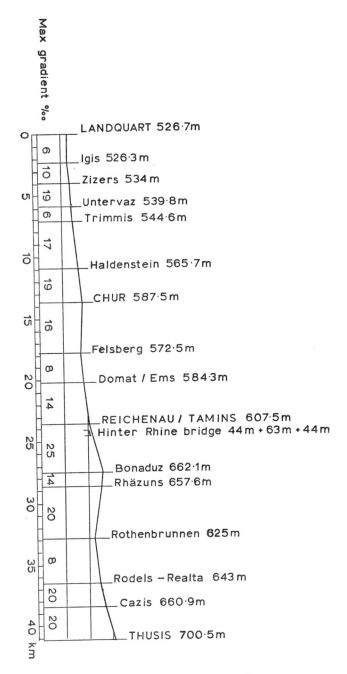

Max gradient ‰

LANDQUART 526·7m
Igis 526·3m
Zizers 534m
Untervaz 539·8m
Trimmis 544·6m

Haldenstein 565·7m

CHUR 587·5m

Felsberg 572·5m

Domat / Ems 584·3m

REICHENAU / TAMINS 607·5m
Hinter Rhine bridge 44m + 63m + 44m

Bonaduz 662·1m
Rhäzuns 657·6m

Rothenbrunnen 625m

Rodels – Realta 643m

Cazis 660·9m

THUSIS 700·5m

Profile of RHB Landquart–Thusis

and from Landquart to Chur on 29 August following. Stations, with heights and distances are shown on the map and gradient profile, pp 56 and 57. The original rails were 12m long, weighing 25kg/m, on steel sleepers.

With the Albula project now firmly established, the Landquart–Davos Narrow Gauge Railway transferred its head offices to Chur on 15 June 1896,[6] and on 2 November 1896 the company adopted the title Rhätische Bahn (RhB) or Rhaetian Railway in English and Ferrovia Retica in Italian.[7] Wetzel then resigned as engineer and took up private practice in Davos until 1898 when he became responsible for the construction and management of the Davos–Schatzalp Railway for twenty years. He died in 1928 aged 71.[8]

W. J. Holsboer, to whose initiative and energy the Rhaetian Railway owed its existence, had to forgo fulfilment of his dream of an international narrow gauge railway through Graubünden. He died in Davos, aged barely sixty-four, on 8 June 1898 just before work began on the Albula tunnel.[9]

KLOSTERS RECONSTRUCTION

Following electrification in 1920–1 (Ch 7) traffic at Klosters built up to such an extent that congestion in the station became intolerable. The longest platform was only 146m and the necessity for changing locomotives as all trains reversed caused considerable delays. In winter snow ploughs had to be turned, and in mixed trains goods vehicles remarshalled to the rear to allow passenger cars to be heated.

Early in 1929 it was decided to build a through station, a new bridge over the Landquart and a loop tunnel of 400m on a radius of 125m and a gradient of 18‰ to link up with the former route above the old bridge. Route selection was simple, but construction presented mighty problems—the ground on both banks of the Landquart at Klosters is waterlogged and unstable.

The entire contract including station, bridge and tunnel was let to Prader & Co of Zurich. The tunnel, begun in November 1929, was bored from the lower end only to assist drainage, and had to be lined throughout in concrete with 60cm walls and roof and a 35cm invert. It was completed in September 1930.

The new bridge was designed in reinforced concrete by Robert Maillart (1872–1940), one of the pioneers of light-weight concrete arch construction and one of the most famous of Swiss bridge builders.[10]

For its lightness and elegance the bridge was an astonishing achievement, with a central arch of 30m span and 7.9m rise, supporting the railway deck which was lying on a curve of 125m radius. In plan the arch decreased from 5.5m wide at the ends to 3.6m in the centre and its thickness varied from only 34cm to 26cm. The bridge was begun in May 1930 and completed in September. Its total length is 75m and it carries the rails 17m above the river bed. It is the only Maillart bridge on the RHB. See photograph on page 51.

The new station was begun on 8 April 1930 and was completed on 24 October. It has five platforms 240m long. On 3 November the complete new layout was brought into use. The old Landquart bridge was retained as a footway.[11] (See diagram p 45.)

Early in 1938 inspection of the new bridge revealed cracks in most of the sections, in fact it was in danger of collapse. The RhB immediately appointed Prof F. Hübner, bridge inspector, to make a report. The foundations on both banks were slipping inwards, and the tunnel was also moving under enormous pressure.

After four years of close observations two solutions were proposed, one of which was to replace the bridge by a steel span. To the eternal credit of the RhB, however, out of respect for Maillart who had died on 5 April 1940, it was decided to retain his bridge and build a concrete footbridge beneath the arch, braced to it by steel wires, to act as a strut between the abutments; to build sole plates between the foundations on the left bank and an additional abutment behind that of the main arch on the right bank. As a safety precaution the bridge was closed to rail traffic during rebuilding. This was begun in September 1943 and completed in August 1944 at a cost of 103,000Fr.[12]

Troubles with the line in the river bed through the Klus led to a decision to avoid this section by a 984m tunnel which would also permit higher speeds. When this was completed in 1965 the old railway formation in the gorge was incorporated in road widening works and it now carries the footway. The tunnel was built large enough to pass standard gauge stock on transporter wagons. Landquart station, RhB and SBB, was completely rebuilt in 1972–3.

Plans envisaged for the period up to 1980 include the doubling of the Utervaz–Trimmis section between Landquart and Chur and straightening between Schiers and Furna to permit speeds of 75kph and standard gauge wagons on transporters as far as Küblis.[13]

The train service is based on main line connections at Landquart. Fast trains take 1hr 10min from Landquart to Davos with stops at Küblis, Klosters Dorf, Klosters and Davos Dorf. Stopping trains take about 1hr 30min. Return times are about the same. Some trains run through to or from Chur and some terminate at Schiers or Klosters. There is a frequent service of local trains between Chur and Landquart, some running through to and from Thusis. The Thusis–Chur–Klosters service is now operated by the new thyristor equipped railcar units running at speeds up to 90kph (Ch 7).

CHAPTER FOUR

The Albula Railway

FROM Thusis there was no alternative but to carry the railway above the Albula River through the Schyn gorge as far as Tiefencastel. Here an alternative route presented itself, southwards up the Julier valley and under the Julier Pass to emerge above St Moritz. The issue was determined by the abrupt steps in the valley floor, mentioned in Chapter 1. In the Julier valley the lowest step occurs at the entrance to the valley with a rise of 226m in the first 3km, requiring heavy development work, followed by a rise of only 20‰.

In the Albula valley the lowest step was further up, affording an opportunity to gain height before reaching it. Also the Albula route facilitated a connection from Filisur to Davos. The first portion from Thusis to Filisur had been surveyed in 1887 by Moser (Ch 3) who had worked out the scheme very fully for his report of 1890, with several alternatives. The final section had to await a decision by the Federal authorities on the site of the station at St Moritz.

The concession for the Filisur–Samaden section, granted in June 1890, authorised either a mixed rack and adhesion line (11.4km rack and 15km adhesion) with maximum gradients of 90‰ for the rack and 30‰ for adhesion; or a purely adhesion line of 32.5km with maximum gradients of 45‰ as on the Davos railway. Both schemes included a summit tunnel of only 2,650m at a cost of 650,000Fr, the estimate for the remainder being 160,000Fr per km for the mixed line or 191,000Fr per km for the adhesion line which would thus cost Fr8 million

Notes to this chapter will be found on p 248

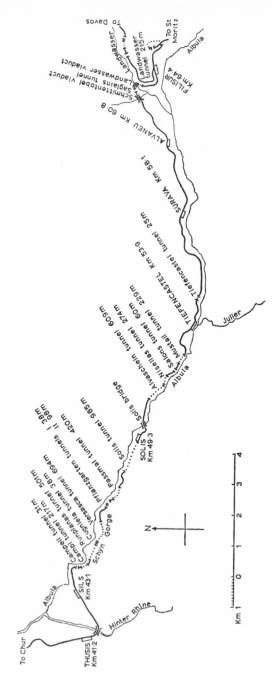

To Davos

To St Moritz

Albula

Landwasser
viaduct

Landwasser
tunnel 215 m

FILISUR
Km 64·4

Schmittentobel viaduct

Stg:ains tunnel

Landwasser viaduct

ALVANEU Km 60·8

SURAVA Km 58·1

Tiefencastel tunnel 25 m

TIEFENCASTEL Km 53·9

Musteil tunnel 229 m

Salons tunnel 274 m

Niseilas tunnel 60 m

Alvescheln tunnel 609 m

Julier

Albula

Solis bridge

Solis tunnel 985 m

SOLIS Km 49·3

Passmal tunnel 420 m

Pilanzgarten tunnels II 98 m

Schyn Gorge

Versasca tunnel 38 m

Cugnela tunnel 69 m

Rumplanas tunnel 277 m

Campi tunnel 50 m

Campi tunnel 31 m

Albula

SILS Km 43·1

Hinter Rhine

To Chur

THUSIS
Km 41·2

Km 1   0   1   2   3   4

N

Map of Albula railway, Thusis–Filisur

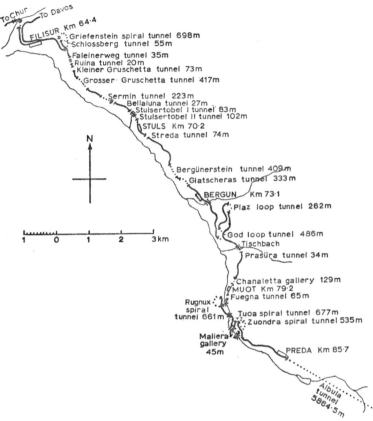

To Chur
To Davos
FILISUR Km 64·4
Griefenstein spiral tunnel 698m
Schlossberg tunnel 55m
Faleinerweg tunnel 35m
Ruina tunnel 20m
Kleiner Gruschetta tunnel 73m
Grosser Gruschetta tunnel 417m
Sermin tunnel 223m
Bellaiuna tunnel 27m
Stulsertobel I tunnel 83m
Stulsertobel II tunnel 102m
STULS Km 70·2
Streda tunnel 74m
N
Bergünerstein tunnel 409m
Glatscheras tunnel 333m
BERGUN Km 73·1
Plaz loop tunnel 262m
1 0 1 2 3 km
God loop tunnel 486m
Tischbach
Prasüra tunnel 34m
Chanaletta gallery 129m
MUOT Km 79·2
Fuegna tunnel 65m
Rugnux spiral tunnel 661m
Tuoa spiral tunnel 677m
Zuondra spiral tunnel 535m
Maliera gallery 45m
PREDA Km 85·7
Albula tunnel 5864·5m

Map of Albula railway, Filisur–Albula tunnel

more.[1] The latter was adopted, but as the project took shape in 1897 it was decided to lower the ruling gradient to 35‰, thereby increasing the length to 36km. It was to prove a wise decision.

Moser prepared two projects on this gradient, with summit tunnels of 7,520m and 5,840m. The second was chosen, offering good operating conditions without excessive cost. The total estimate for the 63.2km from Thusis to St Moritz was 19,600,000Fr. At the same time Moser was engaged on surveys for the branch from Reichenau to Ilanz (Ch 5).

On 9 June 1898 the Federal Council granted a state subvention of Fr8 million towards the construction of the Thusis–Samaden and Reichenau–Ilanz lines on the condition that Graubünden

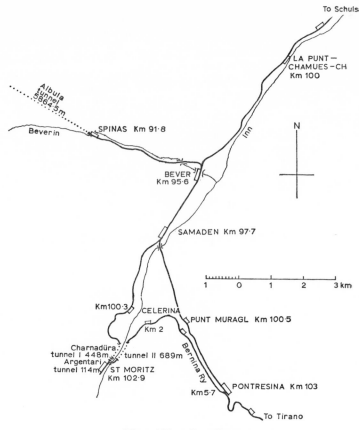

Map of Engadin railways

and the local communities contributed Fr7 million in shares.[2]
The government interest was chiefly concerned with military
movements. With the help of Prättigau and Davos the share capital of 15,850,000Fr was raised and debenture capital of
10,150,000Fr was covered by the cantonal authority.

In the summer of 1898 Fritz Hennings, one of the greatest
European railway engineers, was appointed chief engineer for
the construction of the Albula and Ilanz lines. He was born at
Kiel on 15 December 1838 and, after studying at Hanover and
Zurich, he began his railway career on the Zurich–Zug–Lucerne
line. In 1864–5 he worked on the surveys for the Gotthard Rail-

way. Following further experience in Austria, in 1879–83 he was placed in charge of the construction of the south ramp of the Gotthard line. His appointment to the RhB followed a period with Moser on the Emmersborg tunnel at Schaffhausen. But it was the Albula Railway which was to rank as his greatest achievement.[3]

The resident engineer was G. Gilli and the leading member of the technical staff was Gustav Bener. Bener was to become divisional engineer of the Davos–Filisur and Bever–Schuls lines (Ch 5), but his most outstanding work was to be the Chur–Arosa Railway (Ch 9). He was born in Chur on 17 July 1873 and qualified as a civil engineer in 1897.

Apart from the Rhine bridge at Thusis all bridges on the line are of stone. The building of the largest of these involved the construction of daring timber centrings designed and erected under the supervision of Richard Coray (1869–1946) who achieved an outstanding reputation in the construction of arches.[4]

The most urgent job was the Albula tunnel. So that work could be established before winter set in it was begun at Preda, on the north side, on 15 October 1898 and at Spinas on the south on 1 November, under state management, before the contract was finally settled. The contract for this section comprising Lots 8 and 9, Albula tunnel and 3km of connecting line, was awarded to Ronchi & Carlotti on 16 January 1899.

The remaining work involved thirty-seven tunnels excluding galleries, totalling about 10km, 27km of viaducts, 950,000cu m of earthwork, 75,000cu m of dry walling and a further 18,000cu m with mortar. In July 1900 the work was contracted as follows:

Lots 1 and 2	km0–11	Munari, Cayre & Marasi;
Lot 3	km11–17.5	Caprez & Co;
Lots 4 and 5	km17.5–29.5	Müller & Zeerleder;
Lots 6 and 7	km29.5–41.75	Aebli, Hunerwadel & Maternini;
Rhine bridge, Thusis		Theodor Bell & Co;
Lot 10	km54.1–59.2	(Bever-Celerina) was let in Nov 1900 to Noli & Zanotta.

Thusis–Tiefencastel km0–12.6

This stretch, through the Schyn gorge (see diagram p 66),

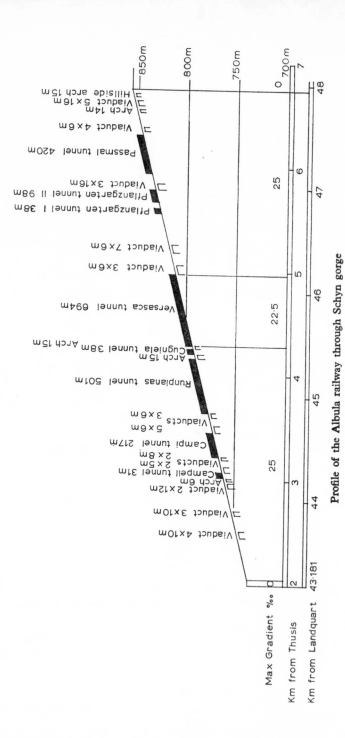

Profile of the Albula railway through Schyn gorge

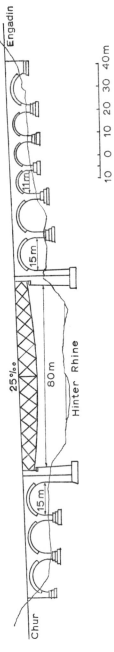

Rhine bridge, Thusis, km0.51

included 4,106m, or 33 per cent, in tunnel, twenty-seven viaducts and 'side viaducts' (Lehnenviadukte) totalling 1,300m or about 15 per cent of the open portion, and it cost about 275,000Fr per km. The three middle piers of the Lochtobel viaduct, of five 16m arches, have foundations 13m deep. The 986m Solis tunnel, the longest on this stretch, penetrated the hardest rock on the entire railway. Two-thirds of the tunnel are unlined. The only steel bridge on the entire railway, over the Hinter Rhine at km0.51 from Thusis, was first tested on 10 December 1901.[5] Its span of 80m is the longest on the RHB. (See drawing p 67.)

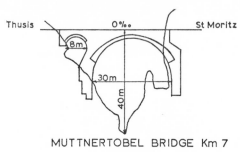

MUTTNERTOBEL BRIDGE Km 7

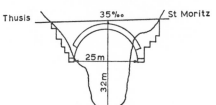

STULSERTOBEL BRIDGE Km 28·466

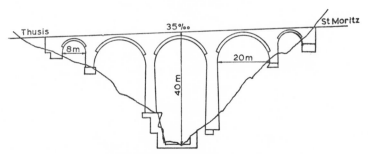

TISCHBACH VIADUCT Km 36·7

Muttnertobel, Stulsertobel and Tischbach viaducts

The Muttnertobel bridge (drawing p 68), abutting into the Passmal and Solis tunnels at km7.011, has a 30m semi-circular arch 40m high above the stream bed. The Solis viaduct (drawing p 70) at km8.651 leaps across the Albula gorge with a central arch of 42m span, 89m above the river. The arch consists of three rings, completed on 31 May 1902, and the total cost was 127,152Fr. The best view of the bridge is obtained from the old road bridge alongside. Beyond Solis viaduct four tunnels totalling 1,240m and seven viaducts totalling 316m were needed to carry the railway through the gorge. The rock through most of this stretch was Grissonian slate, some of it ideal for building.

Tiefencastel–Filisur km12.6–23.0

This section is dominated by two great viaducts, seen in the photograph on p 34. The Schmittentobel viaduct shown below, km21.385–21.522, has seven arches of 15m span, 36m high

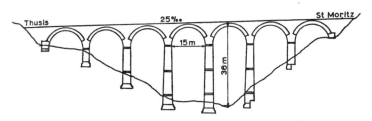

SCHMITTENTOBEL VIADUCT Km 21·454

Schmittentobel viaduct

above the stream, and lying on a curve of 120m radius and a gradient of 25‰. It is immediately followed by a tunnel of 50m beyond which is a brief and exciting glimpse of the Landwasser viaduct curving to the right, and of the river far below.

The Landwasser viaduct at km21.876 is one of the most famous in the world. Its five complete arches of 20m span, with a maximum height of 65m, lie in a curve of 120m radius and on a gradient of 20.25‰. More remarkable is the southern arch which abuts directly into the cliff face at the entrance to the Landwasser tunnel. Emerging from this tunnel on to the full height of the viaduct is a breathtaking experience. The drawing

M.G.R.—E

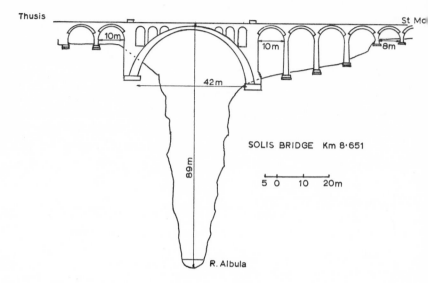

Thusis   St Mo

10m   10m   8m

42m

SOLIS BRIDGE Km 8·651

89m

5 0   10   20m

R. Albula

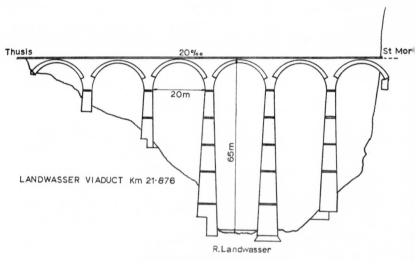

Thusis   20‰   St Mor

20m

65m

LANDWASSER VIADUCT Km 21·876

R.Landwasser

Solis and Landwasser viaducts

on page 70 shows the viaduct in elevation, as if straightened out.

The foundations were begun in late March 1901, the deepest being 3m below low water level. The tallest pier has a sectional area of 91sq m just above the foundations. Construction of the three tallest piers was facilitated by two lattice steel spans which were raised with the masonry work. Two electric hoists on trolleys ran along the spans and lifted stones, timber and other materials. Stone was obtained from a quarry above the left bank of the Landwasser just above the road bridge and was conveyed to the site along a narrow gauge railway which crossed the river twice. Part of this is now a public footpath.

Work was suspended from November 1901 until April 1902, and the viaduct was completed on 15 October 1902, having consumed 9,000cu m of limestone masonry, at a total cost of 257,421Fr. On 21 October the first passenger train from Thusis to Filisur crossed the viaduct.[6] It is worth while breaking the journey at Filisur and walking down to inspect the viaduct from below. There is a direct path from the station.

Filisur station was sited to facilitate connection with Davos by a railway up the Landwasser valley (Ch 5). Geologically, the Grissonian slate continues to km17 and is followed by shell limestone, trias and trap.

Filisur–Bergün km23.47–32.3

Immediately beyond Filisur station is the start of the maximum gradient of $35\%_0$, reduced in longer tunnels to $30\%_0$. To maintain this gradient required a loop of 1,200m just above Filisur, partly inside a 694m tunnel. Above here was the most difficult terrain on the whole railway, but fortunately the trap and limestone provided both good foundations and material for the extensive walling required. In this section are fourteen tunnels totalling 2.3km and eight viaducts totalling 300m. The Stulser gorge with its beautiful waterfall, at km28.47, is crossed at a height of about 32m by a stone arch of 25m span (drawing p 68) sandwiched between the Bellaluna and Stulsertobel tunnels. Along here, where the line is not in a tunnel or on a viaduct, it is built up above and below with massive dry stone walling. At km 29 is a passing loop on a gradient of $15\%_0$.

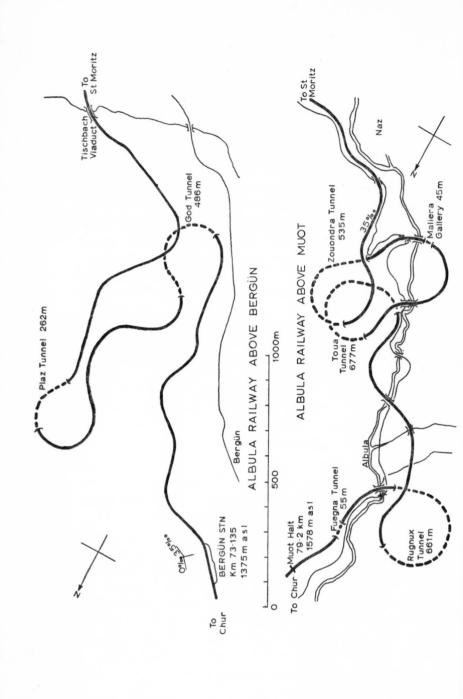

ALBULA RAILWAY ABOVE BERGÜN

ALBULA RAILWAY ABOVE MUOT

Bergün–Albula tunnel   km32.3–44.58

The direct distance between Bergün and Preda is 6.5km, but the height difference of 416m meant that to maintain a maximum gradient of 35‰ the line had to be lengthened by development to 12.2km. A great number of different schemes were worked out and examined before the final course, shown in the diagram on p 72, was adopted. There are seven tunnels totalling 2,718m, the worst of which to bore was the Rugnux spiral tunnel, 622m, in which torrents of water at 4°C poured into the workings, greatly hindering progress.

Viaducts include one 40m high over the Tischbach at km36.72 (drawing p 68), and four over the Albula River. The rocks encountered were dolomite, lias and Grissonian slate. The average cost of construction was 230,000Fr per km.

Allowance had to be made for the heavy snowfall in this region and wherever possible cuttings were avoided and the line placed on embankments. With the help of a Federal Government subvention considerable avalanche protection works were built in the section above the Tischbach. A journey over this section presents a bewildering sensation to the traveller who can easily lose all sense of direction. In fact the railway looks equally bewildering from the road, which is well worth walking. See photograph on page 34.

Albula tunnel   km44.58–50.45

To assist ventilation the section of the Albula tunnel was made 0.3m higher and 0.2m wider than the shorter tunnels and measures 5.0m high and 4.5m wide, half a metre less in both directions than the Simplon tunnels. It is straight in plan, but rises from Preda to the middle at 10‰ and then falls at 2‰ to Spinas. From Preda the tunnel pierced limestone and marly schists for 1,097m, cellular dolomite for 111m, Casanna slate for 52m, granite for 4,346m, moraine for 92m and finally fine granite sand with big boulders for 168m, in its total length of 5,866m.

The method of boring was as used in the Arlberg tunnel, driving a bottom heading using Brandt's boring machines and explosives, and from this at intervals striking up into the top of the tunnel where further headings were driven. At both ends water penetration caused immense difficulties. In April 1900, at 1,006m from Preda, it suddenly increased to 300 litres a second at a temperature of 6°C, and throughout the cellular dolomite the men had to work in great quantities of almost freezing mud. Machine boring was interrupted for fifteen months until September 1901. During this period the contractor gave up and in March 1901 the work had to be taken over by the railway company at which time there were still 4,260m of heading to be driven, in two years. Despite these difficulties an average advance of 100m a month was maintained from each end, increased still further from the Preda end to avoid the Spinas heading going beyond the summit and working downhill.

On 29 May 1902 the headings met at 3,030m from the Preda end, with a horizontal error of 50mm and vertical of 48mm. In February 1903 the tunnel was completed, at a total cost of 7,183,000Fr. Most of the bore is lined except for 1,909m in the granite. With its summit 1,823m above sea level it is the highest of the principal Alpine tunnels.

In all the tunnels refuges were cut every 50m on both sides; in the Albula at every 1km was a large refuge 6m deep and 3m wide.[7]

Albula tunnel–St Moritz   km50.45–62.8

Because of the danger from avalanches in the first 4km of the descent to Bever the line was carried close to the river on a high embankment largely formed of material from the tunnel. On the approach to St Moritz two tunnels had to be bored in the narrow Inn gorge.

On 6 May 1903 the first through goods train ran into Celerina station. The line was inspected and passed on 15 June and on 27 June was ceremonially opened.[8] Regular passenger services between Thusis and Celerina began on 1 July and were extended to St Moritz on 10 July 1904. At St Moritz the trains from the Albula line share the station with those from the Schuls branch (Ch 5) and the Bernina Railway (Ch 8).

The total cost of the railway was 23,957,000Fr, or 388,300Fr per km. There are forty-two tunnels or galleries altogether, with

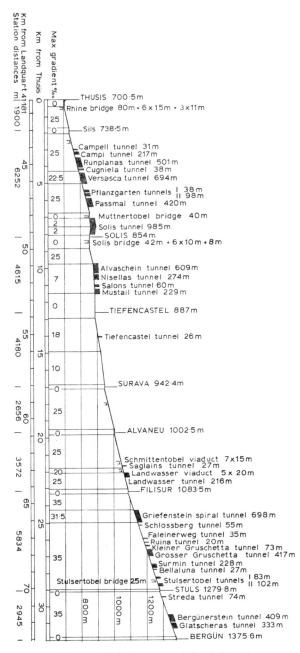

Profile of Albula railway, Thusis–Bergün

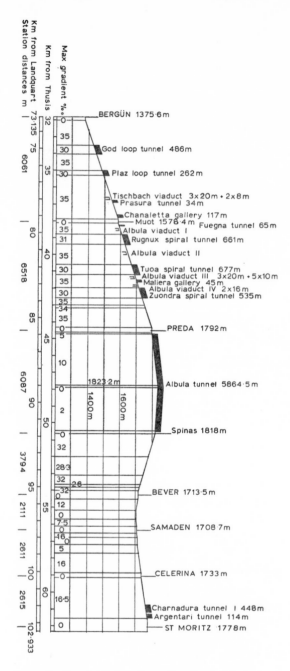

Profile of Albula railway, Bergün–St Moritz

a total length of 16.48km, representing well over a quarter of the total railway length. Of the 108 bridges and viaducts, with a total length of 2,759m, sixty-four are over 10m long. The total cost of the bridges was 250,000Fr. The original permanent way consisted of rails 12m long, 25kg/m below Filisur and 27kg/m from there to St Moritz.

The branch of 5.29km from Samaden to Pontresina, originally projected as part of the Bernina Railway, was built by the RhB when the Bernina line was rerouted to St Moritz. It was begun in June 1906 under the supervision of G. Gilli, but in May 1907 progress was interrupted by a strike of workers in the upper Engadin. The consequent reduction of daily working hours from eleven to ten required the raising of the loan by ten per cent, at the same time lengthening the construction period. Together with a dispute with Pontresina about access roads, this delayed opening until 1 July 1908. The total cost was 1,155,000Fr, or 218,200Fr per km. Permanent way was the same as the Albula railway. The steepest gradient is 20‰ and the sharpest curve 120m radius.

Following the completion of the Albula railway, Fritz Hennings was appointed Professor of Road and Railway Building in the Federal Polytechnic at Zurich. He was again engaged by the RhB to work out the general project and estimates for the Bever-Schuls line (Ch 5), completing this work in July 1905. On his retirement on 29 March 1921 he was presented with a gold medal by Dr A. Schucan, managing director of the RhB. In a firm voice the eighty-two year old engineer said, 'Yes, my finest time was with the Rhaetian Railway. I have never enjoyed anything else so much'. The following year, on 2 February 1922, he died, at the age of eighty-three.[3]

PROPOSED EXTENSION TO CHIAVENNA

The original project as envisaged by Holsboer continued beyond St Moritz, over the Maloja Pass and down the Maira valley, known as the Val Bregaglia or Bergell, entering Italy at Castasegna to connect with the Italian railways at Chiavenna. The cost was estimated at 1,250,000Fr, or 25,000Fr per km, and in 1904 a concession was unsuccessfully sought.[9]

On 10 November 1912 the people of the Bergell unanimously approved a subvention of 700,000Fr towards the construction,[10] but all hope of its realisation was destroyed by World War I.

TRAIN SERVICE

Fast trains from Chur to St Moritz take 2hr 5min to 2hr 10min with stops at Thusis, Tiefencastel, Filisur (where connection is made with trains to and from Davos), Samaden (with connection to or from Pontresina and Schuls), and Celerina. Some also stop at Bergün or Preda. Stopping trains take 2½hr. Return times are about the same. In the summer of 1972 there were eight fast and four stopping trains each way between Chur and St Moritz, also four stopping trains each way between Chur and Filisur. Several of the stopping trains are mixed passenger and freight trains.

CHAPTER FIVE

Rhaetian Railway Extensions

REICHENAU–ILANZ

THE first survey for a railway up the valley of the Vorder Rhine was made in 1851 by Kaspar Welti (1822–89) who pioneered the Gotthard Railway ten years later. This was for a projected line to Italy via Disentis and the Lukmanier Pass.[1] The survey was used in 1897 as a basis for another survey by Robert Moser for a metre gauge line to Ilanz and Disentis. A concession in October 1902 covered this and the Davos–Filisur line. Final details were worked out by Fritz Hennings while he was engaged on the Albula railway.

The only major physical obstacle was the deep gorge that the river had carved for itself through the prehistoric Flims landslip, enormous piles of rubble up to 700m thick, from Reichenau to Sagens. The great heights of Trins, Versam, Valendas and Sagens above the railway involved the company in an additional expense of 300,000Fr for nearly 8km of steeply graded roads linking the stations to the villages including, for Sagens, a bridge over the Rhine with a steel span of 60.8m.

On 26 July 1900 the contract for the formation work to Ilanz was awarded to Galli & Co and in August work began. The only suitable building stone was available near Reichenau and Ilanz where quarries were opened and a 75cm gauge light railway, with temporary bridges over the Rhine, was constructed for loco-motive-hauled trains. This came into use from both ends from November 1900 and on 20 November 1901 was united at km33. (Distances on the RhB are measured from Landquart.)

Notes to this chapter will be found on p 248

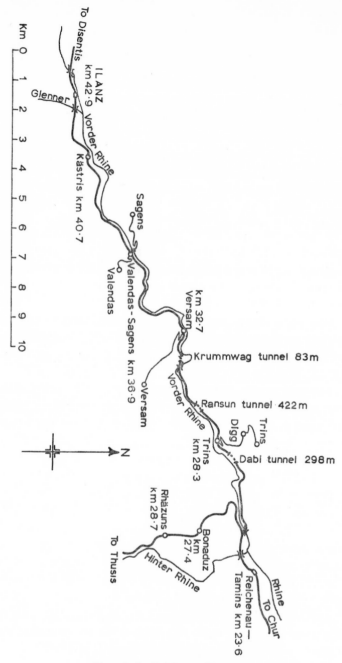

Map of RhB Reichenau–Ilanz

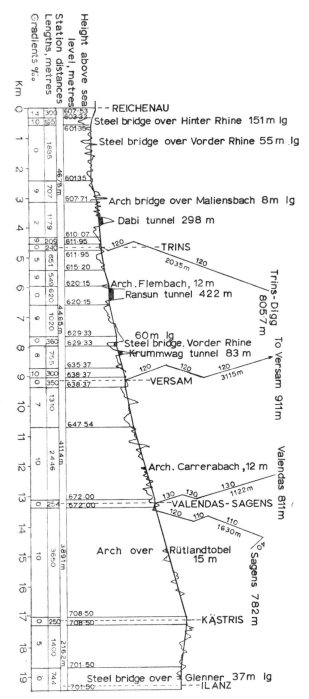

Profile of RHB Reichenau–Ilanz railway, showing also gradients of connecting roads

Because of the remoteness and inaccessibility of the villages, workers had to be housed in eight barracks along the valley. From km25.7 to 39 the railway forms the river wall beside the Rhine, broken into four sections by three tunnels through spurs. Foundations for river walling at km25.6–30.6 and 36.6–39.6 were carried out at low water between November 1900 and May 1901 and the walls were completed in the summer. The volume of retaining walls and footings amounted to 7,100cu m of which 2,240cu m lie between km26.6 and 27.2. Earthwork amounted to 530,000cu m, the greatest being between km31 and 37.

A major job of great urgency carried out in the autumn of 1900 was the draining of the valley slope at km36.6–39.6, great masses of waterlogged shale lying over the Flims breccia. The work involved 2,300m of trenches, a total of 8,600cu m of excavation, 13,950sq m of planking and 7,000cu m of stonework, at a total cost of 95,000Fr.

Tunnelling began in February 1901, and linings were completed in April 1902. The four steel truss spans were erected on timber staging in May and June 1902. The Rhine bridge at km24.74 was built by Wartmann & Valette; that at km31.5 and the road bridge below Sagens by Theodor Bell & Co and the Glenner bridge at km42.6 by Albert Buss & Co.

Station buildings, of timber like the others on the RhB, except Ilanz where stone was used, were built during the summer of 1902 by Maissen Bros. The connecting roads were begun in June 1902 and completed in May and June 1903. Lengths, gradients and heights are shown on the profile on page 81.

The original permanent way consisted of rails 25kg/m in 12m lengths on sixteen steel sleepers 1.8m long each weighing 37kg. It was laid by Galli & Co, beginning in August 1902, and on 22 November the first test train ran to Ilanz. In the autumn, turntable, engine pit and weighbridge were installed at Ilanz and the telegraph was completed. On 1 June 1903 the railway was brought into use, giving access to some spectacular limestone scenery. It cost a total of 4,137,000Fr, or 213,900Fr per km.

DAVOS–FILISUR

Having completed the Albula and Ilanz lines the next objec-

tives of the RhB were to extend the railway up the Vorder Rhine to
Disentis to connect with the projected Furka Railway from Brig
(Ch 11), to link Davos with the Albula railway at Filisur, to
build the Lower Engadin line from Bever as far as the Austrian
border at Martinsbruck and to extend the Albula railway over
the Maloja Pass to the Italian frontier at Castasegna, as mentioned at the end of the previous chapter.

The Davos–Filisur project, originally surveyed in 1898, was
the first to be proceeded with, and was worked out in detail in
1903 by Hennings, who prepared an estimate of 5,440,000Fr.

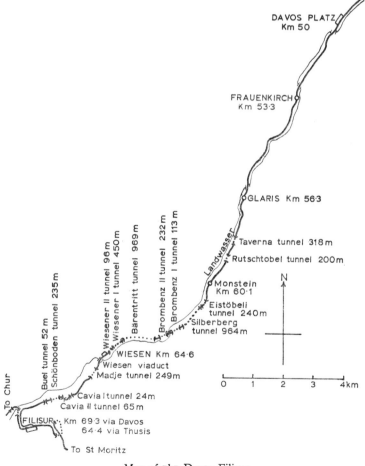

Map of RhB Davos–Filisur

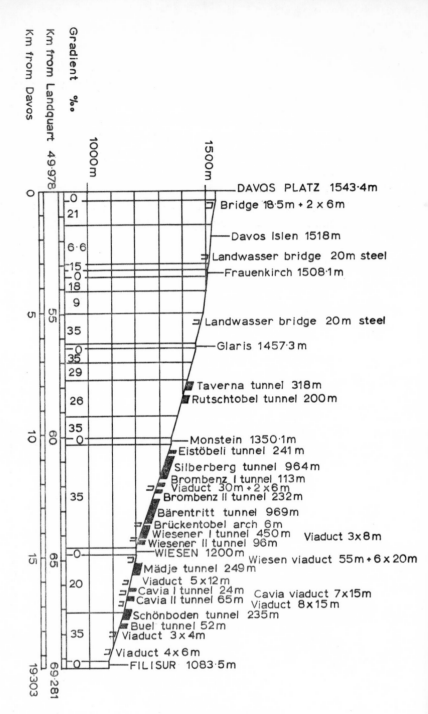

Km from Davos

Km from Landquart 49·978

Gradient ‰

1000m

1500m

DAVOS PLATZ 1543·4m

0 — 0
21 — Bridge 18·5m + 2 × 6m

Davos Islen 1518m

6·6 — Landwasser bridge 20m steel
15 — 0
18 — Frauenkirch 1508·1m

9

5 — 55 — 35 — Landwasser bridge 20m steel

0 — Glaris 1457·3m
35
29
26 — Taverna tunnel 318m
Rutschtobel tunnel 200m
35

10 — 60 — 0 — Monstein 1350·1m
Eistöbeli tunnel 241m
Silberberg tunnel 964m
Brombenz I tunnel 113m
Viaduct 30m + 2 × 6m
35 — Brombenz II tunnel 232m
Bärentritt tunnel 969m
Brückentobel arch 6m
Wiesener I tunnel 450m   Viaduct 3 × 8m
Wiesener II tunnel 96m

15 — 65 — 0 — WIESEN 1200m
Wiesen viaduct 55m + 6 × 20m
Mädje tunnel 249m
20 — Viaduct 5 × 12m
Cavia I tunnel 24m   Cavia viaduct 7 × 15m
Cavia II tunnel 65m   Viaduct 8 × 15m
Schönboden tunnel 235m
35 — Buel tunnel 52m
Viaduct 3 × 4m
Viaduct 4 × 6m

69·281 — 0 — FILISUR 1083·5m

19303

Profile of RhB Davos–Filisur

Page 85. (Above) RHB (former Lanquart–Davos Railway) 2–6–0 tank No 1 *Rhätia* preserved on the Blonay–Chamby Museum Railway near Montreux (p 109); (below) RHB transporter wagon carrying a standard gauge cement hopper wagon

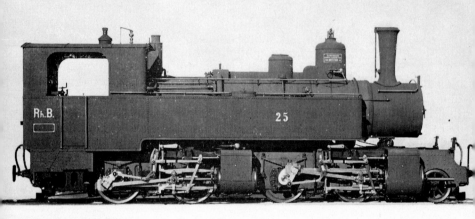

Page 86. (Top) RнB 0–4–4–2 Mallet tank No 23 *Maloja* (p 111); (middle) RнB 2–4–4–0 Mallet tank No 25 (p 112); (bottom) RнB two-cylinder compound 2–8–0 No 104, high pressure side (p 113)

THE CORNISHMAN
Saturday, 8 June

Watford, Harrow, Wembley, Kensington, Ealing, Slough, Reading to Penzance. Optional scenic coach trip to St Ives and Land's End.

THE NORTH DEVONIAN
Sunday, 16 June

Watford, Harrow, Wembley, Kensington, Ealing, Slough, Reading to Exeter for coaches to the Torbay Steam Railway or time at nearby seaside resorts or Barnstaple. Optional scenic coach trips to Clovelly or Exmoor.

THE WELSH BORDERER
Sunday, 23 June

Euston, Harrow, Watford, Hemel Hempstead, Bletchley, Rugby to the Severn Valley, Welshpool & Llanfair or Talyllyn Railways. Optional scenic coach trip to Powys Castle & Shropshire Union Canal cruise.

THE CENTRAL WALESMAN
Saturday, 29 June

Euston, Harrow, Watford, Hemel Hempstead, Bletchley, Rugby to the Central Wales Line, Llanelli & Carmarthen. ...

34081 at Templecombe
18 April 1964

Photo:
N. E. Preedy

You can help to restore "92 Squadron" to working order and enjoy the feeling of achievement when she steams again.

For details of the Society and Share Scheme please write (enclose 3½p stamp) to:

MIKE WATTS

Membership Secretary,
The Battle of Britain Locomotive Preservation Society
53 Yardley, **Letchworth,** **Herts**

ABOVE: No 108, one of the two SLM 2-8-0 locomotives of 1906 retained by the Rhaetian Railway for excursions, approaches Bevers with an enthusiasts' special from Zernez in 1970. [Peter Meyer]

Under the concession half the building capital had to be raised in shares, of which the Canton took up 950,000Fr. Of the remaining 1,770,000Fr Davos council took Fr1 million on 6 December 1903; the remaining share capital was raised by private persons, and by the summer of 1905 financial arrangements were complete.

In connection with this project the RhB ordered ten new 2–8–0 tender engines, Nos 105–14, for main line work, to release the smaller engines for the branches, and thirty-two items of rolling stock at a total cost of 404,000Fr. Details are given in the next chapter.[2] Contracts were let between 15 and 25 September 1906, the section from Davos Platz to km6.615 below Glaris station to A. Baratelli of Davos, and the remaining three sections to Filisur to Froté Westermann & Co of Zurich, and work began at once.[3]

Few railways in Europe have so many major engineering structures per kilometre as this. (See map and gradient profile, pp 83 and 84.) In its 19.303km it has fourteen tunnels totalling 4,211m or 21.8 per cent of the total length, and twenty-nine bridges of which twenty-one are over 10m long, with a total length of 757m. The greatest of these, the Wiesen bridge with a length of 199m, has a central arch of 55m span carrying the railway 88m above the river. Most of these works are crowded into the 8km below Monstein station where the line enters the

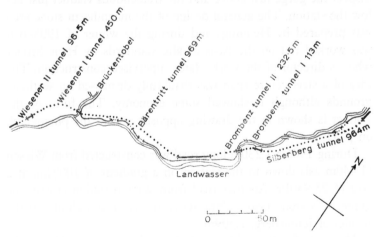

Map of Davos–Filisur line through the Züge gorge

wild and narrow Züge gorge in which avalanches can fall from either side as late as the autumn. Seven of the tunnels are situated on this section. A walk through this gorge from Monstein to Wiesen is highly rewarding both for the scenery and for the views of the railway.

Between Davos Platz and Frauenkirch the line twice crosses the Landwasser. The use of the left bank from km50.606 to 52.64 was the result of a tremendous hailstorm during the night of 28–29 July 1908 when the swollen river washed away part of the uncompleted railway works on the right bank. From km55.353 to 62.12 the line is again on the left bank. The passage of the Züge gorge is memorable for its brief glimpses between the tunnels. Between Brombenz tunnels I and II the Landwasser is crossed by a stone viaduct with a main span of 30m. This was built between 25 August and 22 September 1908. In the brief space between Bärentritt and Wiesener I tunnels is an arch of 6m over the Bruckentobel with an exciting waterfall above.

The tunnelling, mostly in limestone, presented no great difficulties. The upper ends of the Eistöbeli and Silberberg tunnels were extended by rockfall galleries, that at the Silberberg tunnel being 1.5m thick to withstand heavy bombardment from a great height.

The traveller with time to spare should alight at Wiesen to inspect the gorge just above and the tremendous viaduct just below the station. The general design of the magnificent stone arch was prepared by Hennings and during the winter of 1905–6 it was worked out on the basis of RhB standards by Hans Studer who, as director of the works, later supervised construction. The idea of a steel centre span was thankfully dismissed on aesthetic grounds although it showed some economy. The form of the viaduct is shown in the drawing opposite and in the photograph on p 51.

During 1906 a 1,230m long road was constructed from Wiesen (1,440m asl) down to the station on a gradient of 100%o, at a cost of 25,830Fr. Another road from Wiesen station crosses the gorge by a stone bridge 75m above the river and climbs to the hamlet of Jennisberg, 1,509m.

Materials for the bridge and the arch centres could now be

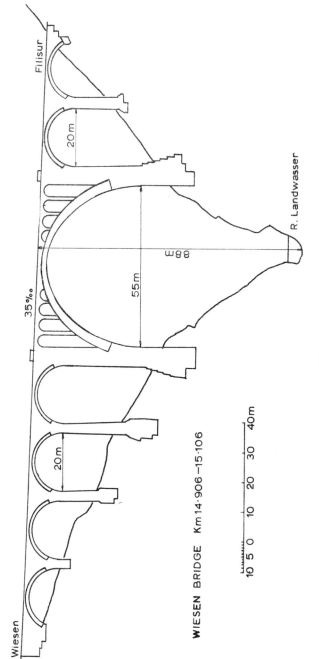

Filisur

20 m

35‰

55 m

88 m

R. Landwasser

20 m

Wiesen

WIESEN BRIDGE Km 14·906 –15·106

10 5 0   10   20   30   40 m

Wiesen viaduct

laid out in the station yard. In October 1906 the foundations were begun, in rough ashlar, carried to depths of down to 14.5m to find secure footings. The main piers were founded on the solid limestone. Building of the piers began on the right (Wiesen) side on 4 June 1907 and on the opposite side on 27 August. To facilitate access a suspension bridge was built across the gorge, and by mid September an aerial ropeway was ready for handling stones.

Quarries were opened in several places where suitable stone could be found and in October 1907 work began on the stones for the arches, in gneiss and granite. In February 1908 a new company was formed with the title of A-G Davos–Filisur to further work as a whole under the direction of G. Marasi, chief engineer of Froté Westermann & Co. Marasi was responsible for the design of the centring for the great central arch. His solution to the problem took the shape of a vast timber structure of astonishing economy yet of great strength.

Erection of the centring began on 22 April 1908 under the supervision of Richard Coray. Each half stood on a concrete foundation and was in nine tiers, 55m high, anchored to a main pier. The structure consumed 494cu m of sawn timber and nearly 600cu m of round timber. Such was his faith in the work that, immediately on its completion on 1 August 1908, Coray walked across on a couple of boards carrying his first baby son.[4]

The main arch, in three rings, was begun on 6 August and was completed on 10 October, after which the centring was carefully lowered and dismantled. The side arches were completed at the same time. The decking was finished early in 1909 and, at the request of the local community who contributed the cost, a footway was cantilevered out on the left side of the viaduct, looking towards Filisur.

Altogether the viaduct consumed 9,950cu m of masonry and cost, without centrings and footway, about 395,000Fr. It is the highest bridge on the RHB, and the central span is almost exactly equal to that of the Ballochmyle viaduct over the Ayr on the Glasgow & South Western main line in Scotland, and so ranks as the second largest masonry arch railway bridge in the world.

Beyond Wiesen viaduct the railway continues high above the

left bank of the Landwasser through wooded country. After several tunnels and viaducts it curves round the end of the hill into the Albula valley and drops down beside the Albula railway into Filisur station. It was opened on 1 July 1909.

Between station limits the total construction length was 18.88km of which 11.466km or 59.4 per cent is straight. Its total fall from Davos to Filisur amounts to 459.95m giving an average gradient of 24.4‰, but it was necessary to use the ruling gradient of 35‰ for 9.711km, or over half the length. The total cost was 6,152,000Fr or 318.200Fr per km.

In the summer of 1972 there were twelve trains each way daily between Davos and Filisur taking about thirty minutes. Trains stop at Islen and Monstein by request only.

FURTHER EXTENSIONS

It was realised that the financing of the remaining schemes, with no wealthy community such as Davos to contribute, could only be achieved with Federal assistance, as a building capital of Fr23 million was required. In view of this the Maloja scheme was postponed and the Inn valley project was cut back to Schuls until the opportunity came to extend it into Austria. It was decided to proceed with the sections between Ilanz and Disentis, for which a general survey had been prepared by Moser in 1898, and between Bever and Schuls, surveyed by Hennings in 1905.

Again government interest was stimulated by the value of these lines for military movements and, following a request from Graubünden Council, the Federal Council, on 28 May 1907, approved a contribution of Fr4 million requiring no dividend until RhB receipts exceeded four per cent of the share capital. By decree of the Upper House on 12 June and of the Lower House on 18 June this contribution was increased to Fr5 million. Deducting share capital of 11,500,000Fr, this left 6,500,000Fr to be raised. Of this the Canton contributed 3,950,000Fr and the remainder was covered by the Chur, Oberland and Engadin communities, hotels and private shareholders, and on 18 February 1909 the financing was complete.

During this period the RhB made an arrangement with a Paris banking firm to enable preliminary work to be carried out.

Constructional details were prepared under the supervision of
Peter Otto Saluz (1847–1914), sectional engineer of the RhB
under Gilli, and by the end of 1908 work was being driven forward on the two longest tunnels, Magnacun and Tasna, on the
Schuls line, under state supervision.

On 27 August 1909 contracts were let as follows:

Ilanz–Disentis
Section 1	Ackermann, Bärtsch & Co; Mels
Section 2a	Angelo Volponi; Kempten, Canton Zurich
Section 2b	Solioz & Perusset; Münster
Sections 3 and 4	Baumann Bros & Stiefenhofer; Altdorf

Bever–Schuls
Section 1	Rodari Gaspare & Co; Ascona
Section 2a	Annibale Lanfranconi; St Pellegrino
Section 2b, 3, 4, 5, 6b, 7	Müller, Zeerleder & Gobat; Zurich
Section 6a	Rolla Bros; Ivrea

In April 1910 the contract for steel bridges on both lines was
let to Theodor Bell & Co, Kriens.

ILANZ–DISENTIS

By the time work began, in March 1910, the Brig–Furka–
Disentis Railway had been financed (Ch 11) and it was hoped
that in a few years a through route would be established. To this
end the station at Disentis was laid out for a future connection.
H. von Kager was resident engineer.

Compared with other sections of the RhB there were no major
difficulties, the principal engineering works being the Val Rusein
viaduct (drawing on page 94) and Val Lumpegna viaduct.
There were three steel spans across the Vorder Rhine and, on the
section from km67.6 to 70.7 twelve smaller viaducts. Some of
these are indicated on the profile on p 95. There were only
two tunnels totalling 338m. The total building length from the
end of Ilanz station was 29.993km of which the forty-seven
bridges totalled 1,582m, or 5.3 per cent, and retaining walls,
1,952m or 6.5 per cent. The original permanent way consisted
of rails 15m long, weighing 27kg/m, on twenty-one steel sleepers

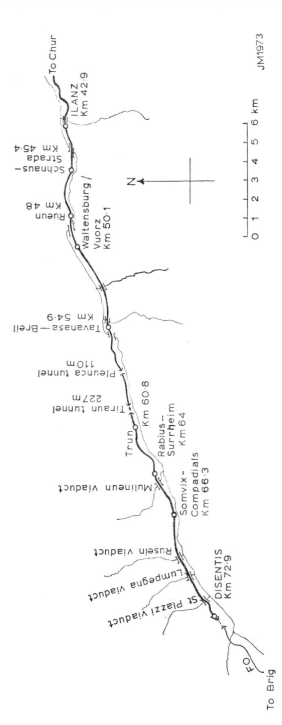

To Chur

ILANZ
Km 42·9

Schnaus–
Strada
Km 45·4

Rueun
Km 48

Waltensburg /
Vuorz
Km 50·1

N

0 1 2 3 4 5 6 km

Tavanasa–Breil
Km 54·9

Pleunca tunnel
110m

Tiraun tunnel
227m

Trun
Km 60·8

Rabius–
Surrheim
Km 64

Mulineun viaduct

Somvix–
Compadials
Km 66·3

Rusein viaduct

Lumpegna viaduct

St Plazzi viaduct

DISENTIS
Km 72·9

FO

To Brig

JM1973

Map of RhB Ilanz–Disentis

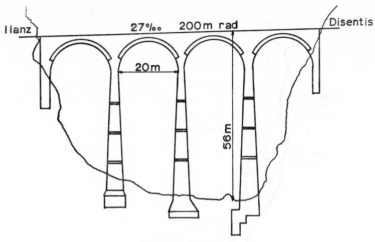

Rusein viaduct km59

1.8m long, weighing 37kg. The minimum radius was 120m.[5] The new railway was opened on 1 August 1912,[6] having cost 5,570,000Fr, or 185,800Fr per km, less than half that of the Albula railway per km.

As shown on the profile, it is a steady climb all the way to Disentis. The lower slopes of the valley are thickly wooded with conifers, but beyond Somvix/Compadials there are some good views across the valley as the line is carried high above the left bank of the river on a rock ledge, crossing the Val Rusein and Val Lumpegna on the lofty viaducts. Disentis, also known by the Romansch name Mustér, is a market town of about 1,700 population with a large Benedictine abbey founded in 614.

The train service in summer 1972 consisted of eleven stopping trains and one fast, the Glacier Express, from Chur to Disentis, and ten stopping trains and two fasts from Disentis to Chur. Fasts take 1hr 15min to 1hr 20min and stopping trains about 1½hr. Seven trains from Chur and six from Disentis connect with Furka–Oberalp trains or carry through coaches to or from Brig. Connection is also made with post buses over the Lukmanier Pass to and from Acquarossa (Ch 10).

BEVER–SCHULS

When it was constructed the Inn valley line was confidently

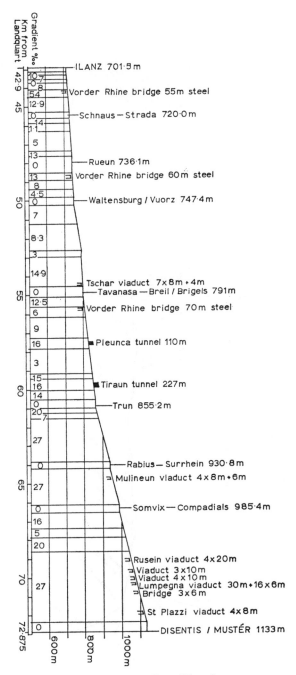

Profile of RhB Ilanz–Disentis

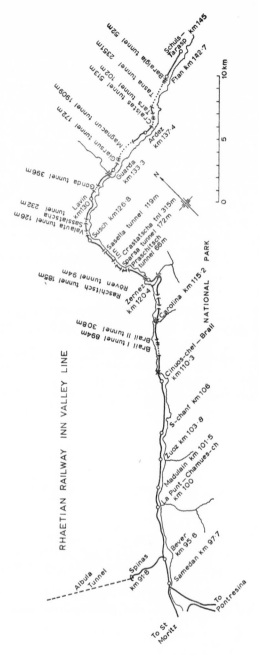

RHAETIAN RAILWAY INN VALLEY LINE

Albula Tunnel

Spinas km 91·8

Samedan km 97·7

Bever km 95·6

To St. Moritz

To Pontresina

La Punt-Chamues-ch km 100

Madulain km 101·5

Zuoz km 103·8

S.-chanf km 106

Cinuos-chel – Brail km 110·3

Brail I tunnel 894m
Brail II tunnel 308m

Carolina km 115·2

NATIONAL PARK

Zernez km 120·4

Reschitsch tunnel 185m
Röven tunnel 94m

Praschitsch tunnel 68m
Sparsa tunnel 172m
U. Crastatscha tnl 315m
Sasella tunnel 119m

Susch km 126·8

Valauta tunnel 126m
Sassletscha tunnel 232m

Lavin km 130

Gonda tunnel 396m

Guarda km 133·3

Giarsun tunnel 172m
Magnacun tunnel 1909m

Ardez km 137·4

Crastais tunnel 513m
Tars tunnel 102m

Tasna tunnel 235m

Ftan km 142·7

Baraigia tunnel 92m

Schuls–Tarasp km 145

N

0   5   10 km

Map of Rhᴮ Inn valley line

expected to form part of a metre gauge route between Austria and Italy via the Engadin, and its terminus at Schuls-Tarasp was regarded as temporary.

Its construction, under the supervision of Hans Studer, involved some of the most difficult and expensive engineering on the RhB, exceeded only by the Albula railway. Its cost per km of 361,000Fr compares with the 388,300Fr of the Albula. The difficulties were caused principally by instability of valley slopes requiring heavy tunnelling and tremendous foundation work for the numerous viaducts across side valleys and gulleys. In spite of the seventeen tunnels totalling 8.009km or 16.2 per cent of the whole length, it is one of the most spectacular scenic routes on the RhB, both to travel over and to look at. Altogether there are seventy-two bridges and viaducts of a total length of 2,194m. All except three are of stone arch construction, some of outstanding elegance. Protective walling amounts to 1,834m. Fortunately good building stone was found all along the line.

Place names in the Lower Engadin, as in the Vorder Rhine valley, are largely Romansch, and for many there are alternative spellings. As far as Cinuos-chel, or Cinuskel, the valley is fairly broad and the railway was kept as far from the hill slopes as possible to avoid avalanches. Below Cinuos-chel, at km111.235, the Inn is crossed by the first major viaduct, shown in the drawing on p 98. This was necessary to avoid the threat of avalanches which occur at nine places on the left bank every spring. The valley now narrows and between here and Zernez are four tunnels through schists, several bridges and a succession of viaducts. The Val Mela viaduct leading straight into Brail I tunnel was the scene of a tragic accident on 29 August 1911, when the centring collapsed during construction, causing eleven deaths.[7] In the brief space between Brail tunnels I and II is the Val Verda viaduct. Val Schura viaduct follows immediately beyond Brail II tunnel and at km116, just beyond the Carolina passing loop, is the lofty Tantermozza viaduct. Dimensions of these viaducts are shown in the drawings on pp 98 and 101. The Raschitsch tunnel at km116.55 was built as a protection against avalanches. It is followed by the Luftobel and Spöl viaducts before the line descends by a great loop into Zernez

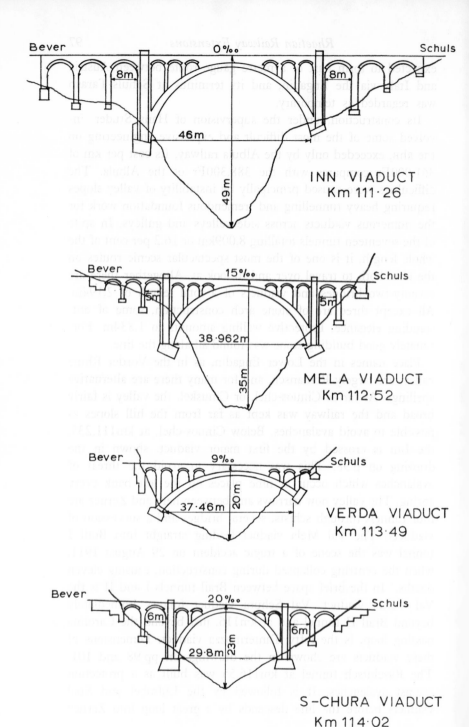

Inn, Mela. Verda. S-chura viaducts

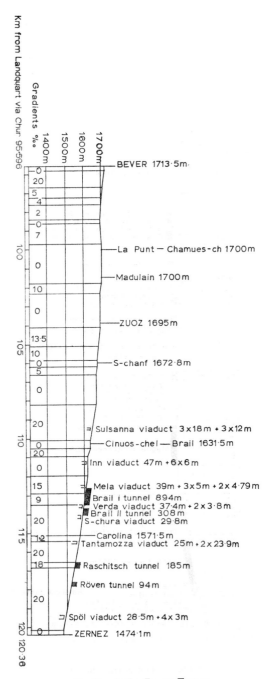

Km from Landquart via Chur 95·596

Gradients ‰

1400m 1500m 1600m 1700m

BEVER 1713·5m

La Punt — Chamues-ch 1700m

Madulain 1700m

ZUOZ 1695m

S-chanf 1672·8m

Sulsanna viaduct 3×18m + 3×12m

Cinuos-chel — Brail 1631·5m

Inn viaduct 47m + 6×6m

Mela viaduct 39m + 3×5m + 2×4·79m

Brail i tunnel 894m

Verda viaduct 37·4m + 2×3·8m

Brail II tunnel 308m

S-chura viaduct 29·8m

Carolina 1571·5m

Tantamozza viaduct 25m + 2×23·9m

Raschitsch tunnel 185m

Röven tunnel 94m

Spöl viaduct 28·5m + 4×3m

ZERNEZ 1474·1m

Profile of RhB Bever–Zernez

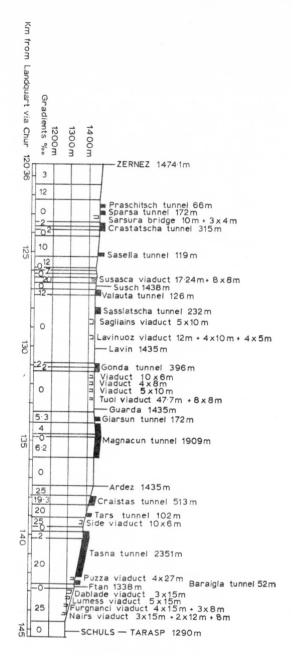

Profile of RhB Zernez–Schuls

where a site was made for the station by diverting the River Spöl. The loop, built at an additional cost of 150,000Fr–200,000Fr. reduced the gradient to 20%₀₀. From Zernez it was expected that a branch would be built via Ofenberg to Meran.

Immediately beyond Zernez station the line recrosses the Inn by a steel truss bridge and remains on the left bank to Schuls. Except for the first 2km from Zernez this was an exceedingly difficult and expensive section as far as Guarda, involving long tunnels, side excavation with heavy walling, and many side viaducts.

The valley slope throughout consists partly of rock and partly of broken moraine, fortunately mostly dry and stable. Protective works were required against avalanches, at km123 by Sparsa tunnel through the debris, at km124.50 by a wall 180m long, at

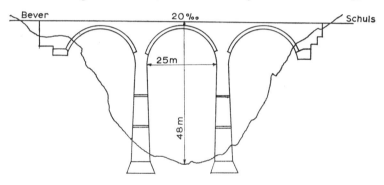

TANTERMOZZA VIADUCT Km 115·9

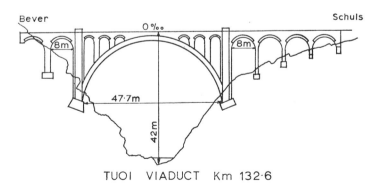

TUOI VIADUCT Km 132·6

Tantermozza and Tuoi viaducts

km125 by Sassella tunnel in hornblend schist, at km127.100 by Vallauta tunnel and gallery in moraine and at km131 by Gonda tunnel again in hornblend schist.

Also in this stretch are several other tunnels and viaducts, as shown on the profile on p 100. At km132.585, just before Guarda station, is the great Tuoi viaduct with the main span identical with that of the Inn viaduct below Cinuos-chel (drawing p 101).

About 500m below Guarda station another stretch of gorge begins. The road, built fifty years before the railway, had moved in several places and was still moving, so to avoid this danger the line was taken through the Giarsun and Magnacun tunnels, heavily lined, in very varied rocks. Two similar gorges through unstable rock between Val Tasna, km139.8, and Val Puzza, km142.2, were likewise avoided by the Tasna tunnel, the second longest on the RhB, again in various rocks. Immediately beyond the tunnel comes the Puzza viaduct, shown below, the highest on

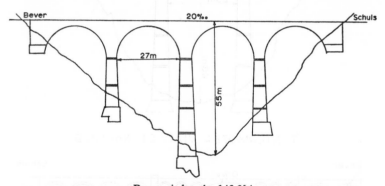

Puzza viaduct km142.214

the line, giving a brief though marvellous view of Tarasp castle on the right before plunging into Baraigla tunnel.

From Ftan to the terminus the line is carried about 130m above the Inn with fine views over the valley. The large embankment at Ftan was formed of material from Tasna tunnel. The terminus at Schuls-Tarasp was placed at a height of 50m above the road to allow a future extension to pass above the village.[8]

Page 103. (Above) RHB thyristor equipped railcar No 513 with trailer and driving trailer at Versam in the deep Rhine gorge through the Flims landslip (p 131); (below) RHB 1–D–1 locomotive No 353 on the Bernina Express at Pontresina. The first two coaches are running through from Tirano to Chur (p 160)

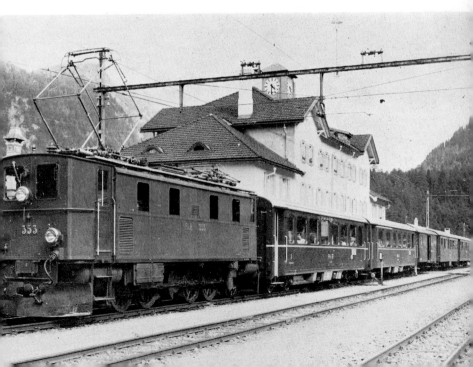

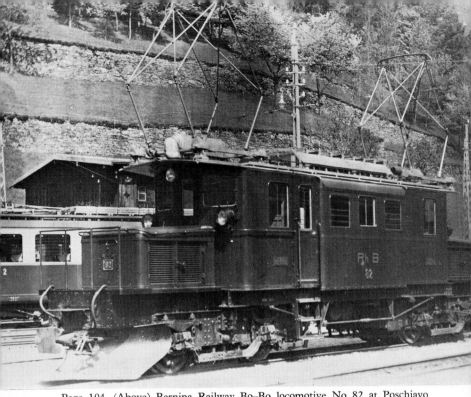

Page 104. (Above) Bernina Railway Bo–Bo locomotive No 82 at Poschiavo (p 157); (below) Bernina Railway steam rotary snow plough at Poschiavo (p 153)

The line is very well laid out with long stretches of straight track and no curve less than 160m radius. Of the construction length of 49.62km, 29.47km or 59.4 per cent is straight. The total fall from Bever to Schuls is 423.5m, an average of 8.6%o. The ruling gradient of 25%o occurs between Ardez and Schuls. The total cost of construction was 17,843,000Fr. Originally steam operation was intended, but in 1910 before construction had proceeded far, the decision was made to electrify the line as an experiment in electric operation at high altitudes, and to continue this through to St Moritz and Pontresina. The electrical equipment and locomotives will be dealt with in Chapter 10. Despite this decision, turntables were installed at Zuoz, Zernez and Schuls, watering facilities also at Zernez and Schuls and an engine shed at Schuls.

The ceremonial opening on 28–29 June 1913 was a significant occasion.[9] Because of the line's importance as a link in a contemplated international route from Landeck in Austria to Chiavenna in Italy, the RhB had invited prominent persons from the Federal Government, the Tirol, the SBB and Graubünden. Lengthy stops were made at Zuoz, Zernez and Schuls, and there were speeches by the hour.

The line was opened throughout to all traffic on 1 July 1913 and on the same day electric trains began running between Bever, St Moritz and Pontresina. This was the last section of the main RhB network to be completed. Magnacun and Tasna tunnels soon gave trouble from rock pressure and water penetration, and from 1914 to 1919 both had to be rebuilt with completely new inverts. To assist drainage in the Tasna tunnel a parallel bore had to be driven on the side farther from the valley.

Following the death of G. Gilli in November 1913 P. O. Saluz became chief engineer of the RhB from 1 January 1914, but his term of office was cut short by his death on 8 September 1914 at the age of sixty-seven.

By this time Europe was plunged into war and although Switzerland remained neutral the country suffered severe economic privations through loss of trade and in these conditions further railway extensions had to be abandoned. After the war attempts were made to revive interest in the Inn valley, Maloja

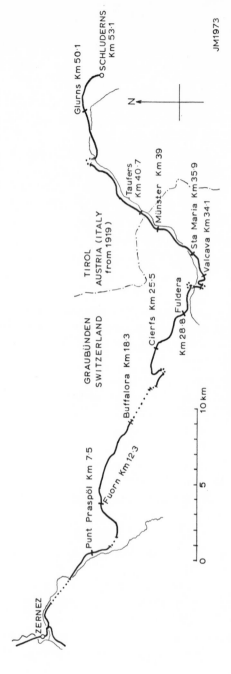

Map of proposed Ofenberg railway

ZERNEZ

Punt Praspöl Km 7·5

Fuorn Km 12·3

Buffalora Km 18·3

GRAUBÜNDEN
SWITZERLAND

Cierfs Km 25·5

Fuldera

Km 28·8

Sta Maria Km 35·9

Valcava Km 34·1

Münster Km 39

Taufers
Km 40·7

TIROL
AUSTRIA (ITALY
from 1919)

Glurns Km 50·1

OSCHLUDERNS
Km 53·1

JM1973

N

0   5   10 km

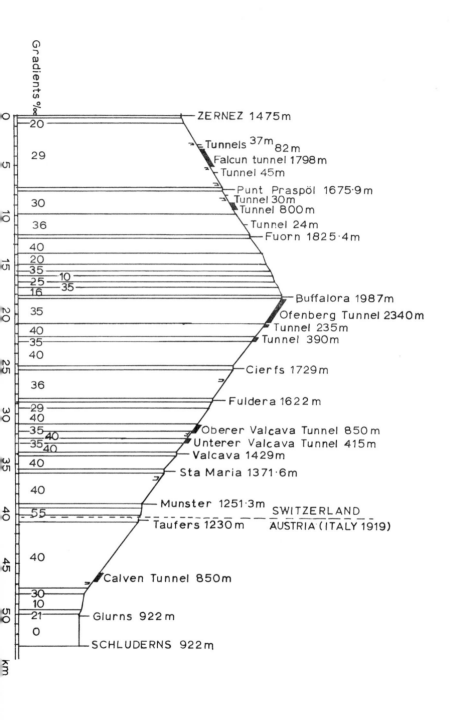

Gradients ‰

0 — ZERNEZ 1475m
20
29
— Tunnels 37m 82m
— Falcun tunnel 1798m
— Tunnel 45m
30
— Punt Praspöl 1675·9m
— Tunnel 30m
— Tunnel 800m
36
— Tunnel 24m
— Fuorn 1825·4m
40
20
35
10
25
35
16
35
— Buffalora 1987m
— Ofenberg Tunnel 2340m
40
— Tunnel 235m
35
— Tunnel 390m
40
— Cierfs 1729m
36
— Fuldera 1622m
29
40
35
40
— Oberer Valcava Tunnel 850m
35
40
— Unterer Valcava Tunnel 415m
— Valcava 1429m
40
— Sta Maria 1371·6m
40
— Munster 1251·3m   SWITZERLAND
55
— — — — — — — — — — — —
— Taufers 1230m   AUSTRIA (ITALY 1919)
40
— Calven Tunnel 850m
30
10
21
— Glurns 922m
0
— SCHLUDERNS 922m

km

and San Bernhardin (Ch 7) projects, but the money was not forthcoming and in 1936 the board of the RhB renounced the extension of the concession. Had it not been for the war there is little doubt that these lines would have been built and that they would have made a useful contribution to the economy of Graubünden.

The projected Ofenberg railway was to have been a metregauge electric line from Zernez to Schluderns, 53.212km long, with fifteen tunnels totalling 7.964km, the longest being 2,340m under the Ofenberg. The line was to climb from 1,475m at Zernez to 1,887m at the west end of the Ofenberg tunnel from where it fell to 922m at Schluderns. Here it would connect with the branch from Meran up the Etsch valley to Mals. The ruling gradient was to be 40‰, and the sharpest curves 120m radius. The cost, including rolling stock and electrical equipment, was estimated at 19,400,000Fr. A concession was granted in 1910, but before any work could begin the war put an end to the project.[10] A map and profile are on pp 106 and 107. Schluderns was in the Austrian province of Tirol until September 1919 when south Tirol was ceded to Italy.

So the Bever–Schuls line has remained a branch, with ten trains each way daily taking about 1hr 40min between St Moritz and Schuls. In summer 1972 the only fast train, 10.53 from Schuls, took 1hr 6min from Schuls to Samaden, stopping at Zernez and Zuoz. There is also a local service of three each way terminating at S-chanf. Stopping trains call at Ftan and Carolina by request only. Some cement traffic originates at Zernez.

CHAPTER 6

Steam Locomotives and Rolling Stock of the Rhaetian Railway

2-6-0 TANK LOCOMOTIVES

FOR the opening of the Landquart–Davos Railway five 2–6–0 tank engines were obtained from SLM in 1889. Their appearance is shown in the photograph on p 85; dimensions and other particulars are given in the tables on p 110. They were numbered 1–5 on the L-D, becoming RhB Nos 1–5 in 1896, and they were the first metre gauge 2–6–0s in Switzerland.

The 1.100m diameter boiler, 3.208m long over tube plates, was large for a metre gauge engine at the time and was necessary to maintain a speed of 15kph up the 45%₀ with a 45 ton train. The maximum speed was 45kph.

Coupled wheels 1,050mm and leading radial wheels 700mm diameter were to become RhB standards for steam locomotives. The engines had outside frames and cranks, Walschaerts valve gear and slide valves.

To work the extension to Thusis three more, Nos 6–8, were obtained in 1896, with greater water and coal capacity. Eight more, bought in 1901–8, had a larger heating surface and grate area.

Because of the Engadin electrification (Ch 7), and the acute coal shortage during the first world war, the RhB found itself in a position to dispose of some of the 2–6–0 tanks. In 1917 Nos 3, 4 and 5 were sold to Luxemburg where they worked on light railways until scrapped in 1954. The remainder were taken out of

Notes to this chapter will be found on p 249

service on the completion of the electrification in 1921. No 1 was preserved and is now on the Blonay–Chamby Museum Railway near Montreux where the photograph on p 85 was taken. Nos 7 and 8 were sold in 1923 to the Ferrovie Regionale Ticinese, Locarno, to operate the Valle Maggia Railway between Locarno and Bignasco during conversion from ac to dc (Ch 10). After being retained in reserve stock they were scrapped in 1943.

Four were sold to the Brünig Railway, Nos 15–16 in 1924 and 9–10 in 1926, becoming SBB Nos 215–18. They were superheated in 1926–7. Small tubes were reduced in number to 37 and the 15 superheater tubes had a heating surface of 18sq m. The maximum

Principal dimensions:

Nos	1–5	6–8	9–16
Cylinders, diameter mm	340	340	340
stroke, mm	500	500	500
Wheelbase, coupled, mm	2,400	2,400	2,600
total, mm	4,500	4,500	4,700
Tubes, 3,208mm long, number	126	124	130
Heating surface, firebox, sq m	4.8	4.8	6.2
total, sq m	62	61	65
Grate area, sq m	0.9	0.9	1.0
Working pressure, atm (kg/sq cm)	12	12	12
Water capacity, cu m	2.6	3.1	3.1
Coal capacity, tons	0.9	1.1	1.1
Weight in working order, tons	30.2	31.7	34.0
Length over buffers, m	7.95	8.384	8.434
Cost, Fr	60,000	37,000	48,500

Class list:

No	Name	Date	Wks No	Wdn	Disposal	Scrapped
1	Rhätia	1889	577	1928	For preservation	
2	Prättigau	1889	578	1925		?
3	Davos	1889	579	1917	Luxemburg	1954
4	Flüela	1889	580	1917	Luxemburg	1954
5	Engadin	1889	581	1917	Luxemburg	1954
6	Landquart	1896	960	1923	Brazil	?
7	Chur	1896	961	1923	Ferrovie Regionale Ticinesi	1943
8	Thusis	1896	962	1923	FRT	1943
9		1901	1369	1926	Brünig Railway (SBB 217)	1941
10		1901	1370	1926	Brünig Railway (SBB 218)	1942
11		1902	1476		RhB reserve stock	
12		1902	1477	1923	Spain	
13		1902	1478		RhB reserve stock	1950
14		1902	1479		RhB reserve stock	
15		1908	1910	1924	Brünig Railway (SBB 215)	1942
16		1908	1911	1924	Brünig Railway (SBB 216)	1942

speed became 55kph. They were withdrawn in 1941–2. In 1923 No 6 was sold to Brazil, and No 12 to the Sagunto Ironworks, Spain, becoming No 207 *Algimia*.[1]

THE MALLET TANKS

The opening of the Klosters–Davos section in 1890 with its 45%o grades soon proved that much more powerful engines were needed; in 1891 two 0–4–4–0 Mallet tanks were obtained from Maffei of Munich, shown in the diagram below. They were numbered 6–7 on the L-D, becoming RhB 21–2 in 1896. Like the 2–6–0 tanks they had outside frames and Walschaerts valve gear and slide valves. As in normal Mallet practice, high-pressure cylinders were on the fixed rear unit, low pressure in front. Wheels were again 1,050mm diameter and the boiler was 1.140m diameter with a barrel length of 3.6m. They were a great advance on the 2–6–0 tanks, hauling 70–80 tons up the 45%o grades at 18kph, and they had a maximum speed of 45kph.

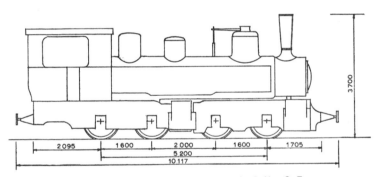

Landquart–Davos Railway Mallet tank L-D Nos 6-7
Maffei Munich 1891

Landquart–Davos Railway 0–4–4–0 Mallet tank locomotive

In 1896 two more Mallet tanks, RhB 23–4, were obtained from SLM. To accommodate a greater water capacity the frames were longer and were supported by a pair of trailing wheels, making them 0–4–4–2s. They had the same size boiler but with the dome in the centre, over the high-pressure cylinders.

The final eight Mallets, Nos 25–32, were delivered from SLM in 1902, in preparation for the extensions to Ilanz and St Moritz, then under construction. The 0–4–4–2 arrangement had not proved entirely satisfactory, so the wheels were rearranged to the 2–4–4–0 type. As on Nos 21–2, the steam dome was again on the front boiler ring, but in other respects they were identical with 23–4. These two types are illustrated on p 86.

In 1910 No 22, and in 1911 No 21, were rebuilt with new boilers and front radial axles, becoming almost identical with 25–32. Dimensions of the Mallets are tabulated below, followed by a class list.[2]

Nos	21–2	23–4	25–32	26–8*
Cylinders, high pressure, diam mm	330	315	315	
low pressure, dia mm	490	490	490	
stroke	550	550	550	
Tubes, small, number	143	139	139	56
superheater, number				15
Heating surface, firebox, sq m	6.1	7.0	7.0	7.0
superheater, sq m				20.0
total	80.2	79.0	79.0	76.9
Grate area sq m	1.4	1.3	1.3	
Working pressure, atm (kg/sq cm)	12	14	14	
Water capacity, cu m	3.0 (3.6)	3.4	3.4	
Coal capacity, tons	1.2 (1.0)	1.2	1.0	
Total wheelbase, m	5.2 (7.01)	6.6	7.01	
Weight in working order, tons	40.5 (47.3)	44.5	47.3	48.4
Cost, Fr	68,400	65,500	76,800	

*26–8 as superheated 1920–1
Figures in brackets for Nos 21–2 applied after rebuilding to 2–4–4–0

No	Name	Type	Date	Maker	Wks No	Wdn
21	Scaletta	0–4–4–0	1891	Maffei	1613	1920
22	Albula	0–4–4–0	1891	Maffei	1614	1920
23	Maloja	0–4–4–2	1896	SLM	958	1926
24	Chiavenna	0–4–4–2	1896	SLM	959	1926
25		2–4–4–0	1902	SLM	1480	1921
26		2–4–4–0	1902	SLM	1481	1920
27		2–4–4–0	1902	SLM	1482	1920
28		2–4–4–0	1902	SLM	1483	1920
29		2–4–4–0	1902	SLM	1484	1921
30		2–4–4–0	1902	SLM	1485	1921
31		2–4–4–0	1902	SLM	1486	1921
32		2–4–4–0	1902	SLM	1487	1921

At the time of withdrawal the engines still had plenty of life left in them, and they were disposed of as follows: Nos 21–2 went to Brazil where their subsequent fate is unknown to the writer;

Nos 23–4 were sold to Oberhasli power station and were scrapped in 1940 and 1937 respectively; Nos 25, 29–32 went to Madagascar and were all scrapped about 1951; Nos 26–8, after being sold to the Yverdon–Ste Croix Railway in south-west Switzerland in 1920, were fitted with Schmidt superheaters, No 28 in 1920 and 26–7 in 1921. (The YSTEC had been using 0–4–4–0 Mallet tanks since 1893 and a massive 0–6–6–0 since 1917.) In 1947 Nos 26 and 28 were sold to Union Española de Explosives (Puertollano–Penaroya), Spain, and were scrapped in 1954 and 1960 respectively. No 27 was scrapped by the YSTEC in 1946.

2–8–0 TENDER ENGINES

Experience during 1903 proved that although the Mallet tanks had fulfilled most requirements, for the heavily loaded fast through trains an engine with a larger boiler was needed. This could be provided only on an engine with a separate tender to avoid exceeding permissible axle loadings. In 1901 SLM built some metre gauge 2–8–0s for the Ethiopian railways which closely followed an earlier design for the Norwegian State Railway. While they stood in the workshops opposite the RhB Mallets being built at the same time it was seen that this was a type which could provide the larger boiler power within the permitted axle loadings.

To make certain that the 2–8–0 was suitable for the curves and that it would run steadily at speeds up to 45kph on all sections, one of the Ethiopian engines was tested on the RhB in autumn 1902 before delivery to Jibuti. The tests were wholly satisfactory and at the end of 1903, when it became necessary to conclude arrangements for increasing the RhB locomotive stock, the management decided to order a batch of 2–8–0s similar to the Ethiopian engines. The tender was made as small as possible, on only four wheels, to permit greater train loads by reducing the deadweight to be hauled up the steep grades. A photograph of No 104 is shown on p 86.

To enable these engines to run from Chur to the Engadin with only one stop at Thusis the tenders from No 105 onwards carried about twice as much water and half a ton more coal. Nos 105–14 were ordered in connection with the construction of the Davos–Filisur line. A total of twenty-nine were built for the RhB, numbered 101–29, in several different batches. Nos 101–6 were two-cylinder compounds with the high-pressure cylinders on the right, using saturated steam. Nos 107–29 had superheated boilers and were simple expansion. The boiler, formed of two rings, had a mean diameter of 1.3m and a barrel length of 4.0m. The 30mm thick plate frames were inside the wheels so that the relatively wide firebox had to be mounted over the frames which were strengthened at the rear. The leading axle was carried in a Bissell truck. The engines had a maximum speed of 52kph and could haul a 90 ton train up a gradient of 35‰ at 22kph.[3]

Following the completion of the RhB electrification in 1922 some of these 2–8–0s were disposed of fairly quickly, as shown in the class list below, but Nos 112–29 were stored until 1927 when they were bought by the Royal State Railways of Siam. I saw some at work in Siam in 1945–6, with the little tenders stacked high with teak logs. In 1972 only Nos 107 and 108 remained in RhB reserve stock for use on occasional steam excursions, or for emergencies. Details of the 2–8–0s and a list of the class are given in the following tables.

Nos	101–4	105–6	107–22	123–8	129
Cylinders, diam, mm	440/660	440/660	440	460	460
stroke, mm	580	580	580	580	580
Tubes, number	176	196	112/18	112/18	112/18
Grate area, sq m	1.9	2.1	2.1	2.1	2.1
Heating surface:					
firebox, sq m	7.6	8.4	8.4	8.4	8.4
superheater, sq m			27.5	27.5	27.5
total, sq m	117.6	131.4	133	133	133
Working pressure, atm	13	14	12	12	12
lb/sq in	180	200	170	170	170
Tender, water, cu m	5.0	9.8	9.8	10.0	10.0
coal, tons	2.0	2.5	2.5	2.5	2.5
Wt in working order, t	58.9	67.3	67.5	68.5	69.7
Length over buffers, m	13.220	13.970	13.970	13.970	13.970
Cost, Fr	61,500	74,000	77,500	83,300	86,500

No	Date	Wks No	Wdn	Disposal	Scrapped
101	1904	1582	1924	Brazil	?
102	1904	1583	1949	Spain*	
103	1904	1584	1924	Brazil	?
104	1904	1587	1950	Spain*	
105	1906	1707	1951	Spain*	
106	1906	1708	1952	Spain*	

107	1906	1709		RhB reserve stock				
108	1906	1710		RhB reserve stock				
109	1907	1813	1920	Spain*				
110	1907	1814	1920	Spain*				
111	1907	1815	1920	Spain*				
112	1907	1816	1927	Royal Siamese Railway			343	1956
113	1907	1817	1927	,,	,,	,,	344	1954
114	1907	1818	1927	,,	,,	,,	345	1950
115	1909	1987	1927	,,	,,	,,	346	1950
116	1909	1988	1927	,,	,,	,,	347	1953
117	1909	1989	1927	,,	,,	,,	348	1950
118	1912	2208	1926	,,	,,	,,	340	1965
119	1912	2209	1926	,,	,,	,,	342	1954
120	1913	2329	1926	,,	,,	,,	341	1954
121	1913	2330	1926	,,	,,	,,	339	1959
122	1913	2331	1926	,,	,,	,,	338	1965
123	1913	2332	1926	,,	,,	,,	336 to Thailand	
				Railway Museum, Bangkok, 1966				
124	1915	2510	1926	Royal Siamese Railway			337	1964
125	1915	2511	1926	,,	,,	,,	335	1953
126	1915	2512	1926	,,	,,	,,	331	1956
127	1915	2513	1926	,,	,,	,,	332	1961
128	1915	2514	1926	,,	,,	,,	333	1958
129	1915	2515	1926	,,	,,	,,	334	1950

*Nos 102, 104–6, 109–11 to F C de la Robla, Spain. Same numbers. Named as follows: 102 *Ceferino de Urien;* 104 *José de Aresti;* 105 *Guillermo Barandiaran;* 106 *Manuel Oraa;* 109 *José Ignacio Ustara;* 110 *José Maria San Martin;* 111 *Victoriano Garay*

RHAETIAN RAILWAY ROLLING STOCK

The earliest rolling stock of the Landquart–Davos Railway, both passenger and goods, consisted entirely of four-wheeled vehicles built by SIG, with a wheelbase of 4.3m. All the vehicles had steel underframes and could take 100m radius curves at 45kph. Passenger carriages were of four types, seating different classes as follows:

Type	First	Second	Third Class
AB	12	12	—
ABC	6	4	14
B	—	24	—
C	—	—	40

Bodies were framed in oak with panels of poplar or softwood. The coaches were described as being 'fitted up in such a way that, while avoiding luxury, they provide solidity, good taste and comfort.[4] Solidity they certainly possessed. Sixty-four four-wheelers out of a total of 258 passenger carriages were still in use in 1967, giving the passenger a lively ride. Since then more have been withdrawn and on 1 May 1970 the total was thirty-three, the oldest, No 2165, dating from 1900. The oldest bogie carriages were built in 1911; of these thirteen of various types were still in use in 1970.

In 1929–30 the Mitropa Company (Mitteleuropäische Schlaf-wagen und Speisewagen A-G, Berlin) put into service three restaurant cars on the RhB which had the distinction of being the first such vehicles in Europe to use electricity for cooking. They were built by SWS and were 16.44m long, 2.7m wide and weighed 27 tons. Current at 220 volts for cooking was provided from the locomotive transformer. They were suitable for use over the Furka–Oberalp Railway. One is used on the Glacier Express as far as Andermatt and the others between Chur and St Moritz. In the 1973 summer timetable two trains each way between Chur and St Moritz had restaurant cars. Two similar cars built for the Bernina Railway in 1928 are described in Chapter 8.

In 1930 a prototype first and second class saloon car was obtained, built by SWS. It measured 15.5m long, seated twelve passengers in a spacious Pullman type section and twelve first class passengers in a separate saloon, and weighed 24 tons tare. It had end vestibules and a lavatory at one end. It was provided with a rack brake gear to enable it to work over the FO and BVZ systems in the Glacier Express. In December 1930 SIG delivered a first class side corridor coach (No 1154), also 15.5m long, seating thirty-five passengers in six compartments again with lavatory at one end. This did not have the rack brake as it was intended for use on the RhB only.

The newest vehicles, of which the first four, Nos 2411–14, were built by FFA/SWP in 1970, measure 18.77m over buffers, weigh only 13 tons tare, and seat sixty-four second class passengers. Doors are electro-pneumatically operated.

The RhB carries a heavy goods traffic in 1,060 wagons of great variety. Many of the original L–D open and covered wagons built in 1889–90 are still in use. A special wagon for bulk cement traffic was introduced in 1956 and by 1970 there were 100 in

Luxury Travel on Metre-Gauge Swiss Railway

Saloon car of Rhaetian Railway, available to first class passengers on payment of small supplement

Interior of non-smoking compartment, showing effect of spaciousness achieved

Box

4" long Fire Box

outside length 2.6 breadth 3.4 1/4 inside

4.10 3/4 x 2.9 3/4 leaving 2 3/4 water space
at the sides and front and 3 3/8 at the
Back. Area of grate 5.32 sq feet. Depth
below boiler 1.9 1/2. from top of fire
bars to bottom of tubes 1.5 1/2 the
bottom of box was made thick

length of smoke box 1.6 Depth below

Page from manuscript book of notes on early Robert Stephenson & Company locomotives, mentioning engine built in 1833 for U.S.A.

Sometimes they ...
job to find him. What's more, says the
attendant, he is not the class of gentleman you can leave behind. I wonder
who is, but refrain from asking. . .

Back in my compartment I read, then
sleep. Occasionally voices drift in from
the outer world. First the blunt accents
of northern England, then the sharp
urgency of Scots. British Railways
achieve their nightly miracle of changing the engine. The delicacy of touch
is the answer to all those who allege
that railwaymen do not care. The new
locomotive makes contact as lightly as
a fly drops on a trout-stream. For
this deftness, born of consideration
for those asleep, a vote of thanks is
overdue. . . .

And so to morning, to the promised
tea, to the newspaper with its plethora
of far-away places and strange-sounding names to remind the Sassenach of
his changed whereabouts. . . Little
stations like Culloden and Aviemore
loom up and fall behind, black-faced
sheep dot the hills, and curlew rise from
the straths beside the line. It has been
a quiet, and wholly typical, night in the
vehicle of drama. But I know that

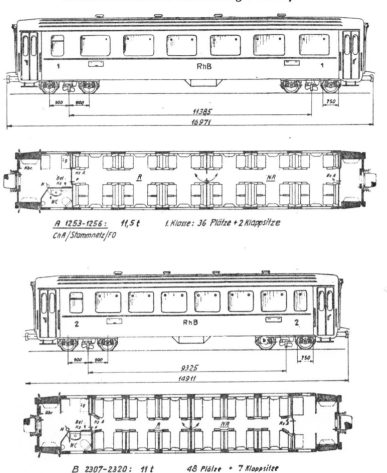

Scale ÷ 1:170

A 1253-1256:   11,5 t   1. Klasse: 36 Plätze + 2 Klappsitze
ChA / Stammnetz / FO

Scale ~ 1:171

B 2307-2320:   11 t   48 Plätze + 7 Klappsitze
Bernina / StN u. BM

RhB coaches; top is a first class coach for RhB main line
services including through workings to the FO, and bottom
a second class coach for the Bernina line (*RhH Chur*)

service. Another important traffic is oil, carried in tanks loaded
at Tirano and worked over the Bernina to unloading points elsewhere on the RhB. The transport of standard gauge wagons west
of Chur began in 1928 when a transporter wagon was obtained
from SIG. There are now twenty in service from Chur to Küblis
and Reichenau. (Photograph on p 85.) In addition there are
74 tank wagons, 55 flat wagons, 29 wagons for gravel and rock,

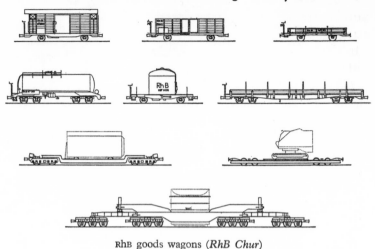

RhB goods wagons (*RhB Chur*)

20 bogie wagons with movable partitions and capacity equal to standard gauge wagons, and a number of well wagons and special vehicles for loads up to 100 tons. Over 300 new wagons were obtained in 1971–2 and more are under construction at the present time.

SNOW PLOUGHS

The RhB must be prepared for routine snow clearance of moderate falls on its main network, for massive falls and drifts on the Bernina section and for avalanches or snow slides anywhere on the system. The simplest frame or bogie-mounted snow ploughs, fitted to locomotives and railcars, can cope adequately with light snowfalls. For heavier work the Landquart–Davos Railway obtained four four-wheeled wedge ploughs from SIG in 1889–90; all were rebuilt at Landquart between 1924 and 1963, and can clear a depth of 0.5m to 0.86m. The RhB obtained four more from SLM in 1897, 1903 and 1908. The wedge ploughs are stationed at Landquart, Davos, Samaden and Reichenau.

The only rotary snow ploughs available for use on the RhB were the three steam machines built for the Bernina Railway (Ch 8), but in 1958 a 220hp diesel rotary plough with twin rotors, No 9216, was built by Martin Beilhack, Rosenheim, Germany, and Robert Aebi, Zurich; it is propelled by a locomotive or railcar and will clear a width of 4m to a depth of 1.94m.

In 1966 a four-wheeled two-directional wedge plough, No 9141, was obtained from E. Stadler, Zurich. The ploughs can be raised or lowered hydraulically, controlled from the propelling locomotive. Three more, Nos 9142–4, were obtained in 1968, and they are stationed at Arosa, Davos, Pontresina and Poschiavo respectively.

The latest machines, Nos 9218–19, built by Beilhack and BBC in 1967, are electric rotary ploughs, with twin rotors each driven by a 350hp motor, used with electric/diesel-electric locomotives Nos 801–2. On the Bernina line they obtain their power from the overhead wire and are propelled by the locomotive or by one of the railcars Nos 41–6. When used on the main RhB network the diesel-electric locomotive both propels the plough and supplies the current for the motors. Both are stationed at Pontresina. (See pp 158–60.)

CHAPTER SEVEN

Electrification and Progress on the Rhaetian Railway

As early as 1898 the Swiss Railway Bank made inquiries concerning the electrification of the Landquart–Davos Railway. Fortunately nothing was done, for by May 1910 when a positive decision was made to electrify the Engadin lines considerable technical progress had been made in electric traction.[1] Even so, the scheme was regarded as an experiment.

The idea was first proposed by Dr A. von Planta, then president of the RhB, at a meeting of the company on 2 March 1905. A report on 6 April urged investigation into the possibility of electrification 'on a level stretch of the system'. Various schemes were studied: Burgdorf–Thun (1899, 750V three-phase ac 40Hz), Bellinzona–Mesocco (1907, 1,500V dc), Bernina (under construction, 750V dc) and Valle Maggia (1907, 5,000V single-phase ac 20Hz).

The original decision was to use single-phase alternating current at 10,000 volts, 15Hz; the system decided upon, however, was 11,000V $16\frac{2}{3}$Hz. The voltage was as high as was practicable, allowing for restricted clearance in the numerous tunnels. The single-phase system required only simple overhead equipment, and the low frequency, a third that of the commercial supply, was necessary because at the time it was only for such a low frequency that a serviceable ac motor could be built for the rigorous demands of railway traction. Suitable rectifiers for locomotives did not exist then, nor for many years after.

Notes to this chapter will be found on p 249

120

A contract was made with the power station at Brusio in the Puschlav for the supply of three-phase current at 23,000V, 50Hz, by lines over the Bernina Pass to a sub-station at Bever, a distance of about 40km. The sub-station was equipped with two converter groups, each consisting of a three-phase motor of 900hp, running at 450–540rpm, coupled to a 1,300kW single-phase generator with a 20 ton flywheel, and a dc motor-generator which could supply or take a current of 2,000 amps at 500V, connected to a large storage battery. The single-phase generator supplied current at 2,500V, $16\frac{2}{3}$Hz, which was transformed to line voltage of 11,000. The battery served to balance uneven loadings and could drive the dc machines which then worked as motors. The ratings shown are nominal.

The catenary was supported by wooden poles, which later had to be replaced by steel, spaced 60m on straights and 35m on curves down to 400m radius. Normal height was 5.5m above rail level, increased to 6.3m in stations and lowered to 4.15m under bridges and tunnels. The catenary equipment was supplied by Siemens-Schuckert Co and the high tension and converter station equipment by Elektrizitätsgesellschaft Alioth.[2] Feeder lines were 50sq mm cross section and contact lines 85sq mm. No trouble was experienced with these in a temperature range of $+30°$ to $-30°$C.

On 1 July 1913, with the opening of the new Bever–Schuls line, electric trains began running over the whole of the Engadin section, from St Moritz and Pontresina to Samaden, Bever and Schuls, a total of 62km. The Engadin electrification was watched with great interest by the Swiss Commission appointed in 1901 to study railway electrification. Its success, together with that of the Lötschberg Railway, also in 1913, influenced the choice of the 15,000V single-phase $16\frac{2}{3}$Hz system adopted by the SBB as a whole, and by other Swiss railways.

EARLY ELECTRIC LOCOMOTIVES

In accordance with the experimental nature of the project, the first electric locomotives were of several types from different makers. The simplest were the 1–B–1 type, Nos 201–7, built by BBC (Brown Boveri) in 1912–13 (see diagram p 122). The

RHAETIAN RAILWAY
SINGLE PHASE ELECTRIC LOCOMOTIVES

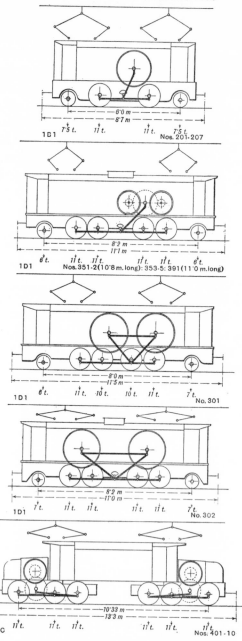

RhB electric locomotives (*The Engineer*)

single Deri motor was directly connected by rods to a jackshaft which in turn drove the outside cranks on the driving wheels. The motor weighed 9,200kg, and developed 300hp at a speed of 28kph. A 415kW transformer provided tappings at 950V for the motor and 300V for heating and auxiliary purposes. The speed of a Deri motor being regulated by brush shifting, extra tappings were necessary for this. Driving wheels were 1,070mm diameter and radial wheels 700mm, and the fixed wheelbase was 2.5m. The locomotives would haul 143 tons at 45kph.

BBC also supplied a 1–D–1 type locomotive, No 301, in 1913, with identical equipment and wheels, but fitted with two motors and deveolping twice the power.[3] (See diagram p 122.) Two further 1–D–1 locomotives, Nos 351–2, were supplied in 1913 by MFO (Maschinenfabrik Oerlikon). They had two 280V neutralised series motors, each of 300hp, with speed regulation from transformer tappings, driving a primary jackshaft through a gear raito of 4.45 : 1. Three more, Nos 353–5, were supplied by MFO in 1913, similar to 351–2 except for two 400hp motors and gear ratio of 4.15 : 1. (See photograph on page 103.)

Another type of 1–D–1 locomotive, No 391, was supplied by AEG (Allgemeine Elektrizitäts-Gesellschaft, Berlin) in 1913. This was similar to 351–5 but had two 350hp series-repulsion motors and a gear ratio of 2.65 : 1.[4] The last of the 1–D–1 loco-motives, No 302, supplied in 1918 by BBC as a stop-gap measure just after the war, was similar to 301 but with two 400hp Deri motors driving through a triangular frame on to a jackshaft. The wheel spacings were as on 351–5 and 391. The general layout of all these locomotives can be seen in the diagrams on p 122. Driving and carrying wheels were as on the 1–B–1 type. On all the 1–D–1 locomotives except 301 the outer coupled axles formed a Bissell truck with the carrying axles. All the locomo-tives were fitted with the Hardy vacuum brake. The weights per horse power varied considerably, as shown in the following table :

Maker	BBC	BBC	MFO	MFO	AEG	BBC
Loco nos	201–7	301	351–2	353–5	391	302
Type	1–B–1	1–D–1	1–D–1	1–D–1	1–D–1	1–D–1
Horse power	300	600	600	800	600	800
Weight, kg	36,700	55,170	49,300	56,370	55,380	57,860
Wt in kg/hp	122	92	82.3	70.5	92.3	72

Current consumption in the AEG locomotive, No 391, was 1 to 2 per cent more favourable than in the MFO locomotives.

COMPLETION OF THE RHAETIAN RAILWAY ELECTRIFICATION

The desperate coal shortage in Switzerland in 1917 and the rapid rise of prices (in 1920 coal cost 4.5 times its pre-war price) influenced the decision to hasten the electrification of the remaining RhB lines as soon as conditions permitted. Under the energetic leadership of Gustav Bener a start was made in 1918 on the Bever–Filisur–Davos lines, 76km in all.

Under a Federal law of September 1918 the RhB received Federal assistance of 17,500,000Fr for electrifying all sections except the Oberland line (Reichenau–Disentis) which was regarded as of lesser importance because at that time there was little prospect of the Furka–Oberalp Railway being completed (Ch 11). Eventually, however, electrification of this line was made possible by the release of a Federal loan in anticipation of the sale of twelve steam locomotives.

The work was carried out with extraordinary speed under the supervision of W. Dürler (d 16 February 1940), and electric operation began on the following dates:

20 April 1919	Bever–Filisur	31.24km
15 October 1919	Filisur–Thusis	23.17km
11 December 1919	Davos Dorf–Filisur ⎫	
22 December 1919	Davos Platz–Davos Dorf ⎬	21.94km
1 December 1920	Davos Dorf–Klosters	14.69km
1 April 1921	Landquart–Thusis (mixed steam and electric)	
1 August 1921	Landquart–Thusis (full electric)	41.18km
7 November 1921	Klosters–Landquart	32.64km
22 May 1922	Reichenau–Disentis	49.39km

Work on the Davos–Klosters line was delayed by troubles with water during the reconstruction of the Cavadürli tunnel, and traffic was interrupted completely from 2 July to 20 August 1919. In 1920, because of the severe gradients on this line, locomotives 353–5 were fitted with equipment for regenerative brak-

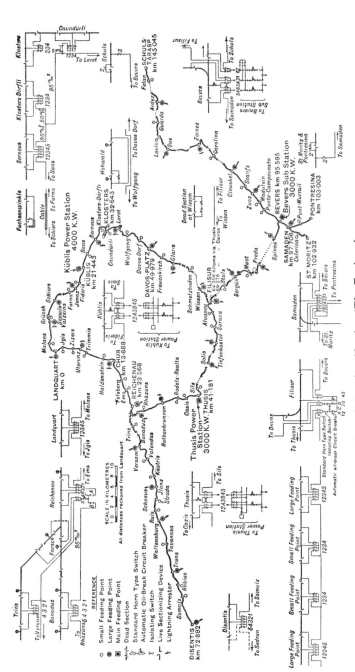

Map of Rhb electrification (*The Engineer*)

ing. The apparatus, supplied by MFO at a cost of 113,500Fr for the three locomotives, weighed 2.5 tons and enabled a train of 95 tons to be held at a speed of 30kph on the 45‰ gradient. On the Reichenau–Disentis section economies were achieved by a lighter overhead system as used on the Swedish State Railways, with a contact line of 80sq mm cross section.

The positioning of the main supply points was arrived at after careful consideration. The general arrangement can be seen on the map on p 125.[5] It was decided to obtain the additional supply from the Rhaetian Electric Works at Thusis, belonging to the Brusio power station, and that at Küblis of the Grisons Power Supply Company. Until Thusis works began supplying power to the railway on 6 September 1921 the whole network except Klosters–Landquart and Reichenau–Disentis had to be run off the Bever sub-station.

Küblis power station began supplying power on 7 November 1921, on which date electric operation began between Klosters and Landquart. It included a three-phase induction motor coupled to a single-phase generator. This both supplied current to the line and recuperated energy from descending trains. If no train was ascending at the time a hydraulic braking nozzle was automatically opened on the turbine.

Küblis and Thusis power stations and the Bever sub-station were arranged to work either in parallel or independently. For this purpose dead sections, long enough for two locomotives and on level track to minimise the danger of stalling, were provided to isolate the systems.

C–C TYPE LOCOMOTIVES

The original assorted locomotive stock of fourteen, increased to fifteen after the war, obviously needed strengthening, and much more powerful locomotives were required for the heavy trains and long gradients of the Albula section. In 1921 six locomotives of a new C–C type appeared, Nos 401–6, illustrated in the drawing opposite and in the photograph on p 52.[6] Electrical equipment was supplied jointly by BBC and MFO, and the mechanical portion by SLM. The locomotive was designed to haul 150 tons at 30kph on gradients of 45‰ and 200 tons on

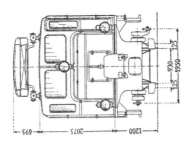

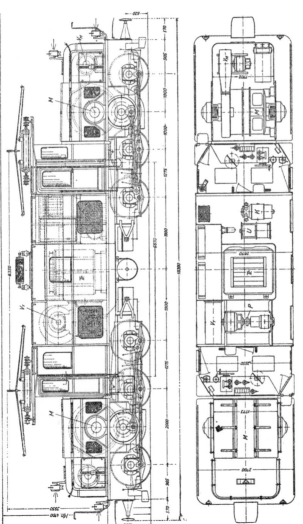

RhB C–C type electric locomotive (*The Engineer*)

gradients of 35%₀. It had two 600hp 500V series motors with rheostat connections driving jackshafts through a reduction of 4.3:1, these being connected by rods to the inner coupled axles. Wheels, as on the other locomotives, were 1,070mm diameter, and the total weight of 65,700kg was entirely available for adhesion. The weight in kg/hp of 54.75 was an outstanding improvement on the best of the earlier locomotives. Hardy vacuum brake equipment was fitted, but was used mainly for the train. To avoid heating of tyres, and metallic dust in the electrical equipment, the locomotives were equipped for electrical braking with resistances. In 1922 four more locomotives, Nos 407–10, were obtained. These and the earlier RhB electric locomotives are painted brown.

The total cost of the completion of the electrification was as follows:

Electrical installation on all sections north of Bever 12,167,900Fr
Alterations to repair shops and locomotive sheds   590,000Fr
Heating of coaches   519,300Fr
Locomotives 302, 401–10 and spares   5,210,100Fr
    Total, including sundries, etc   18,800,000Fr

Following the sale of some of the steam locomotives a further five C–C electric locomotives were obtained, 411–12 in 1925 and 413–15 in 1929.

RECENT DEVELOPMENTS IN MOTIVE POWER

In 1939 four 588hp electric motor coaches were obtained, Nos 501–4, built jointly by BBC, MFO, SWS and SIG. They weigh 37 tons, measure 18m over buffers, seat twenty-eight second class and twelve first class passengers, have a top speed of 65kph, and are used mainly on the Engadin route, between St Moritz and Schuls.

In 1942 a start was made in rebuilding some of the old 1–B–1 locomotives into more modern machines for shunting. The old Deri motor was replaced by a 310hp series motor connected to the jackshaft through double reduction gearing, and a new transformer was installed. The increased space was used for a battery enabling the locomotive to be used for interchange movements at Chur with the Chur–Arosa Railway. The original superstructure was replaced by a single central cab and end bonnets. The wheelbase was increased making room for new brake gear.[7] Nos 201-3 were thus rebuilt and renumbered 211-13. In 1967 211 was again rebuilt with a 320hp diesel engine replacing the battery, so permitting it to be used as a diesel-mechanical locomotive when off the 11kV network. Nos 212-13 were also rebuilt in 1968, but as electric locomotives only without the battery. In 1945 old Nos 204 and 206 were each rebuilt with new transformers and two 502V motors giving a total of 610hp. They retained the old box superstructure, and were renumbered 221-2. The first of the 1–D–1 locomotives, No 301, was withdrawn in 1966. At the time of writing (1972) all the others are still in service.

The slow economic recovery of Graubünden after the second war delayed further necessary improvements for several years. The immense progress in electric locomotive design since 1922 was immediately apparent in 1947 when a new 1,600hp Bo–Bo locomotive was delivered. As with the earlier C–C type the electrical portion was built jointly by MFO and BBC and the mechanical portion by SLM. Each bogie carries two 400hp motors giving a maximum speed of 75kph. With a total weight

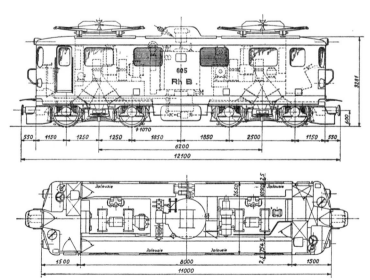

RhB Bo–Bo type electric locomotive No 605 (*RhB Chur*)

of 47 tons it has a weight in kg/hp of under 30. Other dimensions are shown in the drawing on p 129. It can take 220 tons between Chur and Thusis, 165 tons from there to St Moritz or 125 tons up the 45‰ between Klosters and Davos at 46kph. The regenerative brake will stop a train of 145 tons on a gradient of 35‰. Four were obtained in 1947 and six in 1953. They established a new tradition on the RhB by being painted green and carrying names, as follows:

601	*Albula*	606	*Kesch*
602	*Bernina*	607	*Surselva*
603	*Badus*	608	*Madrisa*
604	*Calanda*	609	*Linard*
605	*Silvretta*	610	*Viamala*

In 1958 an even larger locomotive, the ultimate so far in metre gauge power, was obtained. This is the articulated Bo–Bo–Bo type with three motor bogies giving 2,400hp and weighing only 65 tons, about 700 kg less than the C–C type but with twice the power and a weight in kg/hp of 27, half that of the C–C. It was also built by MFO, BBC and SLM and like the 601 type has a top speed of 75kph. Two, Nos 701–2, were obtained in 1958 and five more, Nos 703–7, in 1965. Like the 601 type

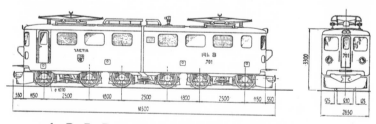

RhB Bo–Bo–Bo type electric locomotive No 701 (*RhB Chur*)

they are green and carry names, some in German on one side and Romansch on the other, as follows:

701	*Raetia*	705	*Pontresina/Puntraschigna*
702	*Chur/Curia*	706	*Disentis/Mustér*
703	*St Moritz*	707	*Schuls/Scuol*
704	*Davos*		

Dimension are shown in the drawing above.

As soon as conditions permitted after the war a start was made with replacing the feeder and contact lines with heavier section material to reduce voltage drop. In 1960 a new 10,000kW feeder station was brought into use to improve the supply arrangements.

In the summer of 1967 the RhB introduced the first 2hr schedule between St Moritz and Chur, including eight stops, with the 7.12 from St Moritz, probably the fastest metre gauge run in the world over such a distance. At Chur connection is made with the 9.22 to Zurich and Basle for the 13.05 Lorelei express from there to Hook of Holland.

In May 1971 four three-car electric multiple unit trains were introduced, three on the Chur local services, Klosters–Chur–Thusis and Disentis, and the fourth between Pontresina and Samaden. They were the first in Switzerland to be equipped with thyristor semi-conductor rectifiers, which combine good traction power with the ability to regenerate for braking. Electrical equipment is by Ateliers de Sécheron, bodies are by Flug & Fahrzeugwerke, Altenrhein, and bogies by SIG, Neuhausen.[8] Each set cost about Fr2 million, and consists of a power car and a middle car, both second class, and a driving end car, first and second class, with a total seating capacity of 165. The total weight is 88 tons and with 1,000hp they can reach a maximum speed of 90kph in 45 seconds. (See photograph page 103.)

In March 1973 the first of ten thyristor equipped Bo-Bo locomotives was delivered. The four motors develop a total of 2,200hp and give a maximum speed of 90kph. They are numbered and named as follows:[9]

611	*Landquart*	616	*Filisur*
612	*Thusis*	617	*Ilanz*
613	*Domat/Ems*	618	*Bergün/Bravougn*
614	*Schiers*	619	*Samedan*
615	*Klosters*	620	*Zernez*

Future plans include a further four railcars in the period up to 1975 and ten more locomotives and four railcars in 1976–80.[10]

RHAETIAN RAILWAY WORKSHOPS AND MAINTENANCE

The rolling stock of the RhB includes about 50 electric locomotives, 3 dual powered locomotives, 34 railcars, 27 shunting and service vehicles, about 270 passenger coaches and about 1,175 goods wagons and 25 snow clearing vehicles. Of the total maintenance work 79.8 per cent is carried out in the main shops at Landquart, 11.35 per cent at Samaden, 4.15 per cent at Poschiavo, 4.15 per cent at Mesocco and 0.55 per cent at Chur Sand on the Chur-Arosa section.[11] Of these Samaden is concerned almost entirely with goods vehicles, and Chur Sand only with railcars. The total working force employed by the various shops is about 320 men including over 50 apprentices of whom 45 are in the main shops at Landquart.

Under Swiss Federal regulations for private railways the periods between general repairs are: for main line locomotives and power cars, passenger coaches, luggage and postal vehicles, 4 years; goods wagons, 5 years; and service vehicles 6 years. In addition to this a considerable amount of daily maintenance, lubrication and cleaning, is undertaken at the various depots. Normally a locomotive will receive an intermediate repair after two years when wheels are turned and various adjustments are made. On average a locomotive receives a general repair, after about 4,000 hours of running, at a cost of around 40,000Fr. Repairs to an average of 1.1 vehicles must be completed each working day to fulfil the year's programme.

Apprentices receive three or four years' training. The first year is spent at the Busch Cantonal Training Workshops at Chur where they receive a thorough grounding in the basic principles of their future careers. During their remaining years in the works they attend classes at the technical schools at Landquart and Poschiavo.

After passing their final examinations many of the apprentices remain with the RhB as engineers and some become train drivers. Driver training involves a year in the main depot or the depot workshops followed by a period in shunting service leading up to an examination. Following this the trainee completes a course of 130 days training on the line. Then success in a further examination leads the apprentice to a year as a reserve driver at the end of which a final examination will qualify him as a driver.

RHAETIAN RAILWAY ECONOMY AND PROGRESS

In its first fifteen years the RhB grew from 92 to 276.6km and later its existence made possible the Bernina and Chur–Arosa railways, described in the next chapters. Its stimulation of the cantonal economy is shown in the total rateable value which rose from 207,800,000Fr in 1886 to 401,600,000Fr in 1912 and Fr648 million in 1936. Earnings in the same period grew from 6,700,000Fr to 70,600,000Fr. By its establishment of a pensions and benevolent fund of 2,500,000Fr and an expenditure of Fr2 million on welfare work during its first fifty years it also contributed substantially to the social development of Graubünden.

During the boom period up to World War I the organisation was enlarged to a working strength of 1,656 under three directors. Increasing road competition compelled reorganisation under a single director after the retirement of Achilles Schucan on 1 October 1918. To this office Gustav Bener was appointed in the autumn of 1919 from the position of director and engineer of the Chur–Arosa Railway. Under Bener's leadership the working strength was reduced to 789 by 1938 with consequent improvement in salaries and security. Bener retired in 1936 and died on 25 January 1946. He was succeeded by Dr E. Branger.

However, the interest of four per cent on the electrification loans imposed a heavy burden, and in the face of increasing road competition and the worsening European situation the most stringent economic measures were unable to restore the railway to financial stability. In 1936 the Federal Council granted a sum of Fr93 million for the development of the cantonal railways and a subsequent mortgage of Fr40 million at a variable interest rate, and also a reduction of the interest on the electrification loan to three per cent.

In April 1939 the cantonal authority made a further loan of Fr125 million to assist in recovery, but the outbreak of war brought further difficulties, leading to amalgamation with the Misox and Chur–Arosa railways on 1 January 1942 and with the Bernina on 1 January 1943, bringing the total route length to 394km.[12] In 1966, of the total share capital of 57,957,000Fr the Canton held 29,752,000Fr, or 51.4 per cent, the Federation

Fr25 million, or 43.1 per cent. A further 800,500Fr, or 1.4 per cent, were held by cantonal communities and the remainder, 2,404,000Fr, or 4.1 per cent, by private shareholders.

On 20 February 1938 Romansch became officially recognised as the fourth language of Switzerland, in which the Rhaetian Railway is referred to as Viafier Retica.

The RhB has been remarkably free from serious accidents. Only one, on 1 August 1952, could be attributed to human failure. A train from Chur to St Moritz took the curve into Bever station too fast and derailed, killing two passengers and a pedestrian beneath a road bridge. The leading locomotive, 1–B–1 No 222, was not seriously damaged, but the train locomotive, the new Bo–Bo No 602, required extensive repair.

Several accidents have been caused by rock slides and avalanches. The worst occurred between Wolfgang and Davos where, on a previous occasion in February 1892, an avalanche blocked the line for a week. At 17.00 on Sunday 29 April 1917 a steam train approaching Davos was suddenly overcome by an avalanche and was wrecked. Ten people were killed and it was 1 May before the line could be reopened.

On 3 August 1931 C–C locomotive No 411 struck a rock slide between Filisur and Stuls. The two leading coaches were derailed, and the locomotive fell down the hillside and broke into three sections, the first two coming to rest about 30m below the line and the rear section another 100m below that. Recovery was a major operation, taking from 19–29 August, under the supervision of Inspector Mäder and Richard Coray of Chur. After extensive rebuilding costing 176,300Fr the locomotive was returned to traffic on 13 March 1932.[13]

From 8–10 March 1945 the Klosters–Davos line was again blocked by an avalanche, near Cavadürli, and on 19 January 1951 another avalanche wrecked the station at Davos Monstein, killing the station master and a lengthman. That winter, for the first time, much of the RhB had to be closed because of the depth of snow and damage to overhead contact lines. Much was learned from these incidents and extensive protection works have lessened the likelihood of recurrences.

Future RhB plans for the period up to 1980 include renewal

of most of the track and the extension of block signalling to the whole system.[14] Happily these improvements are being carried out despite an operating deficit. In 1971 receipts were 58,588,000Fr against an expenditure of 62,472,000Fr. In recent years the track between Chur and Reichenau carrying both Engadin and Rhine Valley services has been doubled and the track on the southern side is laid with a third rail to give standard freight vehicles direct access to the Domat/Ems works from Chur.

RHAETIAN RAILWAY OPERATION AND SIGNALLING

Operation of the Swiss metre gauge railways and mountain lines has always been specialised, and until recently it was considered that they needed little signalling to ensure safety. Indeed on many Swiss local lines of standard and narrow gauge, signalling was, and on some still is, primitive compared with that on Swiss inter-city main lines and the rigid requirements on all British Rail's passenger lines. For example, stations can still be found where there is no interlocking between points and signals and, indeed, where points are controlled by a hand lever at the track-side, and lines may still be worked without the block system or any electro-mechanical means of ensuring the security of single line sections. In these instances trains run under what is known as timetable and train order working.

Normally, trains operate according to the timetable which regulates the crossing places of all trains. The driver's time sheet will also tell him at which points he will cross which trains. If trains run late, however, and services are disrupted, crossing points have to be altered and the station masters concerned must agree by telephone or telegraph which trains are affected, and new crossing places must be arranged. To cover the altered arrangements each driver concerned is given a written train order instructing him to cross the other trains at the revised crossing places. The system works well enough where traffic is light, but it is entirely dependent on the human element.

At some stations there were no signals whatever and station staff had to communicate with the drivers by hand or flag signals. Most stations were, however, and a few still are, equipped with a mechanical home signal in the form of the now obsolete red disc with slanting white stripe. The disc is face on to the driver in the danger position and edge on in the clear position. When clear it permits the train to enter the station, but onward movement into the section ahead can only be made on the personal instruction or signal from the station master or his deputy. The system seems primitive, but speeds are low and most station layouts simple, sometimes no more than a passing loop and possibly a siding. In Swiss practice there has always been much personal contact between station staff and train drivers in signalling matters. On the Continent the station master himself has usually been responsible for train movement and the operation of the block system so that it was inevitable that signalling was supervised from the main station offices. This is why today throughout Switzerland, except at the large junction stations on the standard gauge main lines like Berne, Basle and Zurich, etc modern signalling control panels are centred in an operations room which also includes the ticket office, sometimes the parcels office, and the station master's general office.

Many stations on the RhB and on the other metre gauge lines described in this book are operated by one man who looks after signalling, ticket issue, parcels, shunting, etc. Even so, on lines like these, where operating costs make up a large part of the deficit, measures are being investigated to reduce the labour requirements of railway operation, even using unmanned stations at times during the day. Moreover, Swiss railways are suffering a shortage of staff, particularly in principal operating grades, which means that modern methods of centralised control must be introduced.

The first move towards a modern signalling system on the RhB was in 1952 when a switchboard was installed at St Moritz to control points and signals. It was followed in 1959 by the installation of automatic crossing equipment at Cavadürli above Klosters. The success of this led to a contract with Integra Ltd of Zurich for the installation of electric signalling over the entire main line from Chur to St Moritz and along the Rhine valley to Disentis from where the same system was to be extended by the Furka–Oberalp Railway to Brig. Work began in 1961 and by the

Page 137. (Above) Alp Grüm and the view over the Poschiavo Lake, from above Pozzo del Drago tunnel on the Bernina Railway. An avalanche shelter now covers the railway in the foreground; (below) St Moritz–Alp Grüm train passing Lago Bianco, Bernina Railway (p 149)

Page 138. (Above) Spiral below Brusio, Bernina Railway (p 152); (left) Castieler viaduct, Chur–Arosa railway, after rebuilding. Railcar No 482 on train to Chur (p 169). The viaduct requires periodic correction, carried out by hydraulic jacks. In 1962 the steelwork had to be moved 30cm

beginning of 1969 the section Filisur–St Moritz was completed.

The section from Thusis to the middle of the Albula tunnel is supervised from the Filisur control panel. Of the nine stations in this section Solis, Surava, Alvaneu, Stuls and Muot were rebuilt as automatic crossing stations. Sils is controlled from Thusis, 1.9km away. Tiefencastel and Bergün, with their fairly large passenger traffic, remain staffed and are equipped as block points for local operation with facilities for switching out to enable automatic through working to operate, but without automatic crossing. Preda, which handles sports traffic in winter, was given similar treatment, with the possibility of automatic crossing being installed later. Where distances between stations were long (four are over 6km and four more over 4km) they were divided by intermediate block sections of which the longest is 3.2km. The Albula tunnel was not divided as it can be operated at speeds up to 75kph.

The northern portals of the Rugnux tunnel above Muot and of the Albula tunnel are closed by doors in winter to prevent the formation of ice in the tunnels. These doors and the connected signals are operated automatically by the trains themselves as are several level crossing barriers.

The section from Albula tunnel to Bever is controlled from Samaden. Spinas, at the south end of the Albula tunnel, is equipped as an automatic crossing station. At Bever automatic crossing is available only for Albula trains. The lines to the Lower Engadin are controlled from Samaden. Celerina, St Moritz and Pontresina are operated from local control desks.

Stations with local control are operated from a push-button panel in the station building. From this, indications are automatically communicated to the remote control panel which has direct control only of the block section above and below the station concerned, the switching on and off of point heaters and time switches for station lighting, and the by-pass switching for through or automatic working. When remote control is in use the station is operated entirely from the distant control panel which assumes the function of the local official. Crossing, overtaking and shunting movements are possible.

At automatic crossing stations the points and signals are set by circuits operated by the trains themselves. The first train into the station must stop in the track nearest to the station building so that the crossing train passes behind it. This is to ensure that passengers boarding and alighting (where there is no subway) are not in danger from an approaching train. For arrival and departure without crossing, the track with the simplest arrangement of points is used. Should two opposing trains approach two automatic crossing stations at the same time the most favourable crossing place is automatically selected. The handling of three trains at one automatic station requires operation from the remote control panel.

Because the metre gauge lines are almost entirely on steel sleepers normal track circuiting is not possible and is used only on short sections specially laid on wooden sleepers. Direct current for the block section equipment is provided by a rectifier at each station, the equipment itself being housed in a concrete cabin by the signal and operated from the local or remote control panel. Every station has arrival (home) and departure (starting) signals.

The introduction of automatic train control has resulted in a reduction in journey times and promises considerable economies in operating costs. The next sections to be dealt with will be the Rhine valley, Chur–Arosa and Bernina sections.

The Rhaetian Railway never fails to astonish the interested traveller by its efficiency and punctuality. On a wide ranging network of steeply graded routes, almost entirely single track, it operates about 370 trains a day in the summer season. If trains are late it is generally because of a delayed international connection at Chur, possibly with through coaches from northern Europe. At crossing stations the waiting train will be on the move immediately the passing train is inside the loop. Besides its own connections at Chur, Reichenau, Filisur, Samaden and St Moritz, the RhB connects with SBB trains at Chur and Landquart, with the FO at Disentis, with the Italian railways at Tirano, and with postal motor coaches at numerous other places. At all points changes are convenient, and everywhere the traveller is met with friendly courtesy and helpfulness. A journey in Graubünden is a pleasure indeed.

CHAPTER EIGHT

The Bernina Railway

see also RW NOV & DEC '72

PLANNING

THE south-east portion of Graubünden, known as the Veltlin, like the Misox valley and Tessin or Ticino, belongs geographically to Italy, and the entire population speaks Italian. It is separated from the rest of Graubünden by the Bernina Pass, 2,334m. In 1865 a road was completed over the pass and a horse postal service became established, taking nine hours between Samaden and Tirano. The great height of the pass, the brutally severe weather in both summer and winter, the long distance between villages on each side and the steep gradients made it a hazardous journey even in the best conditions; but the magnificent scenery attracted increasing numbers of tourists, some of whom lost their lives on the journey.

At the end of the nineteenth century plans were prepared for a railway from Samaden to Tirano. A Swiss concession was granted on 22 December 1899 and an Italian concession for the short section in that country on 12 June 1902. Also in 1902 the standard gauge Valtellina Railway was opened to Tirano.

The Bernina project was seen as a link in a metre gauge network following proposals for a line of about 29km from Tirano over the Aprica Pass to the Valcamonica Railway (opened in 1909) at Edolo and thence over the Tonal Pass to Malè, and the extension of the RHB from St Moritz over the Maloja Pass to Chiavenna and down the Inn valley to the Arlberg Railway at Landeck.[1]

The building of the Brusio power station in the Puschlav or

Notes to this chapter will be found on p 249

Poschiavo valley above Tirano in 1904–7 gave further stimulus for an electric railway. A condition of its concession was that it should supply electricity to the Bernina Railway at a reasonable cost.

On 12 November 1904 an association of English, Italian and Swiss financiers was formed in Milan with an obligation upon the Swiss group to raise half the share capital for the Bernina Railway. At the same time preliminary agreements were concluded with the contractors Albert Buss & Co of Basle for the construction of the formation, permanent way, overhead gear and signalling installations and with Elektrizitätsgesellschaft Alioth of Münchenstein for the supply of all electrical equipment and rolling stock.

The railway was originally planned to start from Samaden but later, by arrangement with the RhB whose branch from Samaden to Pontresina was opened on 1 July 1908, the terminus was transferred to St Moritz. By reducing the ruling gradient from 82‰ to 70‰ the length was substantially increased. From a height of 1,778m in the Engadin it had to climb to a summit of 2,256m from which, in a horizontal distance of just over 22km, it had to fall through 1,827m to the terminus at Tirano at a height of 429m. (See map and profile, pp 143 and 144–5.)

Rack sections were considered for the south ramp, but as these would have been in the proportion of 8km of rack to 45km of adhesion line it was decided that the extra dead weight of the rack equipment on the vehicles was not justified. The Bernina Railway was thus to overcome by adhesion a greater difference in height than any Swiss rack railway, of which the greatest height differences are: 1,681.06m on the Brienzer Rothorn, 1,628.45m on Pilatus, and 1,411.06m on the Gornergrat. The Albula Railway, in the 47.5km from Thusis to the Albula tunnel, overcomes by adhesion a difference of 1,122.86m.

A summit tunnel of about 9km was considered, to lower the summit level from 2,256m to 1,900–2,200m and to make winter operation easier, but the idea was abandoned, partly for fear of the loss of tourist traffic to the grand scenery at the summit and also because of the expense. The final estimate was Fr12 million for about 60km of railway, but this cost was later increased by

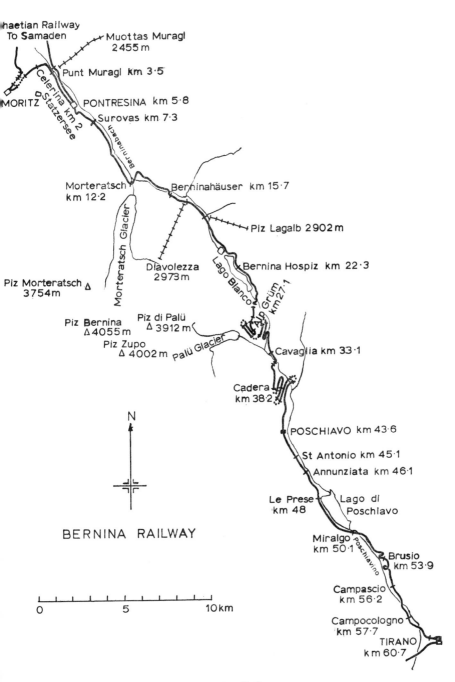

haetian Railway
To Samaden

Muottas Muragl
2455 m

Punt Muragl km 3·5

Celerina km 2

Statzersee

MORITZ

PONTRESINA km 5·8

Surovas km 7·3

Berninabach

Morteratsch
km 12·2

Berninahäuser km 15·7

Piz Lagalb 2902 m

Morteratsch Glacier

Diàvolezza
2973 m

Lago Bianco

Bernina Hospiz km 22·3

Piz Morteratsch △
3754 m

Alp Grüm km 27·1

Piz Bernina
△ 4055 m

Piz di Palü
△ 3912 m

Piz Zupo
△ 4002 m Palü Glacier

Cavaglia km 33·1

N

Cadera
km 38·2

POSCHIAVO km 43·6

St Antonio km 45·1

Annunziata km 46·1

Le Prese
km 48

Lago di
Poschiavo

BERNINA RAILWAY

Miralgo
km 50·1

Poschiavino

Brusio
km 53·9

Campascio
km 56·2

0   5   10 km

Campocologno
km 57·7

TIRANO
km 60·7

Map of Bernina Railway

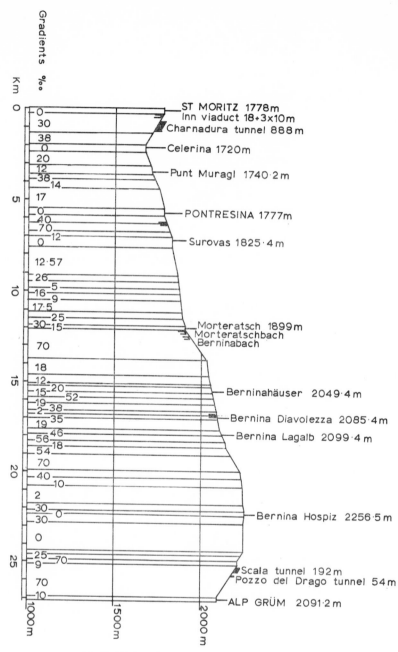

Profile of Bernina Railway, St Moritz–Alp Grüm

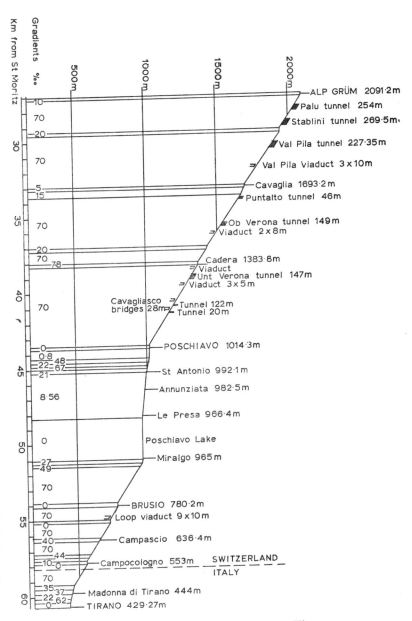

Gradients ‰

500m

1000m

1500m

2000m

ALP GRÜM 2091·2m

10

70

Palu tunnel 254m

Stablini tunnel 269·5m·

20

30

Val Pila tunnel 227·35m

70

Val Pila Viaduct 3 x 10m

5

Cavaglia 1693·2m

15

Puntalto tunnel 46m

35

70

Ob Verona tunnel 149m

Viaduct 2 x 8m

20

70

78

Cadera 1383·8m

Viaduct

Unt Verona tunnel 147m

Viaduct 3 x 5m

40

70

Cavagliasco bridges 28m

Tunnel 122m

Tunnel 20m

0

POSCHIAVO 1014·3m

0·8

48

22

67

45

21

St Antonio 992·1m

Annunziata 982·5m

8·56

Le Presa 966·4m

50

0

Poschiavo Lake

Miralgo 965m

27

49

70

0

BRUSIO 780·2m

70

Loop viaduct 9 x 10m

55

0

70

40

Campascio 636·4m

70

44

Campocologno 553m   SWITZERLAND

10

0

ITALY

70

35

37

Madonna di Tirano 444m

60

22

62

0

TIRANO 429·27m

Profile of Bernina Railway, Alp Grüm–Tirano

alterations to the route to avoid rock slides and snow drifts, extra halts, the widening of rolling stock from 2.4m to 2.5m and additional strengthening works.

The new plans and sections were ready by June 1905. At the same time Italian financial support was suddenly withdrawn and progress was made possible only by the help of the Swiss Railway Bank and the Basler Kapitalisten in Basle. Further help was given by various local authorities along the route who gave the land required by the railway rent free.

CONSTRUCTION

W. Siegrist was appointed chief engineer for the north side and E. Bosshard for the south, with offices at Celerina and Poschiavo. Contracts with Alioth and Buss were concluded early in 1906 and work began on both sides on 16 July following.

Besides the considerable technical difficulties of construction there were problems of housing workers and transporting materials, for on the 37km stretch between Pontresina and Poschiavo there was not even the smallest hamlet. Temporary buildings for workers had to be built to withstand the often violent storms and to provide protection from the extreme cold. At times some 2,500 workers had to be accommodated. South of Alp Grüm where the railway was some distance from the road a mule caravan laden with provisions had to make its way from Poschiavo twice daily over a wretched mule track into the mountains. For this work the company maintained a stud of thirteen mules and three horses, and a team of five oxen for transporting building stone to the inaccessible places. On favourable stretches two 0–6–0 tramway type steam locomotives were used, hired from the Birsigtal Railway at Basle after it changed to electric working on 2 June 1905. They were built by SLM in 1887, and were two of Birsigtal Nos 1, 2, 3 and 5.[2]

The work was hindered by abnormally bad weather throughout the three building seasons of 1908–10; in fact on 14 July 1909 a metre of snow fell on the summit stretch and in all three years the snow lay in some parts until early July. Unfortunately there were no tunnels long enough to provide work throughout the winter, as on the Albula railway. Despite these difficulties the health of the workers was maintained at a high level and the small hospital provision was seldom overtaxed. There were five deaths during construction, all from dynamite explosions. The final cost was 11,698,000Fr, or 192,800Fr per km excluding rolling stock.

Electricity at 50Hz three-phase ac was supplied by Brusio power station at 7,000V along an overhead line on steel masts to a transformer station nearby at Campocologno. Here a portion was transformed to 500V and by rotary converters to 750V dc for line distribution on the adjoining section of railway. The rest was transformed to 23,000V as for the Bever sub station of the RhB and carried by overhead lines on wooden masts to transformer and converter stations at Poschiavo, Bernina Hospiz and Pontresina. To relieve the transformer stations at Poschiavo and Bernina Hospiz of the excessive surge loads imposed by trains climbing the 18km of 70%o between them an accumulator battery station was provided at Cavaglia Halt.

Difficulties with transport of materials on the south side of the summit, variations in the route, bad weather and troubles with the Italian workers who could be persuaded only with difficulty to work at the high altitude, delayed completion of the Hospiz–Alp Grüm section a full year beyond its contract date, but in spite of this the whole line was in operation only four days after the final contract date. The opening dates were:

1 July 1908	Pontresina–Morteratsch, Tirano–Poschiavo
18 August 1908	Pontresina–Celerina, Morteratsch–Berninahäuser
1 July 1909	St Moritz–Celerina, Berninahäuser–Hospiz
5 July 1910	Hospiz–Alp Grüm–Poschiavo

Gradient lengths are:

0–15%o	19,949.5m	32.9 per cent
15–50%o	12,569.2m	20.7 per cent
50–70%o	28,162.2m	46.4 per cent

The original rails weighed 24.3kg/m and were in 12m

lengths. After 1930 the track was relaid with rails of 30.1kg/m in 15m lengths. Steel sleepers were used on the 70%₀ gradients and for the rest of the line wood sleepers were originally used, with oak in tunnels. The entire track now has steel sleepers. There are forty-six bridges totalling 710m, and fourteen tunnels and galleries totalling 4,105m or 6.8 per cent of the total length.

THE ROUTE

At St Moritz the RhB station was enlarged to accommodate the Bernina trains. Outside the station the line crosses the Inn by a stone viaduct and enters the Charnadura gorge. It was originally planned to pass through the Statzerwald, close to the Statzersee, but local objections forced the present longer route, falling through the Charnadura tunnel to Celerina. The line now begins to climb, with beautiful views to the left over the triangle of the Upper Engadin. At Punt Muragl an iron bridge over the Flatzbach connects with the RhB station and the lower terminus of the cable railway to Muottas Muragl. At Pontresina are the carriage sheds and workshops for the north side of the railway.

Above here the line had to be built higher on the mountain to avoid spoiling the beautiful Taiserwald, the additional cost of 50,000Fr being provided by Pontresina. Beyond Surovas Halt the line ascends the left bank of the Berninabach to Morteratsch. After crossing the Morteratschbach by a bow girder bridge it climbs beside the road, crossing the stream again just below the Berninabach Falls which are at their best in the early summer. To the right along this stretch is a splendid view of the Morteratsch Glacier and the peaks of the Bernina range dominated by the Piz Bernina, 4,055m.

An RhB project for a mountain railway from Morteratsch to the summit of the Piz Bernina at an estimated cost of Fr 12 million received a Swiss concession in 1930. In a length of 9.34km including a tunnel of 5,380m it would have overcome a difference in height of 2,119m, but the subsequent war prevented further progress.

Berninahäuser or Bernina Suot station is followed by halts serving the aerial ropeways to Diavolezza and Piz Lagalb. The railway follows the road as far as Arlas from where it follows the old mule track for the next 24km to find a suitable development for the descent to Poschiavo. While the road crosses the pass at a height of 2,334m the railway continues to climb to the east of Lago Bianco, with fine views, reaching its summit level at Bernina Hospiz, or Ospizio station, at a height of 2,256.5m. Lago Bianco was originally four lakes but it was dammed up to form a reservoir for Brusio power station, forcing the railway to be built some 9m higher.

From here the line descends through the Scala tunnel, Pozzo del Drago tunnel (named after a small lake reputed to be the home of a dragon), and beyond an avalanche gallery reaches Alp Grüm. The traveller should spend at least an hour here. The station has a restaurant, and from its balcony there are tremendous views over the Palü Glacier and the surrounding peaks. There is also an interesting alpine garden; but most thrilling of all is the view down the Poschiavo valley to the Poschiavo Lake, 1,290m below and only 11km distant. To reach Poschiavo from above Alp Grüm the railway has to overcome a difference in height of 1,230m in a horizontal distance of 7.5km, and to maintain the ruling gradient of 70‰ the length had to be increased to 17.5km. How this was done is shown in the map on p 150, and the photograph on p 137.

Leaving Alp Grüm the line drops to the right in a semi-circle passing below the station to Palü tunnel in which it describes three quarters of a circle. Emerging lower down the mountain it passes again beneath the station to Stablini tunnel. Now utilising the east slope of Alp Grüm, it threads the semi-circular Pila tunnel, returning to a point below the station where it makes two more semi-circular turns in the open, the last crossing the Val Pila at a height of 22m on a stone viaduct lying on a curve of 50m radius.

At Cavaglia Halt the gradient eases briefly before plunging into the wooded gorge of the Cavagliasco which is crossed to enter Puntalto tunnel. Below is a splendid view over the Poschiavo valley which remains first to the left, then to the right, as the train negotiates the four loops above Poschiavo. First comes the upper Verona tunnel in which the line turns back on itself. The next loop is in the open and brings us to Cadera Halt, below

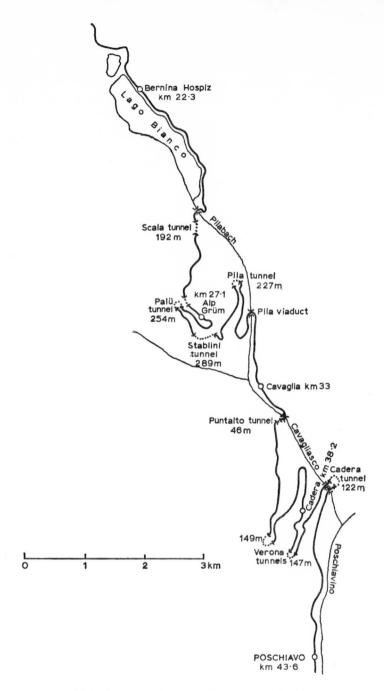

Map of Bernina Hospiz–Poschiavo section, Bernina
Railway

which the line loops round again in the lower Verona tunnel. Still falling, it twice crosses the Cavagliasco on stone viaducts, between which it loops round for the last time in the Cadera tunnel. The piers of the three Cavagliasco viaducts had to be carried down to a depth of 9–12m to find secure foundations in the scree slopes. The developments which have brought the line down from Alp Grüm were adopted upon the advice of Achilles Schucan, engineer and manager of the RhB, but only after several alternative schemes had been fully worked out.

Poschiavo where we now arrive is one of the principal stations, with a restaurant and goods depot, carriage sheds and workshops. The town is an interesting place and a break of journey here is worth while. In 1945 the RhB prepared plans for the rebuilding of Poschiavo workshops but the urgency of other work and lack of money delayed the start of reconstruction until September 1969. The new workshop was completed in 1972 at a total cost of 2,250,000Fr. The main building, with an area of 1,352sq m, provides facilities for the overhaul of all the stock used on the Bernina Railway. The depot employs sixty-six persons of whom sixteen are drivers, and provides a four-year apprenticeship in engineering for eleven pupils.

At St Antonio the main road is joined again, the line passing through Annunziata and Le Prese in grooved rails in the road itself. Along the west shore of Poschiavo Lake a new road has been built above the railway which has been relaid with standard flat bottomed rail along the course of the old road, where it formerly ran in grooved rails. At Miralgo the railway leaves the road, crosses the river, and descends by a couple of loops to Brusio. Disputes over the site of Brusio station, above or below the village, involving the working out of two complete projects, delayed construction of the following stretch. Although the right side of the valley would have afforded a more secure foundation the left side was chosen, despite treacherous scree slopes, to avoid heavy engineering works which would have been needed to cross the valley lower down. Extensive protective works had to be built against rock falls.

Below Brusio the line makes a complete spiral in the open to regain the valley floor and to avoid the insecure mountainside.

The loop, see photograph p 138, includes a stone viaduct 110m long on a curve of 50m radius, beneath the fourth arch of which the line passes about 12m lower. Just below Campascio halt the line crosses the course of a landslide by a bridge of simple steel joists to facilitate restoration if displaced.

At Campocologno passports are examined. About 200m below here a steel truss bridge carries the railway over the five pressure pipes of the Brusio power station. Just beyond here the Italian frontier is crossed. The Italians demanded excessive charges for widening the road below here so that the company had to build the railway on a separate course to La Rasiga. Here it joins the road, which had been already widened, and follows it like a street tramway past Madonna di Tirano to the Tirano terminus.

This is a neat station, with two platform faces and a steel roof. It adjoins the terminus of the standard gauge Upper Valtellina Railway, a private line connecting at Sondrio with the Italian State Railways branch from Lecco on Lake Como. Of the other stations only those at Bernina Hospiz, Poschiavo, Brusio and Campocologno were built with living quarters, offices and goods sheds.

ROLLING STOCK AND LOCOMOTIVES

For its opening the Bernina Railway obtained fourteen 300hp passenger power cars, each with four 75hp motors. Besides rheostat braking positions on the controllers the cars had electro-pneumatic rail brakes, Hardy continuous vacuum brake and hand brakes. Each car seated twelve first and thirty-one second class passengers and weighed 28.1 tons tare. There were also two power baggage cars of which one was withdrawn in 1970. Ten four-wheeled passenger trailers weighing 8.5 tons and some bogie cars weighing 12.7 tons provided extra passenger accommodation. The remaining rolling stock consisted of ten open and ten closed goods wagons, each with vacuum and hand brakes. By 1972 all but a few of the four-wheeled passenger carriages had been withdrawn. Two 340hp Bo locomotives with central cabs and end bonnets, Nos 61–2, were obtained from BBC in 1911 and are used for shunting and pick-up freight work.

Attempts to operate the railway throughout the winter soon proved that the snow protection works and the small ploughs fitted to the power cars were completely inadequate. In the summer of 1910 seven snow galleries totalling 559m were erected. In the same year SLM built a steam rotary snow plough for the Bernina. Its design presented problems, but they were successfully overcome. Steam was dictated by the amount of power required, 500–600hp for the rotary plough and 300–400hp for its propulsion, too much for the contact line which in any event might be broken. The curves necessitated a single-unit machine and the weight restriction of 7.5 tons per axle compelled it to be carried on two six-wheeled bogies, on the Meyer principle. Each bogie had 750mm wheels and two cylinders 300mm diameter by 350mm stroke, at the inner ends of the bogies, with Walschaerts valve gear. The horizontal cylinders for the plough engine were 300mm diameter by 450mm stroke. The working pressure was 12atm (about 175lb/sq in).

The rotary plough was 2.5m diameter, had ten sectors, and worked at 170rpm. The whole machine and the front of the tender were enclosed in a rectangular casing. The four-wheeled tender carried 2.5 tons of coal and contained a device for melting snow by steam. Weight in working order was 45 tons. Another was delivered in 1912 and a third in 1913. They were stationed at Poschiavo and Pontresina, turntables being provided at these places and at Cavaglia and Alp Grüm.[3] (See photograph on p 104.)

In the winter of 1912–13 trains ran to Alp Grüm from the north and to Cavaglia from the south. Traffic between was carried by sledges over the pass road which had been improved by a new bridge built at a cost of 39,000Fr subscribed by the Federal Post Office, Graubünden canton, Brusio electricity works and Poschiavo. Thanks to a mild winter, however, through rail traffic was soon operating again, and 1913 became the first full year of operation. The following winter trains were stopped for only a few days.

Further snow protection works from 1914 to 1918 removed most of the remaining hazards, but some remained as was proved on 16 March 1920 when an avalanche swept down Piz Lagalb and overcame a special train consisting of a steam snow plough and two power cars at Val Minor near Bernina Hospiz, killing eight railwaymen. The power cars were swept from the track and over-turned, and four passengers were injured. Three more railway workers were killed at the end of February 1937 in an avalanche at Alp Grüm. Afforestation carried out since before 1920, and additional snow sheds, have now diminished the likelihood of further disasters of this kind. After World War I sections of the line on the summit stretch were removed from wind-sheltered hollows into the path of north–south winds, so reducing snow clearance.

Heavy goods traffic over the Bernina required a more powerful locomotive, and in the spring of 1916 a new C–C type, No 81, was delivered by BBC. Principal dimensions are shown in the drawing below. Each of the six-wheeled bogies had two motors

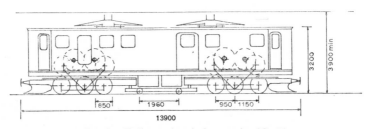

Bernina Railway electric locomotive No 81

geared in a ratio of 910:220 to separate jackshafts which were connected by a triangular frame to the centre coupled axle. The four motors produced a total of 800hp and the locomotive had a top speed of 50kph. It had three braking systems independent of each other: vacuum on all axles, a magnetic rail brake and an electric regenerative brake. The second of these was in the form of a trolley running on rollers 280mm diameter. It had eight mag-nets which could exert a vertical force onto the rail of 20,800kg. Fitted with snow ploughs the locomotive weighed 42.6 tons. Between the two machine rooms was a compartment for three tons of freight.[4] The locomotive was used on both goods and passenger trains. During the 1940s it was rebuilt to B–B type and in 1970 it was sold to the Blonay–Chamby Museum Railway near Montreux and was placed in store at Montbovon on the MOB.

Page 155. (Above and below) Chur–Arosa trains crossing the Langwies viaduct

Page 156 (Above) Railcar No 454 in Mesocco station, Bellinzona–Mesocco Railway; (below) Railcar No 5 at Acquarossa, Biasca–Acquarossa Railway (p 183)

A fourth locomotive, 800hp Bo–Bo No 82, with end bonnets, was built by BBC in 1928. It is powered by eight 100hp motors, two per axle. The total length over buffers is 14.40m, width 2.48m and height 3.76m; bogies have a wheelbase of 2.1m and the total wheelbase is 10.0m. This fine machine (see photograph p 104) weighs 43 tons and has a maximum speed of 45kph. In 1961 the four locomotives had 100 added to their numbers, becoming 161–2 and 181–2.

In 1929 the Mitropa Company introduced restaurant cars on the Rhaetian and Bernina Railways (Ch 6) in connection with the completion of the Brig–Visp link. Because of the sharp curves, of only 45m radius, the two Bernina cars (built by SWS) were made smaller than those of the RhB, only 14.32m long over bodies and 2.5m wide. They seated thirty-six passengers, weighed 18.2 tons, and included toilet facilities. The kitchens were housed in separate four-wheeled cars 5.4m long, rebuilt at Poschiavo from covered goods wagons.[5] The service was withdrawn early in the war period and in 1943 the two cars were rebuilt for use on the main RhB networks, as Nos 3813–14.

About 1930 the line voltage of the Bernina Railway was increased from 750 to 1,000. In the improved economic conditions after 1933, with Federal and cantonal assistance, the line was moved away from the avalanche threatened slopes of Piz Lagalb and the valley floor at Alp Bondo. In December 1934 successful experiments were carried out with trench mortars in dislodging masses of snow before they reached dangerous proportions, a method since used with great advantage. The three steam snow ploughs were completely overhauled in 1940.

Because of economic difficulties during World War II, on 1 January 1942 the working of the Bernina Railway was taken over by the RhB with which it was amalgamated on 1 January 1943. One of the first jobs after the amalgamation was to augment the Bernina snow ploughs by an electric rotary machine, RhB No 9215, built at Poschiavo in 1943, using one of the old RhB wedge plough chassis built by SIG in 1908.

MODERNISATION

After the war the economic recovery of Graubünden lagged

behind that of other Swiss cantons and it was not until the mid 1950s that long needed improvements and replacements could be carried out on the Bernina Railway. Because of a seventeen per cent increase in energy consumption it became necessary after 1957 to overhaul the entire electrical installation. The old rectifying apparatus was replaced by modern equipment of 800kW, and feeder and contact lines of heavier cross section were installed. Also two 1,200kW dc to three-phase ac mains installations were built for recuperation of power from trains descending to Poschiavo, to provide a braking load, because although some trains pass at Cavaglia, there is not always an ascending train to absorb power from the descending one.

Some of the original passenger and goods rolling stock was rebuilt and modernised at the RhB workshops at Landquart from 1963 onwards. To handle the increase of bulk oil traffic six new power cars, Nos 41–6 weighing 41 tons, with 12 first and 24 second class seats, were obtained in 1964–5. Their appearance and principal dimensions are shown in drawing opposite. They resemble those built in 1957–8 for the Chur–Arosa section, Nos 481–6. With 940hp they can haul 60 tons up the 70%o gradients at 27kph and they have a top speed of 65kph. For absolute safety when descending they are equipped with five braking systems: a compressed air brake with one cylinder on each bogie of the cars themselves and vacuum brake for the train operated by the same control; a hand brake operating on both bogies from either end; regenerative brake feeding into the contact line and capable of stopping the car and a 40 ton trailing load from a speed of 20–30 kph on the steepest pitches; an electric rheostat brake, independent of the contact line, and an electro-magnetic rail brake energised from a 36 volt battery. Electro-pneumatic flange lubricators ease the passage of the 45m radius curves. The cars were very much a joint product. Bogies, bodies and interior work were by SWS, other work was carried out by MFO, SAAS and BBC. Like the old cars, the new ones are attractively finished in bright red.

The latest power units, shown in the drawing on p 160, are two electric/diesel-electric Bo-Bo locomotives Nos 801–2, built in 1966–7 by BBC, intended for use on the Bernina as electric locomotives of 940hp or on other lines as diesel-electrics of 1,060hp.

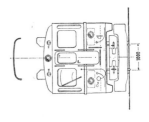

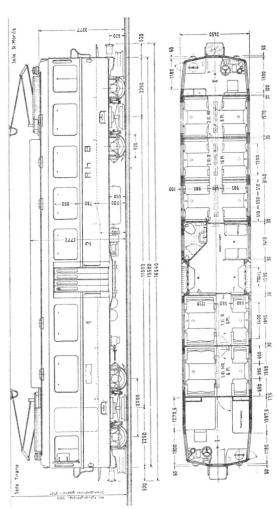

Bernina railcar (Nos 41–6) *(RhB Chur)*

For maintenance work a diesel tower wagon, No 9916, was built in 1963. Six bogie first and second class coaches, Nos 1541–6, with light metal (Unidar) frames were built in 1968 and are used on the through services between Tirano and Chur. Early in 1973 three new power cars, Nos 47–9, were delivered.

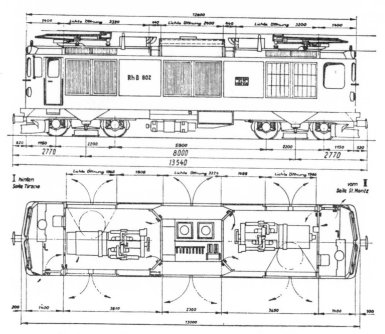

RhB electric/diesel-electric locomotive No 802 (*RhB Chur*)

The passenger service in the summer of 1972 consisted of six trains each way over the whole length with times varying from 2hr 37min to 2hr 58min. In addition there were six each way between St Moritz and Alp Grüm, one each way between St Moritz and Campocologno, three from Tirano to Poschiavo and two back to Tirano, one each way between Poschiavo and Campocologno and four additional trains each way between St Moritz and Pontresina. Fares for the whole journey are calculated as for a distance of 83km. In 1973 a new through train called the Bernina Express was introduced between Chur and Tirano. It was formed by a through portion attached to the 09.15 Chur–St

Moritz train as far as Samaden and taking 4hr 37min for the overall journey in each direction.

Plans for the period to 1980 include block signalling, and the possibility of radio control is being investigated.

CHAPTER NINE

The Chur-Arosa Railway

PLANNING

AROSA, with a population of about 3,500, stands at the head of the Plessur valley 25km above Chur, at an altitude of about 1,750m. Its magnificent setting beside a lake, surrounded by mountains and woods, inevitably made it a popular resort. Because of the steep sides of the Plessur valley, threatened by landslides or avalanches and cut into by deep gorges, it was necessary to build the carriage road to Arosa at a great height above the river with a laborious ascent out of Chur. Carriages over this road took 5hr 55min up and 3hr 35min down.

The first proposal for a railway to link Arosa with Chur was by a Dr Rüedi about 1889–90, but it was not until 1909 that Dr Anton Meuli expounded the idea to a meeting of interested persons in Chur, ending with the words *Wo ein Wille, da ist auch ein Weg* (where there's a will there's a way) which later formed the motto on the station at Lüen–Castiel.

The most astonishing thing about this railway was the speed with which it was carried out. Anton Caflisch, member of the Lower House of the Federal Assembly, at once took up the challenge and through his efforts up to Fr1 million was raised in Chur and Arosa and a further 200,000Fr from the valley communities. On this basis a concession was obtained and on 15 July 1911 the Chur–Arosa Railway Company was established in Chur. At the same time Gustav Bener was appointed engineer,[1] already mentioned in connection with the Albula, Davos–Filisur and Bever–Schuls sections of the RhB.

Notes to this chapter will be found on p. 250.

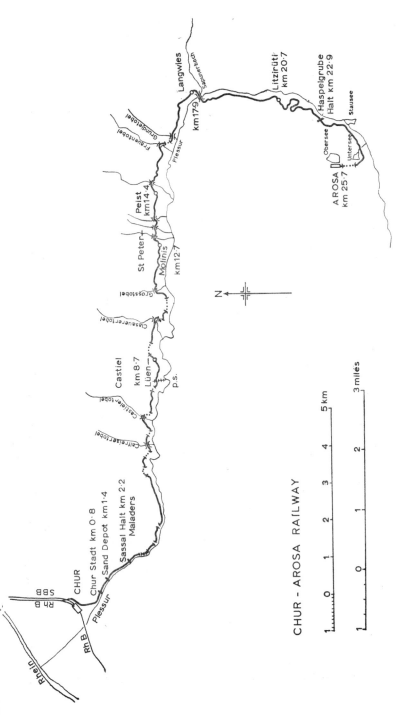

CHUR - AROSA RAILWAY

Map of Chur–Arosa Railway

Obviously a railway to Arosa would need to begin its ascent lower down the valley, but the treacherous nature of the lower slopes below Langwies posed formidable problems. Fritz Hennings, engineer of the Albula Railway, advised on the route, but the construction project was entirely worked out by Bener between 1 August 1911 and 14 March 1912. The estimated cost was 7,618,499Fr.

CONSTRUCTION AND ROUTE

The principal contracts were awarded as follows: to Züblin & Co, Zurich, for the section including Langwies bridge and station (5 July 1912); Baumann Bros & Stiefenhofer for the Sassal–Grosstobel–Peistergrenze section (18 July, 20 August); Müller, Zeerleder & Gobat for the section from there to Arosa, except Langwies (20 September); Bosshard & Co of Näfels for three steel bridges (30 October); BBC for the whole electrical work including rolling stock (18 November); Caprez & Rossi of Chur for the town section (15 February 1913); Löhle & Kern, Zurich, for landslide galleries (11 April).[2]

The lower terminus was made in the street outside Chur station, the line continuing to a goods shed and interchange sidings connecting with the RhB. As far as km2.25 the line is laid with grooved rails along Engadinstrasse and then beside the river along Plessurquai. The additional width required here had to be obtained by cantilevering part of the road and the footway over the river on reinforced concrete brackets.

Along this section is Chur Stadt Halt, nothing more than a 'tram stop', and beyond this, on the left at Sand, are the main carriage sheds and workshops. Shortly beyond Sassal Halt the road crosses the river and the railway strikes off on its own formation up the right bank. It soon begins to rise at the ruling gradient of 60‰ which continues with only short breaks to Arosa. Between the three Sassal tunnels are two avalanche galleries, and a third, above Sassal tunnel III, had to be built following a landslip on 10 March 1914. Above here the views on the right begin to open out and become ever more exciting as far as the Langwies bridge.

Meiersboden and Nesslaries tunnels are followed by Eber

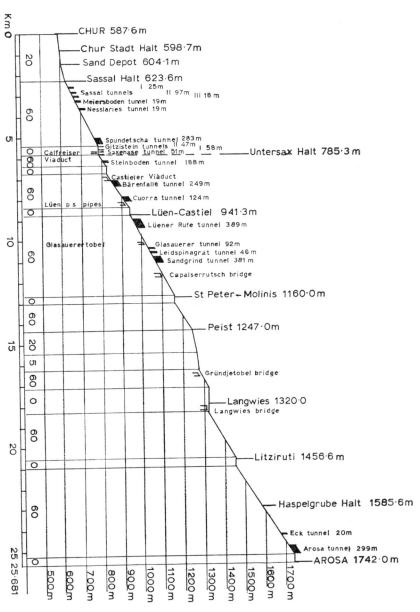

Profile of Chur–Arosa Railway

Km 0

CHUR 587·6 m
Chur Stadt Halt 598·7m
Sand Depot 604·1m
Sassal Halt 623·6m
I 25m
Sassal tunnels II 97m III 18 m
Meiersboden tunnel 19m
Nesslaries tunnel 19m

Spundetscha tunnel 283m
Gitzistein tunnels II 47m I 58m
Calfreiser Saxenase tunnel 51m
Viaduct Steinboden tunnel 188m
Untersax Halt 785·3 m

Castieler Viàduct
Bärenfalle tunnel 249m
Cuorra tunnel 124m
Lüen p.s pipes
Lüen-Castiel 941·3m
Lüener Rufe tunnel 389m

Glasauerertobel
Glasauerer tunnel 92m
Leidspinagrat tunnel 46m
Sandgrind tunnel 381m
Capalserrutsch bridge

St Peter–Molinis 1160·0m

Peist 1247·0m

Gründjetobel bridge

Langwies 1320·0
Langwies bridge

Litziruti 1456·6 m

Haspelgrube Halt 1585·6m

Eck tunnel 20m
Arosa tunnel 299m
AROSA 1742·0m

500m 600m 700m 800m 900m 1000m 1100m 1200m 1300m 1400m 1500m 1600m 1700m

gallery. During the construction of the Nesslaries tunnel at km 3.46 a 10m fracture in the roof necessitated a stronger lining and a retaining wall outside. In February 1914 a retaining wall at km3.78, containing about 740cu m of dry stonework, suddenly sank, although it had been carrying heavy material trains for over six months. The cause was discovered to be waste water from the village of Maladers above running onto the open hillside, and the railway company was forced to build a drain to carry the water to the river. Indeed, all along this next stretch drainage proved one of the major problems.

The course of a landslip here had to be crossed by a steel truss span of 46m of which the lower abutment reaches a depth of 15.5m to the rock where it was secured by steel anchors. During its construction a temporary structure had to be rigged up alongside to facilitate transport of materials to the Lüen power station, upon the completion of which depended the operation of the railway.

Further trouble was experienced at the Dorfbach bridge just above here at km3.85. Originally the bridge had one steel truss span of 24m, the lower abutment of which has its foundation 10.2m below ground. A subsequent movement in the lower wing wall compelled its replacement by three further steel spans, each of 12m (the curve would admit nothing longer) with consequent piers and abutments, all of great depth. From km4.1–4.2 another slip occurred in the spring of 1914, and a wall 4m thick had to be built to hold the slope.

The next problem was the Spundetscha tunnel, km5.0–5.3. An open line was originally planned, and had indeed been built for construction purposes, but it was decided to avoid the worst piece of ground by a tunnel of 148m. This was cut through by 31 October 1912, mostly in scree and broken schist, and a year later was completed, and from then until February 1914 was used by construction trains. Great pressure then began to show in the lining, and a settlement at the lower end in April 1914 forced the section engineer, H. Studer, to make the difficult decision to abandon and to fill in 80m of the lower end of the tunnel and to bore a new tunnel further into the hill in stable schist, curving round to emerge 88m near Chur than the original portal. Foun-

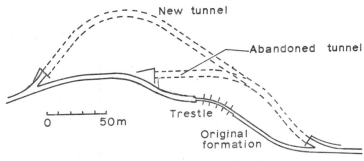

Plan of Spundetscha tunnel (km5–5.3), Chur–Arosa
Railway

dations here were carried 8.5m below rail level and the upper end
was considerably reinforced. The contract for the deviation tunnel was awarded to Baumann Bros & Stiefenhofer, contractors for
this section, on 9 April, and the entire 283m tunnel was ready
early in September. Throughout this work the original open
course was used for transport of machinery to Lüen power
station.[5] Although the course of the open line can still be seen,
there is no trace whatever of the blocked tunnel entrance.

The Schmalztobel viaduct of six spans is followed by three
short tunnels in fairly secure ground, bringing us to the Calfreiser
viaduct at km5.9. The absence of suitable building stone along
here and the difficulty of transporting large girders compelled the
engineer to use concrete. The two main arched spans of 25 and
18m were built of concrete blocks and the four side spans of 12
and 6m of rammed concrete with concrete block facing.

Beyond the Steinboden tunnel is the deep gorge of the Castielertobel, at km6.8. On the lower side of this gorge the beds of
schist dip steeply into the river with a covering of scree, while the
opposite side is a sheer cliff, overhanging in places. One solution
only was available here, a high viaduct leading straight into a
tunnel, like the Landwasser viaduct on the Albula railway. A
three-arched viaduct of great elegance was built, as shown in the
drawing on p 168. Shortage of building stone again dictated the
use of rammed concrete for the pier cores, faced with broken
stone, the arches of 25m span being turned in concrete blocks.
The upper arch abutted into the cliff face beneath the lower portal of the Bärenfalle tunnel.

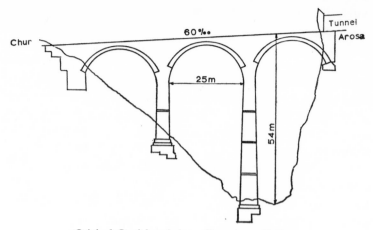

Original Castieler viaduct, Chur–Arosa Railway

After the viaduct had been in use for six or seven years concern was aroused by slight movements of the piers and the lower abutment. On 19 September 1923 a considerable movement was noted, resulting in great pressure along the axis of the viaduct towards the tunnel. Over the succeeding years this pressure increased, forcing the crowns of the first two arches upwards, and from 1929 to 1932 strengthening work had to be carried out in the form of centrings built by Richard Coray beneath arches 1 and 2 which were then reconstructed. In 1935 a further movement occurred, now in arch 3, so far unaffected, and by 1940 it had lifted 150mm. Dr R. Haefeli, a consulting engineer, estimated the pressure of the mountain on abutment 1 to be from a minimum of 5,000 to 15,000 tons and considered that the viaduct was by then beyond rescue. The decision had to be made to rebuild either the whole or part of the viaduct.

There was great reluctance on aesthetic grounds to abandon the arch form, but eventually it was decided to dismantle the arches and to replace them by steel spans on the existing piers. This work was directed by Hans Conrad, chief engineer of the RhB with which the Chur–Arosa and Misox railways were amalgamated on 1 January 1942, as a result of wartime economic difficulties.

From autumn 1941 to summer 1942 centrings were erected

under the arches from the crowns of which a core was removed. Inside this a timber trestle was erected to carry the track and on 26 July 1942 work began on dismantling the arches and placing the girders in position. For this work a mobile crane with a lift of 3 tons was erected on rails on each side of the viaduct. The adapting of the piers and abutments to fit the steelwork was carried out with the material from the arches, and the rebuilding was completed on 25 November 1943. The third span moves on a bracket inside the tunnel. Support for pier 2 was given by a concrete footing in the stream bed. The cost of the original viaduct was 144,000Fr; the early reconstruction cost 146,000Fr and the final rebuilding 365,400Fr. The whole of the rebuilding was carried out without interruption to traffic.[4]

The present form of the viaduct is shown in the photograph on p 138 which shows how any movement of the piers is registered by the indicator hanging over the handrail beside the track. A forward movement of pier 1 will lower the weight and of pier 2 will raise it. The line is carried above the river at a height of 54m and enters Bärenfalle tunnel on a gradient of 60%o and a curve to the right at the minimum radius of 60m. The tunnel is in the form of a reversed S.

Cuorra tunnel leads straight into an avalanche gallery enclosed in the rock slope at km7.85. At km8.1 the line crosses the pressure pipes and adjacent inspection railway of the Lüen power station, seen in the valley far below, and soon reaches the first station, Lüen-Castiel. In Lüener Rufe tunnel the line turns through ninety degrees and after crossing a stone viaduct passes through Glasaurer, Leidspinagrat and Sandgrind tunnels.

From here to Langweis the railway passes through moraine for a distance of 7km, and in only two places was bare rock found. Fortunately the moraine was sufficiently compacted to be built upon and of seventy-five piers and abutment foundations in this stretch fifty-one stand in moraine, fourteen in scree, and only seven are on rock.

The Grosstobel is crossed by a lofty steel bridge of three spans from which, on the left, can be seen some interesting earth pillars. The Capalserrutsch landslip at km11.7 is crossed by another steel bridge. Because of the sharp curve two spans were necessary and the centre pier was taken to a depth of some 15m to find a secure foundation. A high stone viaduct brings us to the second station, St Peter-Molinis.

Two stone viaducts are the only works of importance between here and Peist station. On the following section as far as Langwies the absence of building stone forced the engineer to use concrete even for retaining walls and tunnel linings. Fortunately concrete materials were plentiful. Two more viaducts, a steel bridge over the Frauentobel and the Matten tunnel bring us to the wild gorge of the Gründjetobel at km16.4.

The design for the Gründjetobel bridge presented problems and it was not until 21 June 1913 that approval was given for a concrete arch with a span of 86m. The bridge has a total length of about 145m and a maximum height of 46m. Work on the foundations began on 27 June and by 26 August the centring was complete. This also was designed by Richard Coray and had previously been used at the Halen bridge near Bern. The arch was completed on 15 September. From the bridge some more earth pillars can be seen just above on the left.

The greatest work on the railway, the magnificent Langwies bridge, now appears ahead on the right. (See photographs on page 155.) The line curves into Langwies station, and if time allows it is worth alighting here for a couple of hours to examine the Langwies and Gründjetobel bridges which when built were the longest and second longest reinforced concrete spans in the world. The Langwies bridge has a total length of 287m, with a centre span of 96m carrying the rails 62m above the river. It consumed 6,000cu m of concrete and 250 tons of reinforcing steel. Again Richard Coray designed the centre, producing an enormous fan standing on central piers 22m high, from the tops of which it radiated outwards. It consumed 700cu m of timber. The piers on the Arosa side had to be secured by ribbed sole plates between them and bearing against the main arch abutment to prevent them from sliding inwards. The arch centre was erected by 6 September 1913 and on 6 October the two ribs of the great arch were completed.

Beyond the bridge the views are obscured by trees, and there is little to be seen up to Arosa. Above Litziruti the line bends back on itself twice, climbs above the Stausee, seen on the left, threads the short Eck tunnel and finally Arosa tunnel, emerging into Arosa station. The construction of Arosa tunnel was difficult because instead of the expected gneiss, clay moraine and weathered serpentine were encountered.

Arosa station is a beautifully designed building, on the shore of the Obersee. The station buildings are among the many attractive features of this railway. Their designs were the result of a competition and particular care was taken to conform to the traditional styles of the locality. In common with so many Swiss chalets these stations are decorated with old sayings which, of course, read best in their original German but which, roughly translated, are as follows: Lüen-Castiel, 'Where there's a will there's a way'; St Peter-Mollinis, 'Fear not the world—attack bravely'; Peist, 'Time flies—mankind be prepared!'; Langwies, 'Time levels high and low, but it hurries—understand it and be busy!'; Litziruti, 'For progress and trade, honour the fatherland!'

Despite the shortage of labour caused by the mobilisation of Swiss manpower at the start of the war, work on the railway went ahead with great speed and on 5 September 1914 the directors of the company with a party of guests made the first journey from Chur to Arosa. More remained to be done, however, and it was 12 December before the line could be opened for traffic. It had cost 8,696,000Fr, or 338,600Fr per km. Of this total amount, which was about 1,100,000Fr above the original estimate, rolling stock cost 487,600Fr and electrical equipment 289,700Fr.[5]

In its total length of 25.679km, 12.3km or 48 per cent is curved and almost two-thirds of that at the minimum radius of 60m. There are eighteen tunnels and galleries totalling 2,714m or 10.6 per cent of the length of the railway. The forty bridges and viaducts have a total length of 1,747m. Details of all tunnels and bridges and heights of stations are shown on the profile on p 165. Station distances are shown on the map on p 163.

Electric power was supplied by the Lüen power station to transformer and rectifier stations at Chur Sand (800kW), Lüen and Arosa (both 1,200kW). The installation at Lüen included apparatus for recuperating power from descending trains for which it acted as a braking load. The line supply was 2,000V dc.

In 1909 15,900 people travelled to Arosa in road carriages. In the first year of railway operation 68,570 passengers arrived there. The railway has continued to hold its own against ever increasing road competition.

After 1957 the energy consumption on the railway increased by about 18 per cent, making it necessary to overhaul the electrical plant. The Lüen station has been changed to automatic operation, that at Chur Sand strengthened to 1,600kW and a new 1,200kW rectifier installation has been built at Arosa. The line voltage is now 2,400 at feed points.

The oldest power cars operating on the c–a are now Nos 30 (1911) and 31/2/4 (1908), with four 150hp motors giving an output of 600hp on the c–a, or with 135hp motors giving 540hp on the Bernina. Heavier traffic is handled by the six new passenger power cars Nos 481–6, built in 1957. With four 174hp motors giving a total of 700hp they can haul a 60 ton load up the 60%o gradients at 27kph, and have a maximum speed of 65kph. They measure 17.77m over buffers, wheels are 920mm diameter with a total wheelbase of 13.95m, and the tare weight is 43.4 tons. Electrical equipment was by BBC and SAAS and coachwork was by SWS. Vacuum controlled compressed air brakes and straight Charmilles compressed air brakes are fitted.[6] Nos 483–4, fitted with four 240hp motors, could be used on the Bellinzona–Mesocco section (Ch 10) where, with a total of 960hp they were among the most powerful cars in Switzerland.

Four new lightweight coaches, Nos 1253–6, were built by FFA/SIG in 1967–8, with cast light metal (Unidar) frames. They are 16.97m long, have a tare weight of only 11.5 tons and carry 36 first class passengers. They are used in winter on the c–a and in summer on the main rhb network and for through working over the fo and bvz.

The train service provides fourteen to Arosa and thirteen to Chur including two fasts each way daily including Sundays. An additional train runs each way Fridays to Sundays. Stopping trains take 1hr 15min up and 1hr 10min down and fasts take about 1hr each way. Fares for the 26km are charged as for 36km.

The small amount of goods traffic is mostly handled in wagons attached to passenger trains. In 1969, to reduce the need for power cars to run round the trains in the street at Chur, two baggage cars were equipped as driving trailers.

CHAPTER TEN

The Ticino Lines

JUST north of Bellinzona the River Ticino is joined by the Moesa which rises near the St Bernhardin Pass and flows down through Mesocco, or Misox, and Roveredo. The Misolcina, or Misox valley, lies largely within Graubünden but geographically forms part of the Ticino region. It was an important trade route, particularly after the opening of the St Bernhardin road in 1823, but traffic declined after the opening of the St Gotthard Railway and, since the valley was not very fertile, the population began to decrease.

It was partly to arrest this process and to provide a better route to the new health resort on the St Bernhardin Pass that the metre gauge Misox Railway was projected from Bellinzona to Mesocco.

Following a public meeting on 5 December 1891 a committee was formed to further the project and eventually, on 9 December 1899, a concession was obtained. It was expected that the railway would carry 40,000 passengers and 30,000 tons of merchandise annually.[1]

The Misox valley is flanked by very steep slopes rising in places to peaks over 3,000m high. Tributary streams flowing down these slopes carry large quantities of rubble, the worst being the Calancasca joining the Moesa at Roveredo. On occasions the rubble has actually dammed up the main river and forced it into a new channel. This danger had to be considered when laying out the railway.

Notes to this chapter will be found on p 250

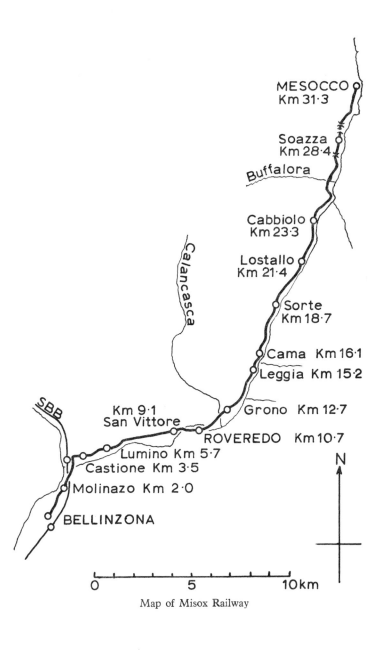

MESOCCO o
Km 31·3

Soazza o
Km 28·4

Buffalora

Cabbiolo o
Km 23·3

Lostallo o
Km 21·4

Sorte o
Km 18·7

Calancasca

Cama Km 16·1
Leggia Km 15·2

SBB

Km 9·1
San Vittore

Grono Km 12·7

ROVEREDO   Km 10·7

Lumino Km 5·7
Castione Km 3·5
Molinazo Km 2·0

BELLINZONA

N

0   5   10 km

Map of Misox Railway

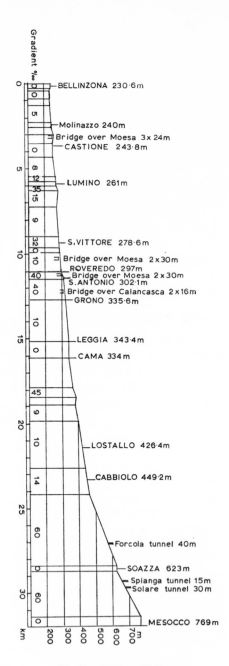

Profile of Misox Railway

Raising the capital proved exceedingly difficult, even on the basis of a most economical estimate of 2,700,000Fr which later proved insufficient. The route was surveyed in March to June 1904 under the engineer S. Berg. Plans were prepared by October, the contract was awarded in January 1905 and in March the staking out of the line began.

By then work had already begun on bridge foundations during low water. The greatest economy had to be exercised as only 800,000Fr had been allowed for formation work. Abundant building materials were available all along the line, which was fortunate because a total of 16,000cu m of walling was required. Earthworks totalled 160,000cu m. The terminus at Bellinzona was a short walk from the main station on the Gotthard railway. To have brought the line into the main station area would have cost disproportionately more.

In its 31.284km the line rises 538.4m which gives an average gradient of 17.4%o. However, the nature of the valley is such that most of the climbing occurs at the upper end and because expensive development was ruled out the line has 4.6km at the ruling gradient of 60%o. The sharpest curve is 80m radius, but straight sections amount to 22.308km.

At km10 a tunnel of 17m accommodates both the railway and a road; the three other tunnels amount to only 85m. The twenty-seven bridges and viaducts totalling 625m include three over the Moesa and one, over the Calancasca, whose two spans of 16m rise only 1.8m. The original rails were 25kg/m in 12m lengths on wood sleepers $1.8 \times 0.18 \times 0.13$m. Since 1942 new rails have been 31.5kg/m, 15m long on steel sleepers.

Excluding rolling stock and electrical installation the total cost of the railway was 1,922,000Fr or 61,400Fr per km. It was opened for freight on 6 May 1907 and to passengers on 31 July. The scenery all along the route is very beautiful; about midway between Cabbiolo and Soazza, to the left on the upward journey, the Buffalora Fall makes an impressive sight.

Electric traction was decided upon from the start, with a hydro-electric station at Cebbia. At first single or three-phase alternating current was considered but at that time single-phase systems were still being developed, and with three-phase the advantage of regeneration on the downward run was outweighed by the fixed speed characteristics. So a 1,500 volt dc system was chosen.

The power station was equipped with two Pelton wheels giving 1,000hp at 500rpm, each coupled to an alternator producing three-phase ac at 10,000V, 50Hz, and a dc generator producing 1,500V for direct line distribution. The ac supply is carried by overhead lines to a transformer station at Roveredo where it is converted to line voltage by two 400hp motor generators with an output of 272kW.

The overhead line was suspended by steel span wires between brackets on wooden poles 30m apart. Each of the original six power cars had four 60hp 750V motors, and had electric lighting and heating. They had two first class compartments with six seats and two second class compartments with fifteen and twenty-four seats, and they were fitted for multiple-unit control. They weighed 34 tons loaded and were designed to pull a 50 ton train up a 60‰ gradient at 19.8kph. Motor goods cars were similar, with a capacity of 10 tons. Most of the electrical equipment was supplied by MFO. All the four passenger trailer cars and twenty-eight goods wagons were four-wheeled vehicles.[2]

In August 1908 the railway was severely damaged by material brought down in mountain streams after a heavy rain storm. The Buffalora River buried the railway beneath 4m of material and some 600m of line had to be relocated at a higher level. At Grono the railway and road were washed away and the river cut a new bed. Both railway and road had to be rebuilt and carried over the new channel on a common steel bridge. Then, after another flood in 1913, the river resumed its old course.

Economic pressure during World War II forced the company to amalgamate with the RhB on 1 January 1942, along with the Chur–Arosa Railway.

In 1958 a new type of power car was introduced, interchangeable with the Chur–Arosa Railway, Nos 483–4, mentioned in the last chapter on p 172.

Latterly the train service consisted of ten through trains each way with times varying from just over an hour to 1hr 27min. Fares for the 31.22km were charged as for 43km. With the opening of the new St Bernhardin road and a through post bus service between Thusis and Bellinzona, the last passenger trains ran on 28 May 1972. Goods traffic is still worked, by the passenger railcars, between Mesocco and Castione where it connects with the SBB. The section from there to Bellinzona has been abandoned.

THE ST BERNHARDIN RAILWAY PROJECT

Mention was made in Chapter 1, p 19, of a projected railway from Thusis to Mesocco via the St Bernhardin Pass. Following the report of a pioneering committee on 28 April 1908 a concession was sought on 10 July 1913.[3] Further progress was prevented by the war, after which the application was renewed and a concession was granted on 2 February 1923.

Details were worked out by the engineer F. Prader of Zurich. Gustav Bener, manager of the RhB, pointed to the benefits which the railway had brought to the communities in the Davos and Engadin valleys, and to the decline of the district between Thusis and the Mesolcina through want of a railway.

As might be expected, enormous development works were required, similar to those on the Bernina Railway, even to maintain a ruling gradient of 60‰. In the first 3.2km from Mesocco station a height difference of 441m had to be overcome by a railway development extended to 8km. Tunnelling would amount to 19.4 per cent of the entire length. Beyond the 5,580m summit tunnel, at a height of 1,669m at the south end and 1,648.6m at the north end, the line would descend through the great gorge of the Hinter Rhine, known as the Viamala, to join the Albula railway at Thusis. The route is shown on the map and gradient profile, pp 175 and 176.

The minimum radius of 100m would allow stock of the RhB and the FO to be used. The estimate of Fr34 million included electrification at the standard RhB voltage of 11,000 ac, conversion of the Misox Railway to this and extension to the SBB station at Bellinzona.[4]

In 1927 a full report with tables, maps, plans, pictures and diagrams, *Die Bernhardin Bahn*, was published in Chur by the Bernhardin Railway Committee under the President Dr A. Meuli. Unfortunately, despite confident support by the various com-

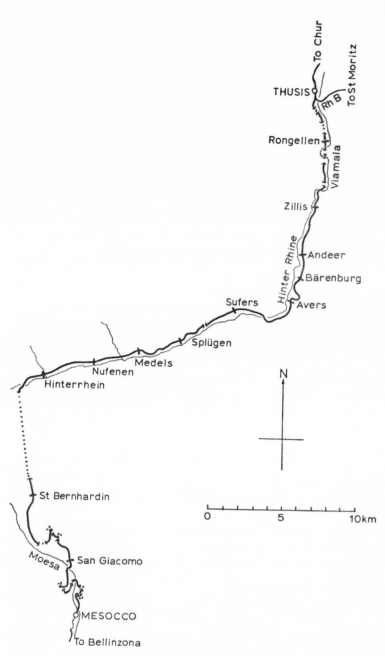

Map of proposed Bernhardin railway

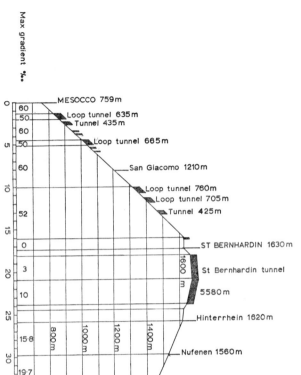

Max gradient ‰

60	MESOCCO 759m
50	Loop tunnel 635m
60	Tunnel 435m
50	Loop tunnel 665m
60	San Giacomo 1210m
52	Loop tunnel 760m
	Loop tunnel 705m
	Tunnel 425m
0	ST BERNHARDIN 1630m
3	St Bernhardin tunnel
10	5580m
15·8	Hinterrhein 1620m
19·7	Nufenen 1560m
15	Medels 1490m
0	Splügen 1461m
13	Sufers 1422m
0	
60	
55	Avers 1165m
	Bärenburg 1060m
0	Andeer 982m
0	Zillis 930m
33	
0	Tunnel 450m
35	Tunnel 570m
0	Rongellen 845m
	Tunnel 680m
55	Tunnel 250m
	THUSIS 700·5m

Profile of proposed Mesocco–Bernhardin–Thusis railway

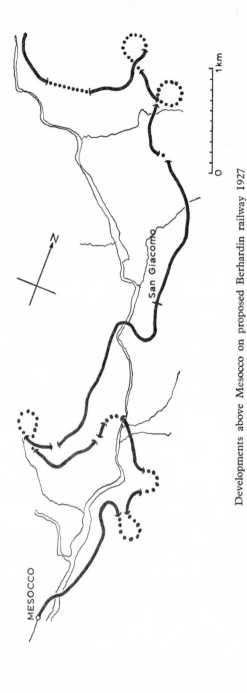

Developments above Mesocco on proposed Berhardin railway 1927

munities concerned, Federal support was not forthcoming and this magnificent project had to be shelved.

The new St Bernhardin road, including the 6.6km tunnel built at a cost of Fr120 million and opened on 1 December 1967, by making possible through traffic all the year, has not only disposed of any possibility of a revival of the railway project, but has brought about the downfall of the Misox Railway itself. Thus we have lost what would have been one of the most wonderful mountain railways in Europe. The Splügen–Bellinzona route has however been considered for a new Trans Alpine base railway tunnel but at a much lower level than the Bernhardin project.

THE BIASCA–ACQUAROSSA RAILWAY

North of Bellinzona the Ticino is joined at Biasca by the Brenno whose valley leads up to the foot of the Lukmanier and Greina passes. It is a valley of great scenic beauty, but thinly populated, and to provide for an increasing tourist traffic a metre gauge electric railway was projected from Biasca to Olivone at the head of the valley. Like the Misox Railway, however, financing was difficult and to begin with construction was limited to the 13.9km to Acquarossa which has remained the upper terminus. (Illustrated on p 156.)

Engineering works were slight but some difficulties were experienced in a landslip area between km1.0 and 2.5. Three steel bridges were needed, of 42.6m over the Brenno, of 30m over the Orino and of 25m over the Leggiuna.

The minimum radius curve of 130m occurs only in the section round Biasca, and of the total length 59.3 per cent is straight; 40.1 per cent rises at between $25\%_0$ and the ruling gradient of $35\%_0$. Rails, 24kg/m, were 12m long. All the original wooden sleepers have been replaced by steel. Stations, distances, heights and gradients are shown on the map and profile, pp 184 and 185.

Single-phase ac at 8,000V, 50Hz, is obtained from the Biaschina power station via a sub-station at Biasca. Here it is transformed by three 150kW transformers to 500V. Three 200hp motor generators convert it to line supply at 1,500V dc. The catenary is supported by wooden masts, and pantograph type collectors are used.

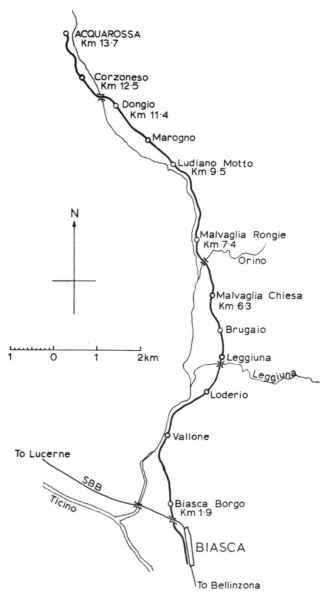

Map of Biasca–Acquarossa Railway

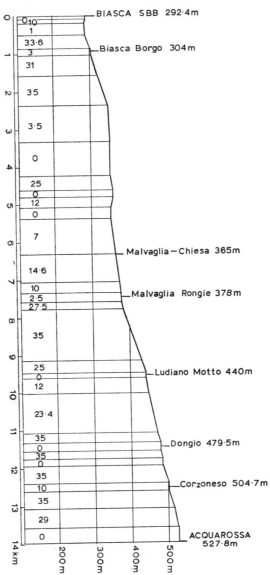

Gradient ‰

0₁₀	BIASCA SBB 292·4m
1	
33·6	
3	Biasca Borgo 304m
31	
35	
3·5	
0	
25	
0	
12	
0	
7	
	Malvaglia—Chiesa 365m
14·6	
10	
2·5	Malvaglia Rongie 378m
27·5	
35	
25	
0	Ludiano Motto 440m
12	
23·4	
35	
0	Dongio 479·5m
35	
0	
35	Corzoneso 504·7m
10	
35	
29	
0	ACQUAROSSA 527·8m

200m 300m 400m 500m

0 1 2 3 4 5 6 7 8 9 10 11 12 13 14 km

Profile of Biasca–Acquarossa Railway

The original rolling stock consisted of three bogie power cars, Nos 1–3 (of which No 2 is now withdrawn), two trailer cars and eight goods wagons. The power cars measure 13.835m over buffers and carry eight first and twenty-four second class passengers, mail and parcels. Bogies have a wheelbase of 2.1m at 7.9m between centres. Only one bogie is driven, by two 75hp series motors. The weight of electrical equipment is about 7 tons, and of the whole car 23 tons. All electrical equipment for rolling stock and fixed structures was supplied by BBC. The four-wheeled trailer cars carry twenty-four second class passengers. All cars are electrically lit and heated. Rolling stock, apart from electrical equipment, was supplied by SWS.[5]

The railway was opened on 6 July 1911, having cost 2,042,000Fr. Of the total share capital of 1,222,000Fr Canton Ticino holds 604,200Fr. Formation work cost about 705,200Fr, steel bridges 96,000Fr, track 307,000Fr, rolling stock 175,000Fr and electrical equipment 182,000Fr.

Two new railcars, Nos 4 and 5, each seating eight first and forty-eight second class passengers, were obtained in 1952 and 1962 from SWS/SAAS. All passenger cars are finished in green and white.

The Biasca terminus is in the street outside the SBB station. The train service in 1972 consisted of ten daily trains from Biasca to Acquarossa and nine back to Biasca, the first leaving Acquarossa at 6.09 and the last arriving there at 22.34. The journey took about half an hour. At Acquarossa the trains connect with the post buses, introduced in 1925, over the Lukmanier Pass to and from Disentis where they connect with trains on the RhB and FO. A new depot and workshop at Biasca, about 1km from the terminus, has recently been completed.

THE VALLE MAGGIA RAILWAY (MAGGIATALBAHN)

The valley of the Maggia River is the largest of the three valleys which converge near Locarno at the head of Lake Maggiore. Although it does not form part of a through route its fertility supports a considerable population in villages or small towns mostly three or four kilometres apart.

In 1904 a power station was built on the left bank of the

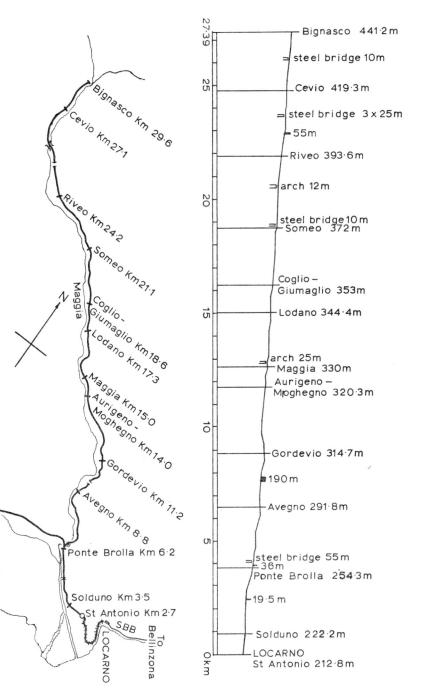

Map and profile of Valle Maggia Railway

Maggia River about 3km from Locarno, and at about the same time work began on a metre gauge electric local railway up the valley to Bignasco, beyond which the valley floor begins to rise steeply. At Locarno connection was made with the town tramway system.

Construction presented few difficulties, and was carried out under the direction of engineer F. Gianella. The maximum gradient was 33%o and the sharpest curve 100m radius. Engineering works were few. Just below Ponte Brolla the old stone road bridge was widened for the railway. Ponte Brolla station was sited on the right bank to provide a connection for the projected Centovalli Railway to Domodossola. Beyond the station the line passed through a 36m tunnel and returned to the left bank by an impressive steel bridge of 55m span. Between Riveo and Cevio at km23.6 the line crossed the river again by a bridge of three 25m steel spans. There were four tunnels, totalling 300.5m, shown on the profile p 187. The total length of the line was 27.388km.

The railway operated on 5,000V single-phase ac, 26Hz, power being supplied by the Locarno power station. Electrical equipment was by MFO. Public traffic began on 2 September 1907 and was provided by three bogie motor coaches 16.00m long and 2.70m wide, each seating forty-four passengers. Each bogie was powered by two 60hp motors, giving a total of 240hp. Transformers were built with primary windings for both 5,000V and 800V to enable the cars to reach the SBB station along the Locarno street tramway, which operated with single-phase ac at 20Hz. The latter was the first ac electric railway in Switzerland. Power cars and trailers were built by Maschinenbau-Gesellschaft Nürnberg.

Goods traffic soon developed beyond the capacity of the power cars, so in 1911 a four-wheeled electric locomotive was obtained. It measured 7.45m over buffers, 2.7m wide, with a wheelbase of 3.3m, and weighed 20.8 tons. It had a single 250hp motor geared to a centre jackshaft driving the wheels through outside cranks and rods. Electrical equipment and gearing were by MFO and the rest by SWS. Like the power cars it could work on both 5,000V and 800V, and on the level could maintain 35.4kph with

Page 189. (Above) Railcar No 12 of 1923 in the street in Locarno near the SBB station with a train for Intragna, Centovalli Railway (p 198); (below) Twin articulated railcar crossing the Isorno bridge at Intragna, Centovalli Railway (p 193)

Page 190. (Above) Railcar and trailer climbing towards Tesserete, Lugano–Tesserete Railway (p 201); (below) Car No 1, Lugano–Cadro–Dino Railway, engaged on the dismantling of the line, July 1972 (p 204)

a train of 84 tons. On the ruling gradient of 35‰ speed was reduced to under 20kph.

For the first time on a single-phase ac system regenerative braking was used, in a system devised by MFO. The Westinghouse brake was used for normal braking.[6]

When the Centovalli Railway was under construction in 1923 the decision was made to convert the Locarno–Bignasco line and the Locarno tramway system to 1,200V dc. During the conversion traffic was operated by two 2–6–0 tank locomotives obtained from the RhB, No 7 *Chur* and No 8 *Thusis* (see Ch 6) which became Nos 7 and 8 of Ferrovie Regionale Ticinesi (FRT, see below). After the conversion they were retained in reserve stock until 1943 when they were scrapped. All rolling stock, including the electric locomotive, was converted to 1,200V dc. A new station was built at Ponte Brolla on the Locarno side of the junction.

From 1 January 1923 the Locarno–Ponte Brolla section (LPB) was leased to the FRT which operated the Swiss portion of the Centovalli Railway, and from 1 January 1952 the two were amalgamated.

The Ponte Brolla–Bignasco section was closed on 29 November 1965 and the service replaced by buses. With the operation of the buses the title of the company became Ferrovie e Autolinee Regionale Ticinesi (FART). Where the railway formation was alongside the road it was incorporated into the road and has thus disappeared, but the tunnels can still be seen, and walked through.

THE CENTOVALLI RAILWAY

The valley of the Melezza known in Ticino as the Centovalli, or Hundred Valleys, and in Italy as the Valle Vigezzo, forms a natural route between the Simplon Railway at Domodossola and the St Gotthard Railway at Bellinzona via Locarno. A railway connecting Locarno and Domodossola was projected at the same time as the construction of the first Simplon tunnel, and on 23 June 1905 the concession was granted for the Swiss portion. Preliminary studies were prepared in 1908 by the engineer J. Sutter for the Swiss company, the Società Ferrovie Regionale

CENTOVALLI RAILWAY

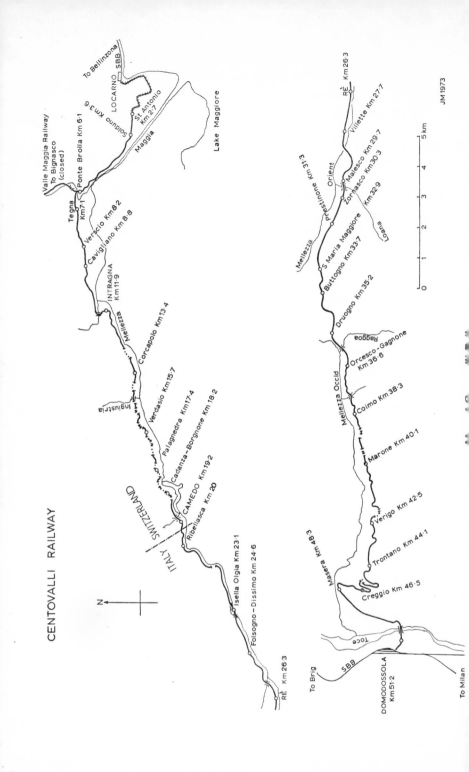

JM 1973

Ticinesi (FRT), (Ticino District Railways Company). The concession for the Italian portion was granted in 1911 under the title Società Subalpina di Imprese Ferroviarie (SSIF). Sutter was appointed engineer to the entire project.

Work began on 1 March 1913, but delays were caused by the international character of the project; then, in November 1913 by the collapse of the Franco–American Bank in Paris which was financing it and lastly, after work had been resumed in March 1914, it was stopped by the war. Thus it was as late as 27 November 1923 when the railway was opened. It had taken over ten years to complete.

From Locarno the trains use the town tramway (closed on 1 January 1933) by a devious route down beside the lake and up to St Antonio where the principal depot and workshops are situated, with the head office of FART in a new building across the road. From here the old Valle Maggia Railway is followed to Ponte Brolla, the best stretch of that line, with good views down into the gorge on the left. The old VM station and yard at Ponte Brolla are still in use as sidings. There is evidence here of a triangular junction at one time.

The Centovalli Railway swings off left, passes through the vineyards of the Tre Terre di Pedemonte, and at km10.565 turns sharply left to cross the Isorno into Intragna by a triple-hinged steel arch bridge of astonishing lightness, 77m high, shown in the photograph on p 189. Another similar bridge carries the line 65m above the Ruinacci valley at km19.015 just before Camedo. Both bridges were built by Löhle & Kera A–G of Zurich in 1915–17. The Intragna bridge has a main span of 86.52m and end spans of 16.48 and 24.72m. The Ruinacci bridge has a main span of 65.92m and two end spans of 16.48m. It is worth breaking one's journey at Intragna and Camedo to see these bridges. Both are in settings of outstanding beauty.

Just beyond Camedo the railway enters Italy. At Rè the valley opens out and the line traverses a high, well wooded plateau, passing a chain of neat villages, reaching its summit of 830m at Santa Maria Maggiore. To see these woods in their autumn colours with the snow covered peaks and glaciers beyond is an unforgettable experience.

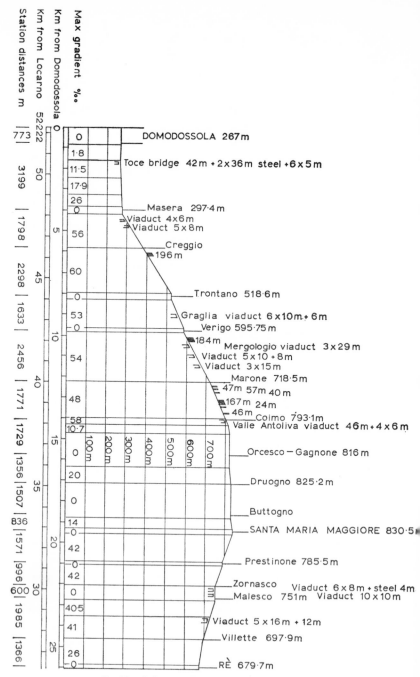

Profile of Centovalli Railway Domodossola–Rè

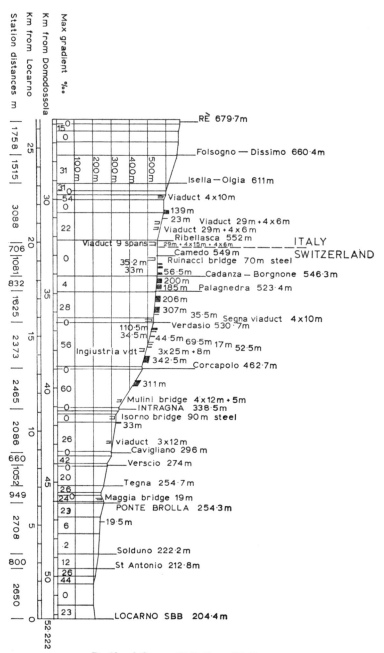

Profile of Centovalli Railway Rè–Locarno

So far the line has followed the Melezza Orient River; it now
follows the left bank of the Melezza Occidental to reach the
gorges leading down to Domodossola. The descent involves bold
engineering; in the fall of 222.2m from Trontano to Masera,
mostly at 60‰, it makes three loops, one in a tunnel of 50m
radius. This section, through the vineyards and groves of chest-
nuts is one of the most attractive on the line. The whole journey
is one of the finest scenic rides in the Alps.

At Domodossola the River Toce is crossed by a steel lattice
girder bridge with two spans of 33.6m and one of 42m. At
Domodossola the line originally terminated just short of the
main line station, but later it was extended under the main line
to the front of the station. In May 1961 a new station was
opened for the Centovalli trains in a subway beneath the main
station. The length from Locarno SBB station to Domodossola
station is 52.22km of which about 20km is in Switzerland. The
maximum gradient of 60‰ totals 3.606km (1.746km in Switzerland and 1.860km in Italy), or about 7 per cent of the entire
length.

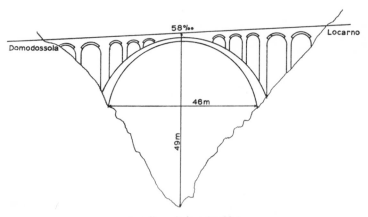

Antoliva viaduct km38.2

There are seventy-two bridges, of which three are steel and
the remainder mostly of gneiss or granite. Of the latter the greatest are Valle d'Ingiustria viaduct between Corcapolo and Ver-
dasio at km14.335, 70m high with three arches of 25m; Valle

Antoliva viaduct at km38.2, between Coimo and Marone, with a main arch of 46m span, 48m high; Margologio viaduct at km42.2, 62m high, with three arches of 29m, and Graglia viaduct at km43.2 between Verigo and Trontano, seven arches of 20m span, 28m above the stream bed.

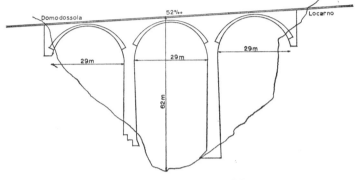

Margologio viaduct km42.2

There are twenty-eight tunnels, eighteen on the Swiss portion totalling 2,093m, and ten on the Italian, 923m, all in gneiss or granite except three which are in moraine.[7]

Electrical equipment and Rolling Stock

The line operates on dc at about 1,200V. As mentioned earlier the Valle Maggia Railway and the Locarno tramways were converted to dc in 1923 to bring the three divisions into line. The FART obtains its supply from Ponte Brolla Power Station as three-phase ac at 6,000V, 50Hz. The SSIF supply comes via a transformer station at Domodossola from where it is carried at 12,500V, 42Hz, to converter stations at Trontano and Ré. There are three sub-stations on the FART section and five on the SSIF feeding dc to the line at 1,300V. A catenary type overhead line is used, except in the street section in Locarno where a simple tramway type suffices. Annual current consumption is about 1,600,000kWh in Italy and 1 million kWh in Switzerland.

The original rolling stock consisted of eight bogie railcars built by Carminati & Toselli, Milan, and numbered 11–18, twelve trailer cars and twenty-six assorted goods vehicles. The

power cars were 14.4m long over buffers on bogies at 8.5m
centres with a wheelbase of 2.2m, they weighed 29.7 tons, had
four motors giving a total of 440hp at 43.5kph giving a maximum
speed of 45kph. All vehicles had Westinghouse air brakes. These
cars were similar to those supplied to the Val di Fiemme and
Dolomite Railways. (See photograph on p 189.)

In 1946 SSIF received two bogie railcars second hand from
an interurban tramway at Zurich; they were built by MFO and
numbered 4 and 5 on the SSIF. Each had two motors developing
a total of 140hp and a maximum speed of 35kph.

At about the same time two completely dissimilar old four-
wheeled tram vehicles built in 1908 were transferred from the
declining Locarno tramway system to FART where they became
Nos 2 and 7. With another old four-wheeled car numbered 6
they are used on maintenance work and for shunting. The tramway between St Antonio and the Piazza was closed on 1 January
1933 and the Solduno–Locarno–Minusio Esplanade route on
24 April 1960.

In 1959 four three-car articulated units, Nos 21–4, were
delivered, Nos 21–2 to FART and 23–4 to SSIF. The cars were
constructed by Schindler of Platteln. They develop 980hp at
43.4kph and have a top speed of 60 and a possible maximum of
80kph. Charmilles air brakes are used, with electric rheostat

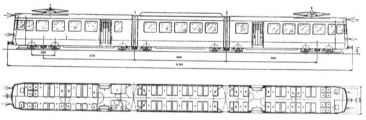

Articulated railcar, Centovalli Railway (*FART Locarno*)

braking on descents. They carry eighty-three second class and
twenty-eight first class passengers, arranged with seven firsts at
one end and nine seconds at the other, to give a good lookout.
The units weigh 60.5 tons tare. Dimensions etc, are shown in the
elevation and plan above. Unusually they have chime whistles,
not the normal 'shriek' whistles standardised on most Swiss stock.

Two 735hp twin articulated units, Nos 31–2, were added in 1963, similar to the 1959 units. The overall length is 25m and the tare weight 45 tons. With the acquisition of these two units Nos 11 and 15 of the old cars, damaged by fire, were withdrawn, as also was No 17. No 18 was rebuilt and remains in SSIF stock, with Nos 12–14 and 16.[8]

All passenger power cars and trailers are finished in the FART livery of blue and white. The present FART stock consists of five railcars and eight trailers, and seventeen goods wagons; that of SSIF of five railcars, seven trailers and thirty-four goods wagons. Each company's stock works the entire length of the line, as do train crews. Since closure of the Valle Maggia Railway the electric locomotive has been used for driver training between Locarno and Intragna.

Fast trains cover the entire journey in under 1hr 40min, stopping at only principal stations. Stopping trains take 2hr 21min. There are nine daily through trains each way and others which cover part of the journey. Good connections are made at Domodossola with trains on the Brig–Milan route, and at Locarno with trains to Bellinzona and the Gotthard line; all connections are well marked in the timetable. There are no customs formalities for passengers travelling through between Brig and Locarno, and for other passengers there is only a cursory examination. Fares for the 52km journey are charged as for 132km, unfortunately making this one of the most expensive train rides in Switzerland, but the interested traveller who plans his journey will feel he has had his money's worth.

THE LUGANO LINES

Lugano, the largest town in Ticino with a population of 18,500, is wonderfully situated on the north of the irregularly shaped Lake of Lugano at a mean height of about 300m. Although it has been Swiss since 1512 it is completely Italian in appearance and language. The opening of the Gotthard Railway in 1882 gave the town a new importance and stimulated its development as a tourist centre. In 1909–12 three metre gauge electric railways were opened to Tesserete and Dino to the north and to Ponte Tresa to the west, shown on the map on

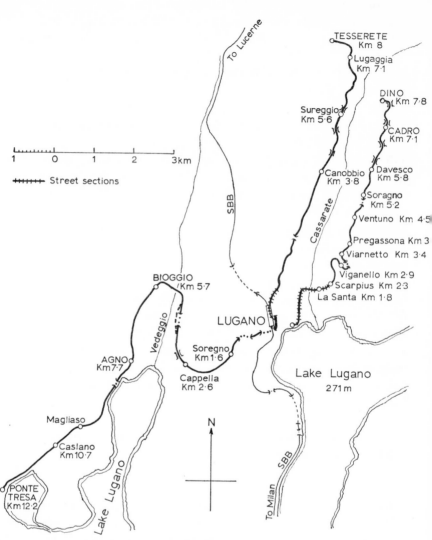

TESSERETE
Km 8

Lugaggia
Km 7·1

DINO
Km 7·8

Sureggio
Km 5·6

CADRO
Km 7·1

To Lucerne

Davesco
Km 5·8

SBB

Canobbio
Km 3·8

Soragno
Km 5·2

Ventuno Km 4·5

Cassarate

Pregassona Km 3
Viarnetto Km 3·4

Viganello Km 2·9

BIOGGIO
Km 5·7

Scarpius Km 2·3
La Santa Km 1·8

LUGANO

Vedeggio

Soregno
Km 1·6

AGNO
Km 7·7

Lake Lugano
271 m

Cappella
Km 2·6

Magliaso

N

Caslano
Km 10·7

PONTE
TRESA
Km 12·2

Lake Lugano

To Milan SBB

Map of Lugano lines

1 0 1 2 3km

+++++ Street sections

p 200. Of these only the last is still running but the others were interesting enough to justify a brief description.

Lugano–Tesserete

The concession for this railway was obtained in 1897; the project was planned in 1905 and construction began in the spring of 1907 under engineer Giuseppe Sona. The ground was mostly bog and soft clay or hard rock and construction was difficult and slow, taking over two years for a bare 8km of route.

The lower terminus was alongside Lugano SBB station. From here the trains ran along the road in grooved rails, weighing 34kg/m, as far as Sassa station, 0.66km. The original intention was for the line to run entirely in the road, but by building it on its own formation beyond Sassa, with four substantial viaducts, the gradients were greatly eased. The steepest pitch of 65%o occurred in the road section for a distance of 213m. Of the total length of 7.9837km, 5.285km or about 66 per cent, was straight. Curves were of a minimum radius of 70m except in the road section where for 38m there was a curve of 50m radius. Rails weighed 22.5kg/m. Gradients and heights are shown on p 202.

Electricity at 25,000V was transformed at a sub-station at Tesserete and converted to line voltage of 1,000 dc by two rotary converters. An accumulator battery of 160Ah, with 485 cells, acted as a buffer. The tramway type contact line, with no catenary, was supported on wooden masts.

Rolling stock consisted of three bogie power cars, with pantograph type collectors, two four-wheeled trailers and four four-wheeled goods wagons. The power cars had four 500V 45hp motors, normally in pairs in parallel. For starting, and on the 65%o gradient, motors were in series, 250V each. The cars measured 14.97m over buffers, were 2.7m wide and weighed 23 tons, and seated 60 passengers. The vacuum brake was used. All electrical equipment was supplied by Alioth. (See photograph on p 190.)

The total cost of the railway was 1,310,000Fr which included 485,220Fr for formation work, 164,130Fr for track and buildings, 188,840Fr for electrical equipment and 183,500Fr for rolling stock.[9] Passenger stock was painted blue and white.

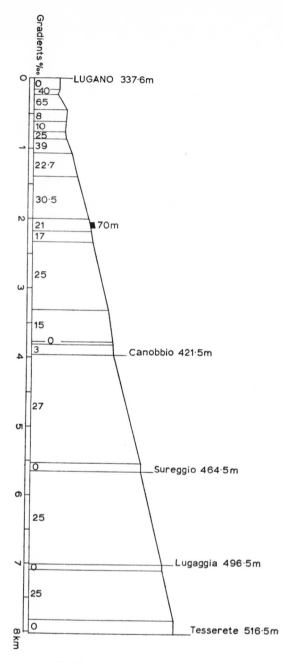

Profile of Lugano–Tesserete Railway

The railway was opened on 28 July 1909. The journey time was 30min up and 26min down, and the maximum speed was 35kph. The normal service was provided by one power car and one goods or passenger trailer. Only on Sundays or at holiday times was a second or even third train needed. On some days as many as forty-eight return trips were run, carrying 4,500 passengers.

On 27 May 1967 the line was closed, largely to eliminate the street section and to avoid heavy replacement costs, and the service is now operated by buses. The railway is dismantled, and much of it too overgrown to walk in comfort, but parts of it make a pleasant walk with good views.

Lugano–Cadro–Dino

Dino is an attractive little town situated high above the Cassarate valley opposite Tesserete at an altitude of 482m. To cater for the residents along that side of the valley, and for large numbers of tourists an electric metre gauge light railway was opened

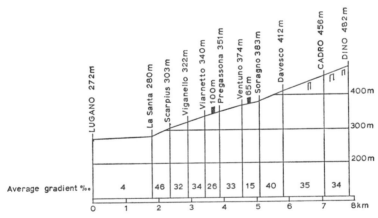

Profile of Lugano–Cadro–Dino Railway

on 5 June 1912. The climb involved some heavy gradients, as shown by the profile above, and to gain height the line had to be looped back on itself twice between Scarpius and Viarnetto.

The railway began at Piazza Alessandro Manzoni beside the lake and ran like a tramway through the streets, some of which were narrow. At La Santa, km1.846, was the main depot and workshops. Grooved rail continued to Viganello, climbing steeply. The first tunnel was on a sharp curve as the line looped up the hillside. The second tunnel was straight. Between Davesco and Cadro was a high viaduct with two stone arches and a centre steel span of 26m. There were two similar bridges with 28m spans between Cadro and Dino. Here there was a two-road car shed.

The track was laid on steel sleepers in stone ballast. The catenary was carried on wooden masts on the open section, but in the street section a tramway type overhead wire was suspended from iron columns. The line operated on 1,200V dc.

Various types of cars were used. The original type, Nos 1–4, had two driving axles and a centre idle axle, and were built by Alioth in 1911. (See photograph on page 190.) They were used with an assortment of four-wheeled open and closed trailers. In 1930 a four-wheeled trailer, No 3, was bought from the RhB. Two bogie trailers were obtained, No 41 (SIG, 1945) and No 42 (Hochstrasser, Lucerne, 1946) and an old Lugano street car which was used on the local service to La Santa. A new car, No 9, was obtained from Ateliers de Vevey in 1955. Car No 10 (SIG, 1937), was built for the Biel–Meinisberg Railway where it ran until 1940. After a period of storage it was bought by the LCD.

Like the Lugano–Tesserete, the LCD was an obstruction to road traffic and, after a period when it was cut back to La Santa at the Lugano end, it was closed on 11 June 1970 for an experimental period of one year and replaced by four buses built in 1947. In some of the village streets the buses creep between buildings with mere centimetres of clearance on each side, and the road with its numerous bends is hardly an improvement on the railway. However, in June 1971 the closure was made permanent and the stock was stored in the tunnels until June 1972 when dismantling of the railway began.

Cars 1–4 and 10 were broken up. No 9 was transferred to the MOB. No 11 was installed in a children's playground near Viganello; No 21 is preserved at Lugano; No 31 was bought for private preservation at Dino and Nos 41–2 suffered the indignity of being bought for use as dog kennels.

Lugano–Ponte Tresa (Società Ferrovie Luganesi)

The background history of this railway dates back to 1873 when the Gotthard Railway was being built between Lugano and Chiasso. A proposal was made for a narrow gauge railway from Menaggio on Lake Como, via Lugano and Ponte Tresa, to Luino on Lake Maggiore. A committee was formed in Lugano and an application was made for a concession, but it was later withdrawn. So matters stood until 30 March 1887 when Leone de Stoppani of Ponte Tresa, a member of the Swiss Lower House, obtained a concession for a standard gauge railway from Lugano to Ponte Tresa, continuing southwards to Varese in Italy. On his death the concession was renewed by his son in 1905 and was taken over by Dr Agostino Soldati (1857–1938) who immediately began negotiations with various railways for the Swiss portion to Ponte Tresa. The engineer Ferdinando Gianella was appointed to make a definitive survey. In the same year a trust was formed to divert the river Vedeggio and a tributary to pass beneath one bridge at Ostarietta; work was carried out between 1906 and 1911.

By now rivals were entering the field and in 1908 two independent committees sought concessions for electric tramways from Lugano to Ponte Tresa and Ponte Cremenaga, about half way between Ponte Tresa and Luino. They were amalgamated to pay for a concession which was granted on 22 December 1908. The tramways took two routes to Agno, via Bioggio and Sorengo, and both had steep gradients and sharp curves. The estimated cost was 1,300,000Fr.

Clearly, however, there was no room for a tramway and a railway so, under the guidance of Luigi Balestra, the two schemes were amalgamated on 21 August 1909 and a new proposal was made for a narrow gauge electric railway from Lugano via Sorengo, Bioggio and Agno to Ponte Tresa. The engineer Giuseppe Magoria (1878–1941) was entrusted with the selection of the route and preparation of the survey. He was assisted by Giuseppe Sona (1867–1929) who prepared a technical report. The total estimated cost was 2,500,000Fr which included installation of the sub-station and transformer at Agno.

On 15 January 1910 the Società Ferrovie Luganesi (Lugano

Railway Company, to be referred to as FL) was formed in Lugano. Money was subscribed by Lugano and Agno (50,000Fr each), Bioggio (25,000Fr), Ponte Tresa (20,000Fr), Magliaso (10,000 Fr) and smaller amounts by other communities and individual persons. A Federal subsidy of 642,000Fr was granted on 15 February 1910. On 3 August the original concession of 22 December 1908 was modified to provide for an electric metre gauge railway from Lugano via Sorengo, Bioggio, Agno and Ponte Tresa to Sessa, about 5km north-west of Ponte Tresa.

Work began in September 1910 on the Sorengo and Montarina tunnels at Lugano to give access to Lugano station, the material from the tunnels forming the embankment in the Tassino valley. At Lugano the rails of the FL are 3.6m lower than those of the SBB and a high wall had to be built between the two levels. With the permission of the SBB, and under the supervision of G. Sona mentioned above, a connecting line was built up an incline of 30%o and across the station forecourt to connect with the Lugano–Tesserete Railway.

Work was completed in 1912 at a total cost of 2,753,000Fr and on 5 June 1912 the railway was opened for public traffic. On 4 April 1914 a new concession, lasting for eighty years from 1 May, authorised the railway to Ponte Tresa only and later to extend to Sessa and to Novaggio, a further 3km to the north-east, but this has never been carried out.[10]

The railway was well engineered, with two tunnels at Lugano and one near Agno, and two viaducts, one 20m high at Brusado, km3.233, and one 16m high at km3.393. The latter disappeared in the construction of the new motorway in 1967 and the railway was cut back into the hillside and through a short concrete-lined tunnel. The Vedeggio is crossed by a steel span of 28m, which had to be replaced after a flood on 8 August 1951, and the Magliasina by a steel span of 24m. The position and details of the tunnels and bridges are shown on the gradient profile, p 209, and station, distances, etc on the map, p 200.

At Agno the sub-station is housed in a portion of the depot and workshop building, and a separate building houses an accumulator battery. Originally the electrical supply to the line was 1,000V dc, transformed from the public supply and rectified. It

Page 207. (Above) Two-car articulated set and trailer at Capella di Viglio, Lugano–Ponte Tresa Railway (p 210); (below) Brig–Disentis train in the Fiescher valley above Fiesch in the Goms, Furka–Oberalp Railway locomotive No 34

Page 208. (Above) Approaching the west end of the Furka tunnel. Furka–Oberalp Railway. The workings of the original alignment can be seen on the left (p 218); (below) Trains on the Schöllenen Railway at Göschenen. On the left is the Gotthard tunnel with the new tunnel for car trains on the far left. This joins the old bore about 900m inside

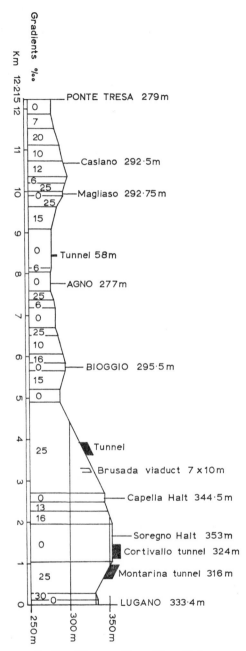

Profile of Lugano–Ponte Tresa Railway

is now fed to the line at 1,100V. The catenary is supported on wooden masts and the railcars have pantograph collectors.

The total length of the railway is 12.21km. In 1948 the only section in a public road, at Ponte Tresa, was replaced by a separate section on its own formation. The original track consisted of Vignoles section rail weighing 24kg/m on oak sleepers 1.8m × 0.13m × 0.18m. From 1931 these were gradually replaced by steel sleepers. The formation is 4.0m wide and the ballast 2.4m wide and 0.3m deep. The ruling gradient on the main line is 25%₀ and the minimum radius curve is 150m, except one of 100m in Lugano station.

Rolling stock at the opening consisted of three electric railcars, three passenger trailers, six goods wagons and one postal van. The annual electricity consumption is about 600,000kW.

The first president of the FL was Giuseppe Soldati, brother of Dr Agostino Soldati. Following his death on 20 January 1913 Luigi Balestra became president on 29 March. Operational difficulties during World War I led Balestra to propose amalgamation with the Lugano–Tesserete and Lugano–Cadro–Dino railways, but because of opposition from the LT this could not take place.

The principal revenue has always come from passenger traffic which increased from 380,158 passengers in 1913 to 798,675 in 1952. This was the year when work began on the modernisation of the railway and during the next six years all the stations were rebuilt, the connection with the LT was renewed, and a new workshop was built at Agno. A tramway vehicle was acquired from the Lugano tramways for maintenance work. Railcar No 3 was rebuilt by SWS at a cost of 102,000Fr and in 1952 a new railcar, No 4, was acquired at a cost of 346,000Fr. Three trailer cars were bought from the RhB and were completely rebuilt at Agno.

On 28 July 1958 another railcar, No 5, was received from SWS for 367,000Fr. At Agno works new machinery was installed, costing 30,000Fr. In 1967 three new articulated railcars, Nos 10–12, were obtained together with three new trailer cars from Schindler Wagons SA, Pratteln, Switzerland. These splendid vehicles now handle most of the traffic. (Photograph on page 207.) Principal dimensions are shown in the diagrams opposite. The

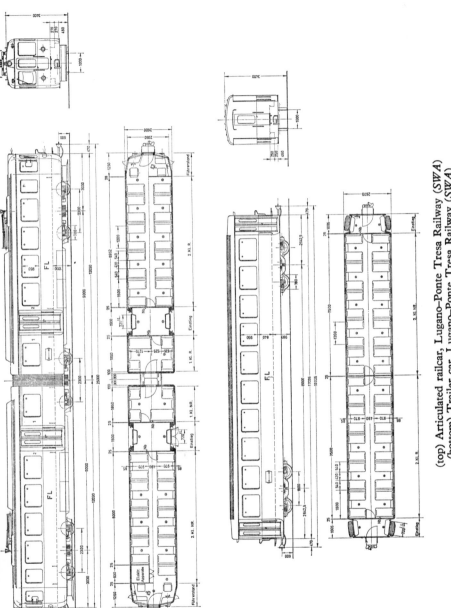

(top) Articulated railcar, Lugano–Ponte Tresa Railway (*SWA*)
(bottom) Trailer car, Lugano–Ponte Tresa Railway (*SWA*)

railcars have a tare weight of 41.6 tons and provide accommodation for ten first class and seventy-two second class passengers. They are powered by four motors consuming a total of 360kW, or producing about 450hp, at 35kph. The maximum speed is 60kph. The trailer cars weigh 15.5 tons tare and seat eighty second class passengers. The present rolling stock consists of seven railcars, five passenger trailers, four closed and five open goods wagons and three vans. Railcars 1 and 6 have been broken up together with all four-wheeled trailer cars. Like the other passenger vehicles around Lugano, the stock is finished in blue and white with black roofs.

The railway employs thirty-seven staff: two in administration, ten at stations, twelve as train drivers and conductors, six on permanent way maintenance and seven maintaining rolling stock.

Although the number of passengers carried has continued to increase, the profit margin has decreased and is now very narrow, as can be seen below:

	1913	1951	1971
Total income from operation Fr	186,663	565,965	1,498,630
Total expenditure Fr	88,730	441,322	1,404,410

In 1971 1,086,808 passengers were carried, an average of nearly 3,000 every day, for a total of 9,199,123 passenger/km. In the same period the railway carried 977 tons of baggage and parcels and 2,287 tons of general merchandise. There are over thirty trains each way daily, taking twenty-two minutes. Clearly the railway serves a local need and justifies its continuing existence. Unlike its former neighbours, the LT and the LCD, the FL occupies no public road, and its future seems reasonably secure.

For the visitor to Lugano the railway provides an enjoyable ride. The view from the station at Lugano is one of outstanding beauty, and beyond Agno there are pleasant views of the lake. Ponte Tresa is an interesting frontier town on the lake, half in Switzerland and half in Italy. The large station building is very Italian in style, and the layout includes a shed for rolling stock. There was no connection with the Italian metre gauge railway which formerly ran from here to Luino, now closed. An interesting scenic tour, for which circular tour tickets are available, can be made by returning to Lugano by the lake steamer.

2 Trailes to C P 1982

CHAPTER ELEVEN

The Furka-Oberalp and Schöllenen Railways

THE FURKA RAILWAY   BRIG–FURKA–DISENTIS

THE upper Rhone valley from Brig to Oberwald is distinguished by its broad floor and steep mountain slopes on each side. Its fertility supports a fairly large population in several villages and small towns despite altitudes of 1,000–1,300m. Dense coniferous forests clothe the lower slopes of the mountains; above these are the alpine pastures beyond which the higher summits are snow covered for most or all of the year. The views that are obtained from some of these peaks, such as the Eggishorn above Fiesch, are highly rewarding and thus the whole region attracts large numbers of tourists.

In common with other glaciated valleys it has a steady rise broken by abrupt steps which occur at Grengiols, above Fiesch, and below Gletsch. Above Grengiols the valley is known as the Goms. At these steps the valley also narrows, forcing the railway engineer to use loops, spirals or a rack, or even all three, to overcome the difference in height. As mentioned in Chapter 1 this valley forms part of an ancient traffic route from Brig over the Furka and Oberalp passes to the Rhine valley above Disentis. The Furka–Oberalp road, providing a through link of 179km between Brig and Chur, was begun in 1850 and completed in 1867. Horse postal services connecting at Andermatt, where the traveller spent the night, were established in 1871 and, following the opening of the Gotthard Railway in 1882, were extended down to Göschenen

---

Notes to this chapter will be found on p 250

at the north end of the tunnel. The travelling time from Brig to Disentis was about 17hr.

The route first interested railway promoters in 1886 when Roman Abt, inventor of the rack rail system, produced a scheme for a standard gauge railway from Brig, then the terminus of the Simplon Railway, to connect with the Gotthard Railway at Airolo. It was to be partly rack operated, with a summit tunnel of 6.3km beneath the Nufenen Pass.

In 1893 a street tramway was projected from the Brünig Railway at Meiringen (Ch 1) to Grimsel, Gletsch, Furka and Andermatt. This in turn was abandoned in favour of a metre gauge electric (dc) line from Meiringen via Grimsel to Gletsch, Brig and Visp where it would connect with the Zermatt line. The scheme, worked out in 1903–4 by the engineers E. Vogt and Karl Probst, was for an adhesion railway, 27.87km long, with maximum grades of 60%o, 71 per cent of the total length, curves of a minimum radius of 60m, and a summit of 1,783.75m inside the 2,300m tunnel under the Grimsel. Heights, etc, are shown on the profile, p 216, and the map, p 215. Excluding rolling stock the estimate for the Meiringen–Gletsch section was 6,040,000Fr and for the Gletsch–Visp 5,760,000Fr.[1]

After failure to achieve a concession, the project was reduced to a mixed rack and adhesion line from Brig to Gletsch for which a concession was granted on 21 July 1907 to engineer Xaveir Imfeld and the Alioth Company, and R. Zehnder, manager of the Montreux–Bernese Oberland Railway (MOB).[2] Another concession was granted on 8 October 1908 to Müller, Zeerleder, Gobat and the Alioth Company for a similar metre gauge electric railway from Gletsch to Disentis, there to connect with the projected RHB extension. The two were united, and on 27 May 1910 the Swiss Furka Railway Company was formed in Lausanne, with headquarters in Berne. The share capital of Fr8 million came mostly from France and the $4\frac{1}{2}$ per cent debenture capital of Fr30 million from west Switzerland.[3]

The strategic importance of this west–east route was recognised by the Federal authorities. With experience of the horse postal service, which for forty years had operated only in summer between Brig and Disentis, the company was urged to lower the

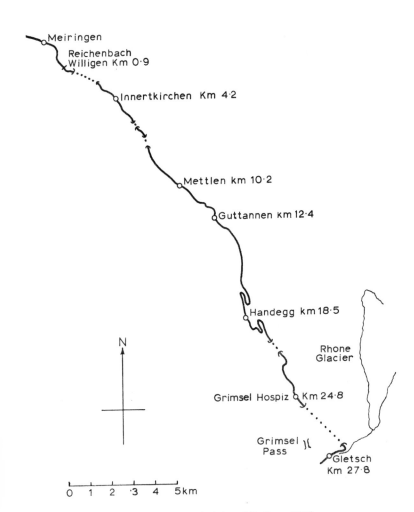

Meiringen

Reichenbach
Willigen Km 0·9

Innertkirchen Km 4·2

Mettlen km 10·2

Guttannen km 12·4

Handegg km 18·5

N

Rhone
Glacier

Grimsel Hospiz Km 24·8

Grimsel
Pass

Gletsch
Km 27·8

0 1 2 ·3 4 5km

Map of proposed Grimsel Railway 1905

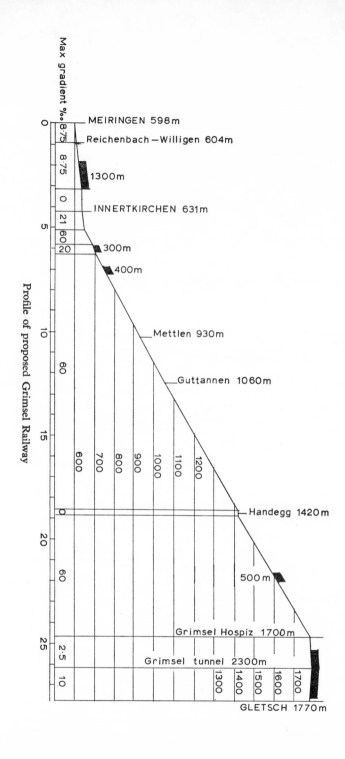

Max gradient ‰

Profile of proposed Grimsel Railway

MEIRINGEN 598m
Reichenbach—Willigen 604m
8·75
8·75
1300m
0
INNERTKIRCHEN 631m
21
60
20
300m
400m
Mettlen 930m
60
Guttannen 1060m
600
700
800
900
1000
1100
1200
0
Handegg 1420m
60
500m
Grimsel Hospiz 1700m
2·5
Grimsel tunnel 2300m
10
1300
1400
1500
1600
1700
GLETSCH 1770m

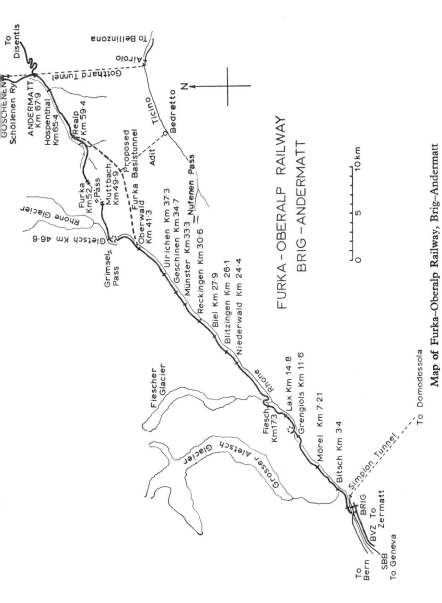

FURKA - OBERALP RAILWAY
BRIG - ANDERMATT

Map of Furka–Oberalp Railway, Brig–Andermatt

altitude of the Furka and Oberalp summits to secure all the year round operation. Regrettably this was not done and consequently ever since through traffic has been possible only in summer.

In 1908 the contract was awarded to the Société des Constructions des Batignolles, but another two years elapsed before work began. The original scheme for a purely adhesion railway was later changed to a mixed system with gradients of 40%₀–90%₀ with centre rails and friction rollers on the Hanscotte system.[4] This system, similar to that of J. B. Fell, would have made it impossible to run RhB stock over the line and, on the advice of the Swiss Railway Department, this was changed to the Abt rack to facilitate connection with the Rhaetian, Visp–Zermatt and Schöllenen railways.[5] Despite the rack, amounting to 31.75km or a third of its length, permitting maximum gradients of 110%₀ and shortening the line from just over 100km to 97.4km, the two spiral tunnels envisaged in the earlier route were still needed to surmount the abrupt steps above Grengiols and below Gletsch, in addition to three curved tunnels above Andermatt. In the 1910 plan and section the second spiral tunnel was shown above Gletsch station which was to be 20m lower.

The major task was the Furka tunnel. Quite apart from the major physical difficulties of boring a long tunnel at an altitude of over 2,000m, there was the human one of keeping the Italian workmen on the job through the winter. Many fled for home at the first sign of snow, even in September. Work began in the summer of 1911 without adequate geological exploration. By the spring of 1912 about 160m had been bored at the west end when the heading ran into moraine material under great pressure. The workings had to be abandoned and a fresh start made in compacted gneiss on a new centre line about 100m to the south. This caused serious delay and additional expense.

By the end of 1913 20,400,000Fr had been consumed, including 830,000Fr for rolling stock. To reduce expense it was decided to use steam locomotives as a temporary measure and ten were ordered from SLM. Nos 1–4 (SLM 2315–18) were built in 1913 and Nos 5–10 (SLM 2415–20) in 1914. The engines cost 82,000 Fr each. They were 2–6–0 four-cylinder superheated tank engines as shown in the drawing opposite, designed by Hans Stutz of

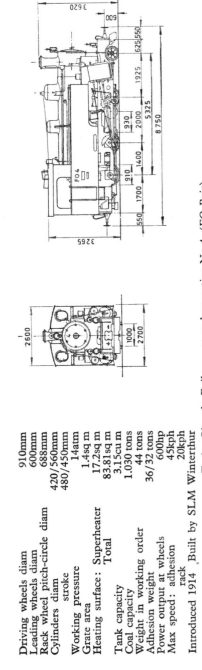

Driving wheels diam	910mm
Leading wheels diam	600mm
Rack wheel pitch-circle diam	688mm
Cylinders diam	420/560mm
stroke	480/450mm
Working pressure	14atm
Grate area	1.4sq m
Heating surface: Superheater	17.2sq m
Total	83.81sq m
Tank capacity	3.15cu m
Coal capacity	1,030 tons
Weight in working order	44 tons
Adhesion weight	36/32 tons
Power output at wheels	600hp
Max speed: adhesion	45kph
rack	20kph

Introduced 1914 Built by SLM Winterthur

Furka–Oberalp Railway steam locomotive No 4 (*FO Brig*)

Winterthur who subsequently became workshop superintendent on the Furka Railway, and later of the Furka–Oberalp until 1952.

On adhesion stretches the engine worked simple. At the approach to a rack live steam would be admitted to the low pressure rack engine between the frames and when this was turning the engine would be changed to compound working before entering the rack. Outside frames were used to provide space for the low-pressure cylinders. Steam distribution was by piston valves actuated by Walschaerts gear. The rear driving wheels were given 23mm lateral play. On adhesion sections the engine could pull 60 tons up a $40\%_0$ gradient at 45kph, and up a rack incline of $110\%_0$ 60 tons at 12–14kph. The engines were painted black and carried the initials BFD for Brig–Furka–Disentis.

Rolling stock consisted of thirty passenger cars, all on bogies except for a few second (then third) class on four wheels, built by SIG. The bogie cars had lavatories, steam heating and electric lighting. Third class bogie cars seated fifty-four and weighed 13.4 tons; first and second class bogie composites seated forty-two and weighed 14.3 tons. One of these is illustrated in the drawing opposite. Ten luggage and thirty goods wagons were supplied by Chantiers de la Buire, Lyons. All the rolling stock had Hardy vacuum brakes and a rack brake.

On 19 June 1914 the first train travelled up as far as the Rhone bridge below Gletsch and on 30 June, after a celebration in Brig, the line was brought into use between Brig and Gletsch to assist in the mobilisation of troops in the anxious weeks preceding the war. After three months trains were suspended for the winter, but for the benefit of the people in the Goms goods trains with passenger accommodation ran between Brig and Oberwald on several days of the week. Regular services between Brig and Oberwald began on 1 June 1915 with two daily return trains, and were extended to Gletsch on 1 July with three daily trains, taking 2hr 12min for the 46km. The local people were given a fare reduction of 50 per cent.

In June 1914 work on the Furka tunnel was suspended after a collapse at the Uri end when an Italian worker was killed. At the Wallis end work had been stopped for some time by shortage of building timber and cement. Early in 1915 boring was resumed,

Tare weight	14.3 tons	
Seating: 1st class	18	
2nd class	24	
Total	42	
Max speed	55kph	
Placed in service	1914	
Built: frame SIG	bogies SWS	
Rebuilt at Brig	1949	

FO composite coach No 4162 built in 1914 (*FO Brig*)

Picture & aisled coach R.W. May 1970

Scale 1:152

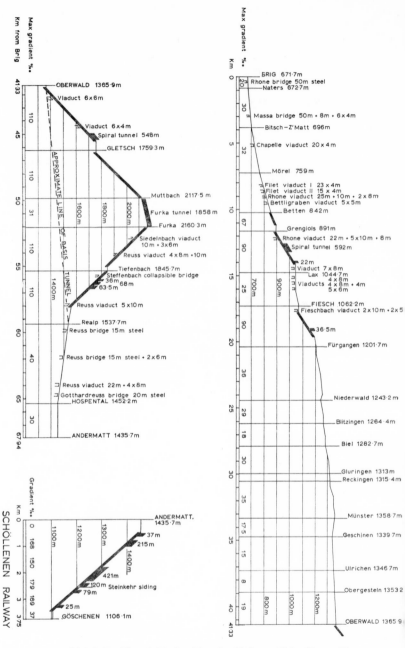

The figure contains the following labels:

Right profile (Furka–Oberalp Railway Brig–Oberwald):

Max gradient ‰
Km

BRIG 671·7m
Rhone bridge 50m steel
Naters 672·7m
Massa bridge 50m + 8m + 6x4m
Bitsch–Z'Matt 696m
Chapelle viaduct 20x4m
Mörel 759m
Filet viaduct I 23x4m
Filet viaduct II 15x4m
Rhone viaduct 25m+10m + 2x8m
Bettligraben viaduct 5x5m
Betten 842m
Grengiols 891m
Rhone viaduct 22m+5x10m + 8m
Spiral tunnel 592m
22m
Viaduct 7x8m
Lax 1044·7m
4x8m
Viaducts 4x8m + 4m
5x6m
FIESCH 1062·2m
Fieschbach viaduct 2x10m+2x5
36·5m
Fürgangen 1201·7m
Niederwald 1243·2m
Blitzingen 1264·4m
Biel 1282·7m
Gluringen 1313m
Reckingen 1315·4m
Münster 1358·7m
Geschinen 1339·7m
Ulrichen 1346·7m
Obergesteln 1353·2
OBERWALD 1365·9

Left profile (Oberwald–Andermatt and Schöllenen Railway):

Max gradient ‰
Km from Brig

OBERWALD 1365·9m
Viaduct 6x6m
Viaduct 6x4m
Spiral tunnel 548m
GLETSCH 1759·3m
APPROXIMATE LINE OF BASIS TUNNEL
Muttbach 2117·5 m
Furka tunnel 1858 m
Furka 2160·3m
Siedelnbach viaduct 10m + 3x6m
Reuss viaduct 4x8m +10m
Tiefenbach 1845·7m
Steffenbach collapsible bridge
36m 68m
63·5m
Reuss viaduct 5x10m
Realp 1537·7m
Reuss bridge 15m steel
Reuss bridge 15m steel + 2x6m
Reuss viaduct 22m + 4x8m
Gotthardreuss bridge 20m steel
HOSPENTAL 1452·2m
ANDERMATT 1435·7m

Schöllenen Railway:

Gradient ‰
Km

ANDERMATT. 1435·7m
37m
215m
421m
120m Steinkehr siding
79m
25m
GÖSCHENEN 1106·1m
SCHÖLLENEN RAILWAY

(right) Profile of Furka–Oberalp Railway Brig–Oberwald
(left) Profile, Oberwald–Andermatt and Schöllenen Railway

but with Italy now in the war the supply of workers was much reduced. On 25 September 160m remained to be bored. Laying of rails between Disentis and Andermatt was suspended in November. Work began again in the spring of 1916 but by July all the building capital was exhausted and for the next nine years further work was suspended.

Until the end of 1923 an annual deficit of 800,000Fr was made up by the Swiss Railway Department on condition that the railway was fully maintained. On 2 December 1923 the Federal Court of Justice ordered a meeting of the creditors of the company which then went into liquidation, but throughout this period traffic was maintained through advance payments by the Federal and Cantonal authorities.

THE SCHÖLLENEN RAILWAY

When work on the Furka Railway was suspended, the Schöllenen Railway, after many years of creeping progress, was nearing completion. With the opening of the Gotthard Railway in 1882 the horse postal service over the pass (which in 1880 had carried 61,000 passengers) was withdrawn and the town of Andermatt, then developing as a summer and winter resort, was cut off from much of its north–south trade. The postal service, established between Andermatt and Göschenen station, making two to three journeys daily and taking one hour on the upward trip, offered a small measure of compensation.

On 10 October 1890 a concession was granted for a metre gauge rack railway from Göschenen station up the wild Schöllenen gorge to Andermatt, but the 1,300,000Fr required for construction was not forthcoming. Other similar schemes were put forward until, in 1904, another concession was granted for a 2,600,000Fr project by engineer Richard Zschokke. Again financial difficulties prevented progress until a consortium of Swiss bankers made it possible to constitute a company in Altdorf on 24 June 1912. A Federal subvention was granted in the same year, and in May 1913 work began.

Progress was delayed following the outbreak of war, but as soon as the strategic importance of the railway was realised military help was given. The military authorities, however, required that the line should be made suitable for the rolling stock of the Rhaetian and Furka railways, for which purpose a further subvention of 300,000Fr had to be obtained for making larger tunnels and galleries and altering the minimum radius from 60 m to 80m.[6] Little did they realise that connection with the Furka Railway was still twelve years ahead.

On 12 June 1917 the line was opened for traffic. In its length of 3.729km, in which it climbed 336m, 2.735km were equipped with the Abt double rack. The three tunnels totalled 627m, with the addition of a gallery of 210m. From the SBB station yard at Göschenen the railway crossed the river Reuss twice and ascended the left bank on a ruling gradient of $179\%_0$. The rack ended at the top of the gorge where the gradient eased. Gradients, etc, are shown on p 222. A photograph of Göschenen is on page 203.

From opening the line was operated electrically, at 1,200V dc. Four small pusher locomotives were obtained from BBC and seven passenger coaches and six goods wagons from SWS. An accumulator battery was obtained at a cost of 669,000Fr of sufficient capacity to act as a buffer to relieve the main supply of excessive surge loads.

The railway operated in summer only and in the first year 28,600 passengers and 2,555 tons of goods were carried. In 1924 some 517m of extra avalanche galleries were built to make winter operation possible from 1925. In the first full year of operation 75,000 passengers and over 7,000 tons of goods were carried. Fares are based on a distance of 20km, making this a very expensive journey per km.

THE RESCUE OF THE FURKA RAILWAY

After the war the prospects for the Furka Railway were grim. Even abandonment was considered until, encouraged by a group of prominent people including Gustav Bener, managing director of the RhB, a syndicate was formed in October 1924 to acquire and complete the railway under the leadership of August Marguerat (1880–1952), director and engineer of the Visp–Zermatt Railway. The syndicate consisted of the VZ, RhB and Schöllenen, Canton Vaud and various local bodies in Cantons Vaud, Graubünden, Uri and Wallis. Through its efforts, Federal assistance

*for details see G Scale Journal Autumn 1995

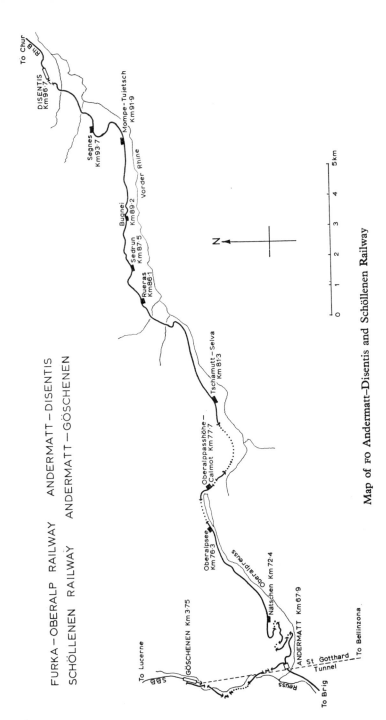

FURKA–OBERALP RAILWAY   ANDERMATT–DISENTIS
                        ANDERMATT–GÖSCHENEN
SCHÖLLENEN RAILWAY

Map of FO Andermatt–Disentis and Schöllenen Railway

M.G.R.—O

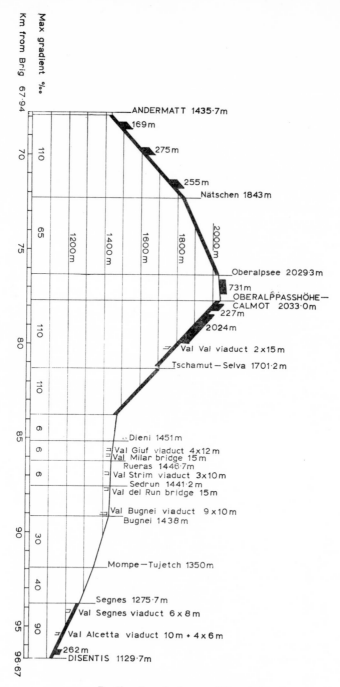

Max gradient ‰

Km from Brig

67·94

ANDERMATT 1435·7m

169 m

70

110

275 m

255 m

Nätschen 1843 m

65

75

1200 m

1400 m

1600 m

1800 m

2000 m

Oberalpsee 2029·3m

731 m

OBERALPPASSHÖHE—
CALMOT 2033·0m

227 m

110

80

2024 m

Val Val viaduct 2×15m

110

Tschamut—Selva 1701·2m

110

85

6

Dieni 1451m

6

Val Giuf viaduct 4×12m
Val Milar bridge 15m
Rueras 1446·7m

6

Val Strim viaduct 3×10m
Sedrun 1441·2m

Val del Run bridge 15m

Val Bugnei viaduct 9×10m
Bugnei 1438m

90

30

Mompe—Tujetch 1350m

40

Segnes 1275·7m

95

90

Val Segnes viaduct 6×8m

Val Alcetta viaduct 10m + 4×6m

96·67

262 m

DISENTIS 1129·7m

Profile of FO Andermatt–Disentis

to the extent of 3,350,000Fr was obtained on 23 March 1925. This was made up to nearly 5,400,000Fr by Canton Wallis (850,000Fr), the syndicate (700,000Fr), Graubünden (199,000 Fr) and the RhB (300,000Fr).

A new company known as the Furka–Oberalp Railway was constituted on 17 April 1925, the board including representatives from the syndicate. In the same year the VZ, Gornergrat, FO and Schöllenen railways combined in an operating partnership. The chief engineer for the completion of the Andermatt–Disentis portion was E. Bernasconi of the RhB.

Work went ahead with such expedition that on 18 October 1925 an experimental train ran through from Brig to Disentis. On 19 June 1926 the section from Andermatt to Disentis was opened to traffic and on 4 July the railway was opened throughout. From then until 30 September four daily trains ran each way throughout the 97km, the two fastest taking 4hr 33min and 4hr 55min. One each way provided a through service between Brig and St Moritz, 295km, taking 9hr 35min to St Moritz and 8hr 58min to Brig, with connections via the SBB to and from Visp and Zermatt.[7] Although at the end of the first fully operational year, in 1927, 143,700 passengers had been carried, including 83,000 between June and September, the receipts of 97,000Fr were 63,000Fr below the total expected.

Under a concession of 1 April 1927 the FO was obliged to operate the Brig–Oberwald and Disentis–Sedrun sections throughout the year. For working the winter traffic as economically as possible SLM designed and supplied two four-wheeled rack and adhesion petrol railcars with a wheelbase of 4.6m and length over buffers of 11.076m. They had eight-cylinder Boxer engines developing 145hp at 1,200rpm, and fluid transmission giving 5, 14, 26, and 43kph at maximum engine speeds, with reverse beyond the transmission. The cars, numbered 21–2, were very advanced for their time and gave good service until years after electrification of the railway. No 22 was sold to the RhB in 1947 and after removal of the rack mechanism it was used on late night turns in the Prättigau until scrapped in 1959. No 21 was withdrawn in 1965 and is preserved at Lucerne Transport Museum.[8]

From Brig to the 2,160m summit in the Furka tunnel, about 250m from the east portal, the railway climbs 1,483m. It then drops 724m to Andermatt, climbs 597m to the Oberalp Pass and drops 900m to Disentis. Heights, gradients, etc, can be seen on the profiles on pp 222 and 226, and distances, etc, are shown on the maps, pp 217 and 225.

With the opening on 6 June 1930 of the vz extension from Visp to Brig (Ch 2) a new service began between Zermatt and St Moritz which developed into the famous Glacier Express. In the same year the vz was electrified. The rhB electrification to Disentis had been completed in 1922, so that the most difficult section of the journey, over the fo with its two summits of over 2,000m, had to be operated by slow, labouring steam engines, albeit of modern design.

ELECTRIFICATION

Electrification of the fo was considered in 1930, but it was the desperate coal shortage in 1939 which at last compelled the company to electrify with haste in order to survive. The entire system was electrified between April 1940 and the end of June 1942, at 10,500V single-phase ac, $16\frac{2}{3}$Hz, to conform closely to the vz and rhB systems. At the same time the Schöllenen Railway was converted from 1,200V dc to 10,500V ac.

In connection with this work the railway was adapted for winter operation between Disentis and Andermatt by realignment of track and the building of large avalanche galleries and tunnels at Oberalpsee and above Tschamut, and mountainside protection works and afforestation below Tschamut. This work was carried out under Paul Schneller, fo engineer since 1925 and later assistant manager and then manager.

The total cost of electrification and construction work, Fr12 million, was subscribed by the Federal government. Electric trains began running between Andermatt and Oberalpsee on 5 July 1941 and throughout on 1 July 1942, with the completion of the Oberalp–Realp section. Conversion of the Schöllenen Railway was carried out in 1940–1 with Federal assistance in view of its military importance. It made possible a reduction in journey time from 25min to 15min. Electric motor coaches were introduced in

Driving wheels diam 940mm
Rack wheel pitch-circle diam 688mm
Weight 46.6 tons
Number of traction motors 4
Max driving force at wheels 19,000kg
Tractive effort at 27kph 11,600kg
Power output at 27kph 1,200hp
Max speed: adhesion 55kph
rack 30kph

Placed in service
31–4 1941
35* 1943
36 1949
37 1956

Built SLM/MFO
*No 35 broken up 13.6.1970

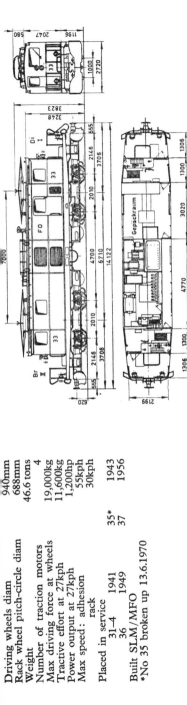

FO Bo-Bo type electric locomotive (*FO Brig*)

Driving wheels diam 790mm
Rack wheel pitch-circle diam 688mm
Number of traction motors 2
Weight, tare 36 tons
Max driving force at wheels 12,000kg
Tractive effort at 27kph 5,600kg
Power output at 27kph 586hp
Max speed: adhesion 55kph
rack 30kph

Seating: 1st class 8
2nd class 32
Standing 6
Total 46

Placed in service
41–3 1941
44–5 1942

Built SLM/BBC

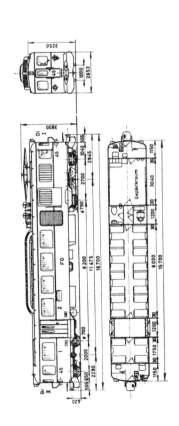

FO electric railcar (*FO Brig*)

1943. Travelling time for fast trains between Brig and Disentis was reduced from $4\frac{3}{4}$hr to $3\frac{3}{4}$hr or $3\frac{1}{2}$hr.

The Bo–Bo type electric locomotives (see drawing on p 229) were modelled on those of vz, with various improvements. The FO and vz locomotives have identical circuits, but twelve years of experience with the latter made it possible to increase the power by some 85 per cent, and at the same time to reduce the weight from 48 to 45 tons. The air cooled transformer of the vz locomotives was replaced by an oil cooled transformer. The superstructure was remodelled, without the end bonnets. Their 1,200hp allows them to haul 100 tons up a gradient of $110\%_0$ at 27kph; they have a maximum speed on the rack of 30kph and on adhesion sections of 55kph, compared with 25kph and 45kph of the rebuilt vz locomotives. In addition to the rheostatic brake, as on the vz locomotives, they have a compressed air brake, a hand brake and a rack-wheel brake, each of which can hold an entire train on the steepest gradient. On the train the automatic vacuum brake works on all running wheels and rack wheels.[9] Nos 31–4 were built in 1941, 35 in 1943, 36 in 1949 and 37 in 1956. No 35 was broken up in June 1970.

Five 586hp motor coaches, Nos 41–5, were built by SLM/BBC in 1941–2; they were equipped with two motors driving on one bogie at the luggage end and can seat thirty-two second class and eight first class passengers. (See drawing p 229.)

Of the ten steam engines, Nos 1, 2, 8 and 9 were sold in 1947 to French Indo–China, now Vietnam; No 6 went to Grenoble in 1946 and No 7 was sold to the Biere–Morges Railway in 1941 on which it worked until that was electrified in 1943 when it was sold to Turkey. Nos 3, 4, 5 and 10 were retained for maintenance work and special trains, though No 4 was used by the RhB for shunting at Chur in 1958–60. No 10 was destroyed in an avalanche in 1965. Nos 3 and 5 were withdrawn, the latter in 1968, leaving only No 4 which is kept at Brig.

The SchB pusher locomotives were rebuilt in 1941 to work on 10,500V ac and were renumbered 21–4. They produce 584hp and weigh 25.1 tons, measure 6.24m over buffers and have a wheelbase of 2.7m. The maximum speed on the rack is 20kph and on adhesion 30kph.

schB receipts were severely reduced in 1955 when the new Schöllenen road was opened for all-the-year-round traffic. The schB, however, was too valuable to the FO to be allowed to fail, so by an amalgamation agreement of 16 December 1961 it was taken over by the FO for 341,000Fr with effect from 31 December 1960. At the same time the FO company wished to become independent and the operating agreement with the BVZ and GGB was ended.

After the amalgamation with the schB there was a need for a locomotive which could work down to Göschenen on the 179‰ grade and the 80m radius curves as well as over the main line. This the FO electric locomotives could not do. Also a power unit was needed to replace the steam locomotives for use on maintenance work when the electric power was off, or for traffic in the event of power failure or damage to the overhead line.

Thus, in 1966, the FO ordered from SLM/BBC/MFO two 1,540hp diesel-electric locomotives with two Cummins 770hp diesel power plants, which were delivered in 1968 and numbered 61–2. (See drawing on p 232.) At 12kph they can push 60 tons up the 179‰ from Göschenen or pull 100 tons up the 110‰ on the main line. Should the occasion arise they have a possible maximum speed of 70kph. In summer they are frequently used in regular traffic.

The newest motive power units are five motor baggage cars, Nos 51–5, delivered in the summer of 1972 from SIG/BBC/SLM. These splendid machines equipped with four traction motors giving a total output of 1,450hp, shown in the drawing on p 232 and in the photograph on page 33, like all FO passenger rolling stock and locomotives, are finished in bright red similar to the BVZ stock, but they are unique in carrying names as follows: 51 *Disentis*, 52 *Tavetsch/Sedrun*, 53 *Urserne*, 54 *Goms* and 55 *Brig*. Like the passenger power cars and the diesel-electric locomotives, they can also work down to Göschenen. To avoid the necessity for running round, four trailers Nos 4151–4 (drawing p 233) were also obtained in 1972. They have electro-pneumatic doors, and twenty-four first class and fifteen second class seats, with a total weight of 13.8 tons.

In addition there are three electric rotary snow ploughs with twin rotors on a body which can swivel right round on the four-

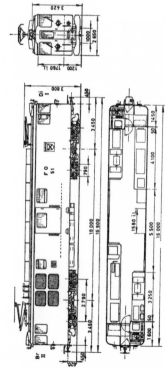

Driving wheels diam	790mm
Rack wheel pitch-circle diam	688mm
Number of traction motors	4
Weight in working order	54 tons
Fuel capacity	1,500 l
Output of diesel engines at 2,100rpm	2×770hp max
Power output at wheels	950hp
Max tractive effort at wheels	22,500kg
Max speed: adhesion	50kph
rack	30kph

Introduced 1968
Built: Mechanical SLM
Diesel engines Cummins (RACO)
Electrical BBC MFO

FO diesel-electric locomotive (FO Brig)

Driving wheels diam	790mm
Rack wheel pitch-circle diam	688mm
Number of traction motors	4
Weight empty	48 tons
Max load	2 tons
Load capacity	11.5cu m
Max driving force at wheels	25,000kg
Tractive effort at 30kph	12,000kg
Power output at 30kph	1,450hp
Max speed: adhesion	60kph
rack	30kph

Type Deh 4/4 Nos 51–5
Placed in service 1972
Built by SIG BBC SLM

FO electric baggage car of 1972 (FO Brig)

Driving data for power baggage cars

Tare weight   Nos 51-5   13.8 tons
Seating capacity: 1st class smoking   12
       non-smoking   12
   2nd class smoking   15
   Emergency seats   4
   Total   43
Brakes: vacuum, hand brake, rack wheel brake
Electro-pneumatically operated doors
Max speed   60kph
Placed in service   1972
Built by: Mechnical SIG
      Electrical BBC
Running Nos 4151-4

FO driving trailer composite coach to work with electric baggage car and another second class car as a push-pull formation (*FO Brig*)

Clearance width
4931, 3450mm   4932, 3600mm   4933, 3605mm
Overhang on curves about 5cm
Weight   16 tons
Continuous rating of motors 2×180hp
Max output of motors 2×275hp
Max speed of motors   1,500rpm
Max speed of rotary ploughs   305rpm
Speed at circumference of rotor   21.7 m/sec
Brakes: hand brake on 2 running wheels and rack
Max running speed   45kph
Placed in service
4931 1941   4932 1942   4933 1945
Built SLM/SIG

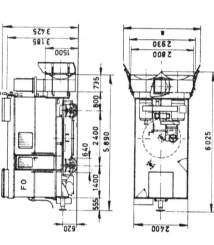

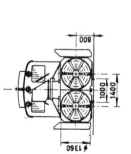

FO electric snow plough (*FO Brig*)

wheeled chassis, as shown in the drawing on p 233. They obtain their electrical supply from electric locomotives Nos 31–7 or from diesel-electric locomotives Nos 61–2 which are used to propel them.

OPERATIONAL PROBLEMS

Because operation throughout is restricted to summer only, traffic receipts suffer proportionally; a difficulty which is increased by the annual expenditure in dismantling and re-erecting overhead equipment in stretches threatened by avalanches, and in snow clearance every spring. Sometimes snow masses up to 20m deep have to be cleared. Snow clearance alone can cost from 20,000Fr to 50,000Fr. Between Tiefenbach and Realp where the line crosses the Steffenbach a stone viaduct of three 10m spans was built originally. On 16 May 1916 it was demolished by an avalanche and swept down into the Furka Reuss valley. When construction was resumed in 1925 Theodor Bell & Co built a collapsible steel bridge at a cost of 20,000Fr. It is in three portions each 12m long which can be drawn back against the two abutments. It was ready for use on 5 August 1925. Every October the bridge is dismantled and is re-erected at the end of May. All this work demands a force of about 200 resident FO employees and represents a total loss.

For many years the company wanted to construct a 'Furka Basistunnel', that is a 12km long low level tunnel from Oberwald to Realp, to eliminate both the climb of 749m between Oberwald and the summit of the Furka tunnel, and the unproductive expenditure in autumn and spring. Also it would enable the whole line to remain open throughout the year, greatly increasing the value of both the FO and the SCHB and the total receipts. The journey time of the Glacier Express over this stretch would be reduced from 42 to 12 minutes, though the train would thereby lose the reason for its title. Gletsch would still be served by the post buses operating over the Grimsel and Furka passes. It would also allow work to proceed on a dam and power station project at Gletsch which would submerge part of the present FO formation.

From 1927 to 1971 the annual number of passenger journeys increased from 143,700 to 1,511,623. Freight tonnage rose from

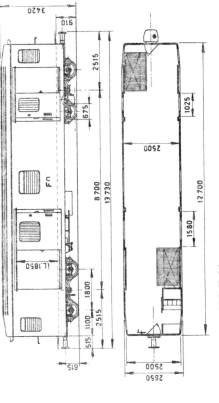

FO baggage car (*FO Brig*)

Capacity   63cu m
Floor space   31.4sq m
Load   6 tons
Tare weight   12.6 tons
Max speed   55kph
Placed in service   1961
Built: frames FFA   bogies SIG

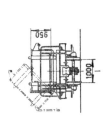

Capacity   2×3cu m
Load   9.5 tons
Tare weight   6.58 tons
Weight of one container   700kg
Max speed   45kph
Placed in service   1914
Built Lyon   Rebuilt 1969   Nos 4720-3

FO box container wagon (*FO Brig*)

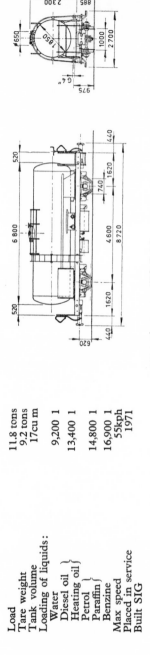

Load — 11.8 tons
Tare weight — 9.2 tons
Tank volume — 17cu m
Loading of liquids:
Water — 9,200 l
Diesel oil — 13,400 l
Heating oil ⎱
Petrol ⎰
Paraffin ⎱ — 14,800 l
Benzine — 16,900 l
Max speed — 55kph
Placed in service — 1971
Built SIG

FO tank wagon (*FO Brig*)

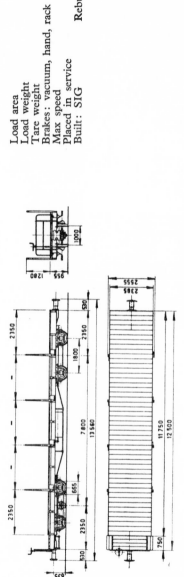

Load area — 28sq m
Load weight — 10 tons
Tare weight — 9 tons
Brakes: vacuum, hand, rack
Max speed — 45kph
Placed in service — 1914
Built: SIG   Rebuilt: 1942, 1970

FO bogie flat wagon (*FO Brig*)

Loading of liquids:

Water	29,000 l
Diesel oil } Heating oil }	35,000 l
Petrol } Paraffin }	36,600 l
Benzine	39,700 l

Tare weight: Flat 15 tons; with tank 21 tons
Load: Flat 35 tons   tank 29 tons
Total: 50 tons
Load area   34.6sq m
Tank volume   44cu m
Brakes: vacuum, hand, rack
Max speed   50kph
Placed in service   1967
Built: J. Meyer AG

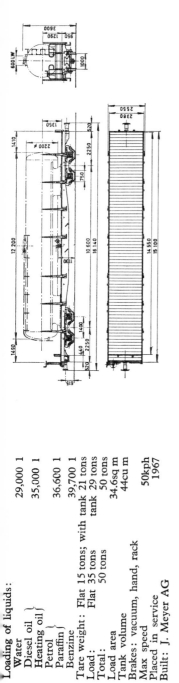

FO bogie flat/tank wagon (FO Brig)

Tare weight   12 tons
Seating: Smoking   32
       Non-smoking   32
       Emergency   3
       Total   67
Max speed   60kph
Placed in service:
     4263–8   1965
     4269–72   1968
Built: bogies SIG   1965
     frames FFA   lighting BBC

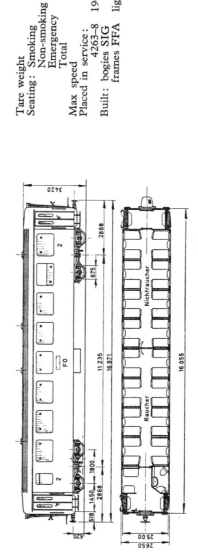

FO passenger second class coach 1965 built by FFA
(FO Brig)

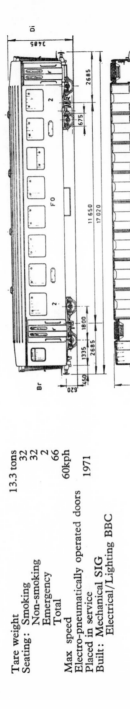

Tare weight	13.3 tons
Seating: Smoking	32
Non-smoking	32
Emergency	2
Total	66
Max speed	60kph
Electro-pneumatically operated doors	
Placed in service	1971
Built: Mechanical SIG	
Electrical/Lighting BBC	

FO passenger coach 1971 built by SIG (*FO Brig*)

5,580 to a maximum of 137,727 in 1965, but varies enormously. In 1968 it was 23,179 and in 1971 34,141. Out of these years only 1927–30 and 1940–7 were without deficit, the best being 1928 with a profit of about 153,000Fr and 1943 with 699,000Fr. Rising receipts cannot keep pace with rising costs. Traffic receipts in 1960 were 2,890,000Fr, but amounts written off to cover depreciation and maintenance totalled 3,540,000Fr. In 1961, with the schB, receipts totalled 3,990,000Fr but expenditure was 4,490,000Fr. By 1971 total receipts had risen to 7,423,368Fr, but expenditure was 11,811,704Fr. Fares are charged for a distance of 136km over the total length of 96.67km.

The pasenger timetable for summer 1972 showed seven daily through trains each way between Brig and Disentis, some with through coaches to or from Chur, including the Glacier Express which takes 3hr 18min eastwards and 3hr 36min westwards. Stopping trains take 3hr 52min to 4hr. Another through train each way included a return trip between Andermatt and Göschenen. In addition there were three return trips from Oberwald to Brig, two from Münster and two from Fiesch. At the other end there was an early morning return service between Andermatt and Realp, two from Andermatt to Disentis and one back, and three return trips between Disentis and Rueras. On the schB there were altogether twelve up to Andermatt taking 13min and thirteen down taking 15min, all connecting with trains on the Gotthard line and with trains to or from Brig and Disentis. Two examples of recent FO second class coaches are shown in the diagrams on pp 237 and 238.

Despite the operating losses the railway is constantly being improved. On 16 October 1971 one of the worst sections, between Oberalp Pass and Tschamut, was avoided when trains began running through the new Calmot gallery and tunnel begun in 1969. It consists of 40m of gallery, 835m of tunnel and a further 55m of gallery linking it to the existing 1,094m gallery above Tschamut. Near Andermatt, on the climb to Nätschen, the new Gändli gallery was completed in 1971. The new 360m Blitzingen gallery was completed in seven months and opened on 20 November 1971. At Andermatt a new depot, and a beautifully designed new station, were almost completed in the summer of 1972.

In 1960 Canton Wallis appointed a committee to examine again the Furka Basistunnel project. Uri and Graubünden added representatives in 1962 and a geological survey was carried out under a syndicate including representatives of the three cantons, engineers, and S. Zehnder, manager of the FO. After receiving their report, the Federal government appointed three experts to report on the project. In July 1969 this report was accepted and on 24 June 1971 a Confederation decision was made to authorise the tunnel and to contribute Fr70 million.

The new line will begin just short of Oberwald, and will enable a station to be made in the middle of the village. The present station is well outside the village because of the rack section. The tunnel will now be 15.5km long rising from the west at $27\%_0$ to a point east of the centre from which it will fall slightly at $2\%_0$ to the Realp end which is now further east than originally planned. It will be for single line but may have one or two passing loops inside. For geological reasons it will not be straight, and of two possible routes the slightly shorter southern one has been selected. Construction began in the spring of 1973 and is expected to take five and a half years and to cost 65,700,000Fr. To facilitate construction, ventilation and drainage, and in the interests of workers' safety, a 6.1km adit is being constructed from Bedretto in the Ticino valley above Airolo, as shown on the map on p 217, so making possible four working faces, and considerably shortening the construction period. It is not expected that the Bedretto tunnel will be enlarged to provide access to Airolo because this would simply duplicate the Schöllenen Railway at the other end of the Gotthard Tunnel.

Although the route of the FO hardly compares in scenic splendour and beauty with the Centovalli Railway, it is by no means devoid of interest. (See photograph on page 207.) Above Gletsch the view of the Rhone Glacier is still striking, despite the diminishing size of the glacier, which a century ago extended to within a few hundred metres of Gletsch and, as proved by my own camera, has considerably shrunk in the last twenty-five years. Unfortunately this view will be lost to rail passengers when the 'Basistunnel' comes into use. The climb out of Andermatt affords some startling views with the town appearing almost vertically below the train, first on one side and then on the other. Beyond the Oberalp Pass there are some fine views over the Vorder Rhine valley as the train descends towards Disentis on a ledge high above the river.

Since 1934 the FO has operated road motor coach services between Fiesch and Binn and up the Fiescher valley, and it now operates one over the new road over the Nufenen Pass, between Ulrichen and Airolo. Post bus connections are also made at Brig with the Simplon–Domodossola service (1919) and to Blatten (1934), at Gletsch with the Grimsel–Meiringen (1921) and Furka–Andermatt–Gotthard service (1921–2) and at Disentis with the Lukmanier–Acquarossa bus (1925) mentioned in the previous chapter.

The FO has opened up numerous winter sports facilities in the area it serves and it now makes convenient connections at many points with aerial ropeways and ski lifts. They were opened as follows:

1938   Ski lift, Nätschen–Gütsch (1958 Gütsch–Stöckli)

1950–1 Aerial ropeway, Mörel–Greich–Riederalp, and Mörel–Riederalp (amalgamated 1956)

1951   Ski lift, Riederalp–Blausee
         Aerial ropeway, Betten–Bettmeralp

1954   Aerial ropeway, Blatten–Belalp

1956   Aerial ropeway, Fürgangen–Bellwald
         Chair lift, Sedrun–Cungieri

1960   Ski lifts, Oberalp Pass–Calmot, Hospenthal–Winterhorn

1962   Ski lifts, Ernen–Mühlebach, and at Realp, Sedrun and Disentis

1963   Aerial ropeway, Andermatt–Gemstock with ski lift to Gurschenalp
         Ski lift, Sedrun–Dieni–Milez–Cuolm Val
         Aerial ropeway, Fiesch–Kühboden, extended to Eggishorn 1970

The administrative board of the FO consists of fifteen members, including eight from the Swiss Confederation, two representatives from Canton Wallis and one from each of Cantons Uri and Graubünden. Since 1925 the FO has had only three managing directors: 1925–49 the engineer Dr Auguste Marguerat; 1949–60 engineer Paul Schneller, and since 1 January 1961 Stefan Zehnder. The main offices, workshops and locomotive depot are at Brig.

Conclusion

FOR the traveller wishing to explore these and other Swiss railways the best bargain is the 'Swiss Holiday Pass', obtainable in any country outside Switzerland, for one or two weeks or a month, first or second class, giving unlimited travel on other than purely mountain railways, post buses and lake steamers. It does not generally include free travel on cable lines or such railways as Pilatus or Jungfrau although it allows tickets to be purchased at a discount, but is valid on most of the lines described in this book. Details of the holiday pass can be obtained from Swiss National Tourist Offices in countries outside Switzerland. On most Swiss railways the same services operate on Sundays as on weekdays. Principal station restaurants open between 6.0 and 7.0 every morning and usually remain open until late evening.

It has been seen that the completion of the metre gauge network as originally planned, particularly in Graubünden, was thwarted by the two world wars. The extensions down the Inn from Schuls to Landeck on the Arlberg railway and from St Moritz to Chiavenna in Italy, and the branch from Zernez to Schluderns via the Ofenberg, which could have given the Inn valley route international main line status, were abandoned because of World War I. As a result the Inn valley line with its expensive tunnels and viaducts has remained a lightly used branch serving small scattered communities and unable to pay its way. Similarly the Thusis–Mesocco link beneath the St Bernhardin Pass, which could have converted the Bellinzona–Mesocco section into part of a main line, was killed by the financial troubles preceding World War II, and as a result the entire route has succumbed to road competition. Many of the troubles of the Furka–Oberalp Railway spring directly from World War I which delayed its completion and then forced the original company into liquidation. The promise of the Furka Basistunnel is the most hopeful sign in a bleak prospect.

However, had the extensions of these railways been made they could hardly have delayed the extensive road construction now taking place all over Switzerland. Even a long established and heavily used railway like the St Gotthard is being threatened by a new road tunnel under the pass, being constructed at vast expense when the railway has proved that it could well carry all the road traffic through the existing tunnel speedily and efficiently. At peak times it carries 8,000 vehicles a day with ease.

In the territory covered by this book a new road has been completed from Thusis to Bellinzona under the St Bernhardin Pass, and another is being constructed through the Schyn Gorge from Thusis, crossing the Albula at Solis close beside the RhB viaduct. Another from Davos is being cut through a great tunnel parallel to the Züge Gorge to Wiesen. The cost of these roads, many of four-lane width, through the gorges and passes and over valleys, involving immense tunnels and bridges, makes metre gauge railway construction look cheap by comparison. The result is bound to be a sharp increase in the volume of road traffic with a corresponding increase in the railways' deficits. The underwriting of the latter from public funds must make a heavy addition to the cost of the roads. Further, many of these roads are being used by traffic passing through Switzerland between Italy and France, Germany or Austria, adding to the congestion inside the country without bringing any benefits.

It seems inevitable that restrictions will eventually have to be placed on road traffic before it chokes itself into immobility and kills even more of us. Atmospheric pollution in the alpine gorges and long tunnels in high summer is a problem in itself, with the strong sun acting on concentrated motor fumes in the gorges on still days producing toxic gases by photochemical reaction. In a tunnel of 8km with vehicles spaced at only ten to the kilometre there are constantly 160 vehicles inside the tunnel, all pumping out poisonous fumes. At busy times there could be well over 200 vehicles. The installation, running and maintenance of an adequate ventilation system adds enormously to the cost of the tunnel. Crashes inside the tunnels are not infrequent and can prove serious health hazards from prolonged exposure to a build-up of gas. Lay an isolated stretch of double track railway through the tunnel and take the vehicles through by train, perhaps on payment of a toll, and the ventilation equipment will not be required, and there will be almost no danger to health, life and limb.

Swiss railways, using hydro-electric power, produce no atmospheric pollution whatever, and are considerably less noisy than road traffic, to say nothing of their greater safety, speed and efficiency. In the USA the Association of American Railroads has established that a railway, even using diesel locomotives, can carry seven times as much freight per employee, and can move an item of freight or a number of passengers for a fifth of the fuel, a sixth of the accidents and a tenth of the land compared with the movement of the same traffic by road. On Swiss railways the economy in fuel is even greater.

Zermatt has retained its freedom from cars and lorries only by a determined effort, and today passengers on the BVZ between the terminal car park at Täsch and Zermatt far outnumber those travelling through from Brig or Visp. It is largely this precarious situation which makes it possible for the BVZ to operate at a profit. With the exception of the Lugano–Ponte Tresa, the other metre gauge railways suffer operating deficits and are in receipt of ever increasing grants from public funds. Of the six purely local lines described here only two, the Biasca–Acquarossa and the Lugano–Ponte Tresa, still operate. If a proposal by the Swiss Federal Bureau of Transport comes into effect it is likely that the BA will close at the end of 1973.

Even if the metre gauge network had been completed it would have been handicapped by breaks of gauge at exchange points, involving transshipment of through freight. Only on short stretches is it possible to carry standard gauge wagons on transporters. The extension of this facility is precluded by the numerous tunnels. Passengers can transfer themselves, but even this can cause delays. Yet, despite these snags, the metre gauge railways continue to make a real contribution to the districts they serve.

Not the least notable part of this contribution has been the manner in which aesthetic considerations were placed before economy in the design of bridges, viaducts and stations. In many situations, as at Filisur and Wiesen, the railway viaducts enhance the scenery, and on the Chur–Arosa Railway for example the station buildings form attractive architectural features of the district. In this respect Switzerland sets an example which could well be followed elsewhere. The country's main detraction is its habit of festooning itself with overhead wires, apart from the unavoidable railway catenaries.

The obvious solution to the transport problem is an integration of road and rail, letting each do the work for which it is best suited. Indeed, this is already operated by the Swiss railways and postal buses, providing an example of transport integration in a sparsely populated rural area which must be unique in western Europe. The carrying of road vehicles through the long tunnels provides another example. But this solution depends upon the survival of the railways. Expensive as it may be to support them out of public funds, this may yet prove to be to the advantage of us all. Perhaps some of us may live to see a railway through the St Bernhardin tunnel after all.

References

NOTES TO CHAPTER 1

1 *Schweizerische Bauzeitung* (S Bz), Vol 31, 18 June 1898, pp185–8
2 S Bz, Vol 31, 16 April 1898, p116

NOTES TO CHAPTER 2

1 S Bz, Vol 12, 27 October 1888, pp108–11
2 *Zeitschrift des Vereines deutscher Ingenieure* (Z), Vol 36, 19 March 1892, pp342–4
3 S Bz, Vol 13, 5 January 1889, p5
4 S Bz, Vol 17, 28 March 1891, p81; June 1891, pp145–6, 152–3
5 Moser, Alfred. *Der Dampfbetrieb der Schweizerische Eisenbahnen 1847–1966*, Basle 1967
6 S Bz, Vol 31, April–May 1898; Z, Vol 42, 27 August 1898, pp959–63
7 S Bz, Vol 32, 3 September 1898, p77; *Gornergrat–Chronik*, GGB 1958, p30
8 *Bergbahnen der Schweiz*, Basle 1959, pp451–9
9 *Gornergrat–Chronik*, GGB 1958, p49
10 *The Engineer*, 21 March 1930, p318
11 S Bz, Vol 94, 19 October 1929, pp193–6; *The Engineer*, 21 March 1930, pp318–19
12 *Railway Magazine*, July 1933, pp57–60
13 S Bz, Vol 103, 24 February 1934, pp98–9

NOTES TO CHAPTER 3

1 S Bz, Vol 16, August–September 1890, pp51–4, 57–60, 63–6
2 S Bz, Vol 13, 2 February 1889, pp26–7, and article by C. Wetzel, 23 February 1889, pp43–4
3 S Bz, Vol 14, 26 October 1889, pp101–2
4 S Bz, Vol 14, 7 December 1889, p134

5 Moser, R. *Report on the laying of an Albula Line and the most convenient link with the Engadin Region* (in German), Casanova Bros, 1891

6 S Bz, Vol 27, 13 June 1896, p174

7 S Bz, Vol 61, 15 February 1913, p91

8 S Bz, Vol 91, 18 February 1928, p91

9 *100 Jahre Schweizer Eisenbahn*, Zurich 1947, p112

10 S Bz, Vol 115, 11 May 1940, pp244–6

11 S Bz, Vol 95, 20 December 1930, pp337–41. Article by P. J. Bener

12 Article by C. Mohr of the RHB in S Bz, Vol 129, January 1947, pp 5–8, 20–4, 32–7

13 *Railway Gazette*, 5 June 1970, p402

NOTES TO CHAPTER 4

1 S Bz, Vol 16, 5 July 1890, p7

2 S Bz, Vol 31, 16 April 1898, p120; Vol 32, 2 July 1898, p10

3 S Bz, Vol 79, 18 February 1922, pp87–8

4 S Bz, Vol 128, 19 October 1946, p211

5 S Bz, Vol 38, 7 December 1901, p255

6 S Bz, Vol 43, 16–30 January 1904

7 Hennings, F. Article in S Bz, Vol 38, 6 and 13 July 1901; Vol 42, 17 and 24 October 1903; *The Engineer*, Vol 97, 1904, pp226 et seq; Vol 98, 1904, p82 et seq

8 S Bz, Vol 41, 9 May and 27 June 1903

9 S Bz, Vol 44, 3 September 1904, p108

10 S Bz, Vol 60, 16 November 1912, p273

NOTES TO CHAPTER 5

1 S Bz, Vol 38, 27 July 1901, pp41–3; Vol 41, 30 May 1903, pp243–7; 6 June 1903, pp258–62

2 S Bz, Vol 45, 20 May 1905, p254

3 Extensive illustrated articles on the Davos–Filisur Railway appear in S Bz, Vol 47, 24 March 1906, pp141–4; Vols 53–4, 1909, 5 June, pp291–4; 12 June, pp305–7; 19 June, pp319–24; 26 June, pp336–40; 3 July, pp3–10

4 S Bz, Vol 128, 19 October 1946, p211

5 Saluz, P. Article in S Bz, Vol 59, 20 April 1912, pp209–12

6 S Bz, Vol 60, 3 August 1912, p69

7 S Bz, Vol 58, 2 September 1911, p133

8 S Bz, Vol 59, 4 May 1912, pp239–43

9 S Bz, Vol 62, 5 July 1913, pp10–11

10 S Bz, Vol 55, 1910, p41; Vol 57, 14 January 1911, pp25–7

NOTES TO CHAPTER 6

1 Moser, Alfred. *Der Dampfbetrieb der Schweizerische Eisenbahnen 1847–1966* (Moser), Basle 1967, pp338–40, 405–6; S Bz, Vol 16, 13 September 1890, pp64–6; Vol 42, 29 August 1903, pp99–103
2 S Bz, Vol 42, 29 August 1903, pp99–103; *The Locomotive*, 28 November 1903, p316; May 1931, p171; Moser, 1967, pp339–43, 349; Wiener, Lionel. *Articulated Locomotives*, New York 1930, 1970, pp348–59
3 S Bz, Vol 45, 7 January 1905, pp2–6; Moser, 1967, pp341, 345–6, 349
4 S Bz, Vol 16, 13 September 1890, pp64–6

NOTES TO CHAPTER 7

1 *Electric Railway Journal* (USA), 23 July 1910, p148; S Bz, Vol 75, 15 May 1920, pp217–20
2 *Electric Railway Journal*, 27 June 1914, p1430; S Bz, Vol 79, April 1922, pp181–3, 194–8, May, pp249–54, 267–9, June, pp279–80; *The Engineer*, May 1923, pp464–6, 492–4; June 1924, pp634–6, 653–4
3 *The Engineer*, 3 October 1913, pp359–60
4 *Electric Railway Journal*, 31 January 1914, p273, and 4 April, p760
5 *The Engineer*, 4 May 1923, p465
6 *The Engineer*, 11 May 1923, pp492–3
7 S Bz, Vol 120, 28 November 1942, p261
8 *Modern Railways*, June 1969, p322, and February 1970, p86
9 *Modern Railways*, March 1971, p132; *Modern Tramway*, April 1973, p144
10 *Railway Gazette*, 5 June 1970, p402
11 Since the reconstruction of the Poschiavo workshops and the withdrawal of passenger services on the Bellinzona–Mesocco section (Ch 10), these percentages (4.15) may have altered slightly
12 '50 Jahre Rhätische Bahn', S Bz, Vol 115, February 1940, pp58–61, 66–70
13 S Bz, Vol 100, 16 July 1932, p41
14 *Railway Gazette*, 5 June 1970, p402

NOTES TO CHAPTER 8

1 S Bz, Vol 59, 1912, pp73–8, 87–91, 99–102, 143–6, 157–9, 169–
M.G.R.—Q

73, 181–4. Article by E. Bosshard
2 Moser, 1967, pp327, 333–5
3 S Bz, Vol 58, 29 July 1911, pp59–62
4 S Bz, Vol 71, 23 February 1918, p95
5 S Bz, Vol 97, 21 February 1931, pp88–90

NOTES TO CHAPTER 9

1 S Bz, Vol 60, 16 November 1912, pp263–4; '25 Jahre Chur–Arosa Bahn', S Bz, Vol 115, 9 March 1940, pp109–12
2 Bener, G. Article in S Bz, Vol 62, 22 November 1913, pp281–6; *The Engineer*, 1 May 1914, pp478–9
3 Bener, G. Article in S Bz, Vol 65, June 1915, pp265–70, 277–80
4 Conrad, H. 'Der Umbau des Castieler-Viaduktes der Linie Chur–Arosa der Rhätischen Bahn', S Bz, Vol 124, November–December 1944
5 S Bz, Vol 64, 19 December 1914, p273
6 Bryner, K., in *Bergbahnen der Schweiz*, 1959, pp359–60

NOTES TO CHAPTER 10

1 *Rivista di Bellinzona*, Anno IV, June 1972, pp15–19
2 *Electric Railway Journal*, Vol 35, 19 February 1910, pp306–10; Berg, S. Article in *The Engineer*, Vol 122, December 1916, pp480–4, 523–5
3 S Bz, Vol 63, 2 May 1914, p263; Vol 80, 1 July 1922, pp9–10
4 S Bz, Vol 90, 22 October 1927, pp213–16
5 S Bz, Vol 58, 21 October 1911, pp223–6; 28 October 1911, pp235–7
6 S Bz, Vol 58, 15 July 1911, pp29–33
7 Passet, Max. Article on the Centovalli Railway in S Bz, Vol 94, 6 July 1929, pp1–6; 13 July, pp14–17
8 Cornolo, G., *La Ferrovia Elettrica Domodossola–Locarno*, Ital. model–Ferrovie, Milan nd
9 S Bz, Vol 56, 10 December 1910, pp317–18; 17 December, pp333–6
10 Chiesa, Virgilio, *Il 40mo di esercizio delle Ferrovie Luganesi*, Lugano 1953

NOTES TO CHAPTER 11

1 S Bz, Vol 45, 21 January 1905, pp38–9; 22 April, pp197–201
2 S Bz, Vol 49, 18 May 1907, p251
3 Volmar, F. A., *Die Furka–Oberalp Bahn*, FO, Brig, 1965. Much

material in this chapter is from this book
4 S Bz, Vol 57, 10 June 1911, pp317–20
5 S Bz, Vol 64, 19 December 1914, pp269–72
6 S Bz, Vol 69, 23 June 1917, p291
7 S Bz, Vol 88, 10 July 1926, p53
8 Hefti, Walter. *Zahnradbahnen der Welt*, Basle 1969, pp141–3
9 *Bergbahnen der Schweiz*, p212

Gradient Conversion Scale

To convert a 'pro Mille' or per thousand gradient into a ratio, or vice versa refer to the left column first. A gradient of 60‰ is equal to 1 in 16.67. A gradient of 1 in 55 is equal to 18.2‰. Other gradients are found by multiplying one column and dividing the other by 10. A gradient of 1 in 500 is equal to 2‰, or 5‰ is 1 in 200.

‰ 1 in	‰ 1 in
125–8	50–20
100–10	45–22.22
95–10.5	40–25
90–11.11	35–28.57
85–11.76	30–33.33
80–12.5	25–40
75–13.3	20–50
70–14.3	15–66.67
65–15.4	10–100
60–16.67	5–200
55–18.2	0–Level

Tables of Comparative Measurements

Inches	Millimetres (mm)	Millimetres	Inches
1	25.4	10	$\frac{3}{8}$
2	50.8	20	$\frac{3}{4}$
3	76.2	30	$1\frac{1}{8}$
4	101.6	40	$1\frac{5}{8}$
5	127.0	50	2
6	152.4	60	$2\frac{3}{8}$
7	177.8	70	$2\frac{3}{4}$
8	203.2	80	$3\frac{1}{8}$
9	228.6	90	$3\frac{1}{2}$
10	254.0	100	$3\frac{7}{8}$
11	279.4	110	$4\frac{3}{8}$
12	304.8	120	$4\frac{3}{4}$
13	330.2	130	$5\frac{1}{8}$
14	355.6	140	$5\frac{1}{2}$
15	381.0	150	$5\frac{7}{8}$
16	406.4	160	$6\frac{1}{4}$
17	431.8	170	$6\frac{3}{4}$
18	457.2	180	$7\frac{1}{8}$
19	482.6	190	$7\frac{1}{2}$
20	508.0	200	$7\frac{7}{8}$
21	533.4	250	$9\frac{7}{8}$
22	558.8	300	$11\frac{3}{4}$
23	584.2	350	$13\frac{3}{4}$
24	609.6	400	$15\frac{3}{4}$
		450	$17\frac{3}{4}$
		500	$19\frac{5}{8}$

Feet	Metres	Metres	Feet	Miles	Km	Km	Miles
1	0.30	1	3.28	1	1.61	1	0.62
2	0.61	2	6.56	2	3.22	2	1.24
3	0.91	3	9.84	3	4.83	3	1.86
4	1.22	4	13.12	4	6.44	4	2.49
5	1.52	5	16.40	5	8.05	5	3.11
6	1.83	6	19.69	6	9.66	6	3.73
7	2.13	7	22.97	7	11.27	7	4.35
8	2.44	8	26.25	8	12.87	8	4.97
9	2.74	9	29.53	9	14.48	9	5.59
10	3.05	10	32.81	10	16.09	10	6.21
11	3.35	11	36.09	11	17.70	11	6.84
12	3.66	12	39.37	12	19.31	12	7.46
13	3.96	13	42.65	13	20.92	13	8.08
14	4.27	14	45.93	14	22.53	14	8.70
15	4.57	15	49.21	15	24.14	15	9.32
16	4.88	16	52.49	16	25.75	16	9.94
17	5.18	17	55.78	17	27.35	17	10.56
18	5.49	18	59.06	18	28.97	18	11.19
19	5.79	19	62.34	19	30.58	19	11.81
20	6.10	20	65.62	20	32.19	20	12.43

1 yard=0.91 metre   1 metre=1.09 yard
1 Kilometre (km)=0.62137 mile=$\frac{5}{8}$ mile approx

1 kilogramme (kg)=2.21lb
1,000kg=1 metric ton=0.9842 ton

kg/sq cm	lb/sq in
1	14.223
5	71.115
10	142.23
11	156.453
12	170.676
13	184.899
14	199.122
15	213.345

Abbreviations used in the Text

ac	alternating current
AEG	Allgemeine Elektrizitäts-Gesellschaft, Berlin
Alioth	Elektrizitätsgesellschaft Alioth, Münchenstein
BA	Biasca–Acquarossa Railway
BBC	A-G Brown Boveri & Cie, Baden
BLS	Berne–Lötschberg–Simplon Railway
BVZ	Brig–Visp–Zermatt Railway
C-A	Chur–Arosa Railway
dc	direct current
FART	Ferrovie e Autolinee Regionale Ticinesi (Ticino District Railways and Buses)
FFA	Flug- und Fahrzeugwerke Altenrein, Staad
FL	Società Ferrovie Luganesi (Lugano Railway Company)
FO	Furka–Oberalp Railway
FRT	Ferrovie Regionale Ticinesi (Ticino District Railways)
GGB	Gornergrat Bahn (Railway)
Hz	hertz, or cycles per second
LCD	Lugano–Cadro–Dino Railway
L-D	Landquart–Davos Railway
GS	Luftseilbahn Gornergrat–Stockhorn
LPB	Locarno–Ponte Brolla Railway
LT	Lugano–Tesserete Railway
MFO	Maschinenfabrik Oerlikon, Zurich
MOB	Montreux Oberland Bernois (Montreux Bernese Oberland Railway)
RhB	Rhätische Bahn (Rhaetian Railway)
SAAS	Ateliers de Sécheron SA, Geneva
SBB	Schweizerische Bundesbahnen (Swiss Federal Railways)

S Bz	*Schweizerische Bauzeitung*, Zurich
schB	Schöllenen Railway
SIG	Schweizerische Industrie-Gesellschaft, Neuhausen
SLM	Schweizerische Lokomotiv- und Maschinenfabrik, Winterthur
SSIF	Società Subalpina di Imprese Ferroviarie (Centovalli Railway)
SWP	Schweizerische Waggonfabrik, Pratteln
SWS	Schweizerische Waggonfabrik, Schlieren
VM	Valle Maggia Railway
VZ	Visp–Zermatt Railway
YStec	Yverdon–Ste Croix Railway
Z	*Zeitschrift des Vereines deutscher Ingenieure* (Journal of the Society of German Engineers)

Sources and Acknowledgements

MOST of the historical material was obtained from *Schweizerische Bauzeitung* (S Bz), the Swiss Building Journal published weekly in Zurich from 1883. For anyone with a good working knowledge of German this is a mine of useful information on Swiss railways. For access to files of S Bz I must thank the staff of Bolton Public Libraries who obtained copies for me from the National Lending Library for Science and Technology, Boston Spa, Yorkshire; and also the librarian of the Christie Library, University of Manchester. Here I was also able to consult the massive volumes of the *Zeitschrift des Vereines deutscher Ingenieure* (Z), the Journal of the Society of German Engineers. The librarian of UMIST (University of Manchester Institute of Science & Technology) Civil Engineering Library kindly allowed me to consult the files of the *Electric Railway Journal* (USA). For files of *The Engineer* and other publications I must thank the staff of the Social Sciences Library, Manchester Public Libraries.

Through the co-operation of Mr J. Schmid of the Swiss National Tourist Office, London, I was able to visit offices and workshops of the various railways in Switzerland, and I should like to express my gratitude to the staff of the Furka–Oberalp and Brig–Visp–Zermatt railways at Brig, the Rhaetian Railway at Chur and at the RhB workshops at Landquart, Sand and Poschiavo, at the FART office, Locarno, and the Ferrovie Luganesi, Lugano. Everywhere I was shown great kindness, my numerous technical questions were all answered, and I was given quantities of useful material. I should like to thank SLM, Winterthur, for the photographs on page 86. Information on signalling was kindly supplied by G. M. Kichenside.

My friends J. F. Thomas and K. I. MacFarlane have been the means of bringing to my notice many useful pieces of information, and Mr J. A. Patmore has given valuable advice on the arrangement of the material. Finally I must record my gratitude to the late Cecil J. Allen who inspired my enthusiasm for Swiss railways over forty years ago.

Index

Page numbers in italics refer to plates